Mostly Veggies

Mostly Veggies

Easy Make-Ahead Meals
for Healthy Living

Brittany Mullins

Photographs by Kristin Teig

VORACIOUS
LITTLE, BROWN AND COMPANY
New York Boston London

Voracious / Little, Brown and Company
Hachette Book Group
1290 Avenue of the Americas, New York, NY 10104
littlebrown.com

First Edition: April 2023

Voracious is an imprint of Little, Brown and Company, a division of Hachette Book Group, Inc. The Voracious name and logo are trademarks of Hachette Book Group, Inc.

The publisher is not responsible for websites (or their content) that are not owned by the publisher.

The Hachette Speakers Bureau provides a wide range of authors for speaking events. To find out more, go to hachettespeakersbureau.com or call (866) 376-6591.

Photography by Kristin Teig
Book design by Mia Johnson

ISBN 9780316427920
LCCN 2022943554

10 9 8 7 6 5 4 3 2 1

RRD

Printed in China

For my family:
everything I do is for you.

Contents

11 Introduction ● 17 The EBF Meal Prep Method
23 Best Kitchen Tools for Meal Prep ● 27 EBF Pantry, Fridge, and Freezer
Essentials ● 28 Storage and Reheating Tips ● 31 EBF Meal Plans

41 ● **Breakfast**

79 ● **Smoothies**

99 ● **Meal-Size Salads**

125 ● **Bowl Meals**

153 ● **Sheet Pan Meals**

175 ● **One Pan Meals**

213 ● **Snacks + Treats**

249 ● **Meal Prep for Littles**

265 Acknowledgments ● 266 Index

Mostly Veggies

Introduction

My healthy eating journey started in college, when most of my meals were eaten at the dining hall and the term "meal plan" simply meant which meal package I had signed up for at the start of the semester.

Before heading off to college I had no real knowledge of nutrition or how to eat healthy, but I was determined not to gain the infamous "freshman 15," so I started doing my own research and used this new environment as a way to dramatically change the way I was eating.

That year I lost 20 pounds of extra weight *without* restrictive dieting. I made healthier food choices. I chose whole, real foods instead of packaged foods whenever possible and ate a ton more vegetables and fruit. It was a big change from the food I grew up eating, which involved traditional Southern fare and a lot of processed foods.

The salad bar was my new best friend, and it was here that I learned how having a bunch of healthy ingredients prepped and ready to combine was the key to making delicious, satisfying meals that didn't get boring: with so many options I could switch up the flavors easily so I didn't feel like I was eating the same thing every day.

I was able to maintain that weight loss throughout college by keeping up with the healthy food habits I had established that first year. This journey not only boosted my self-confidence, it also piqued my interest in nutrition and healthy cooking, which later inspired me to start my website and become a holistic nutritionist so I could share what I learned and help others.

After college, things changed a bit when my husband, Isaac, and I moved in together and I took it upon myself to be in charge of planning out what we were going to eat every week. At the time, I didn't know the first thing about meal planning or meal prep. Plus, I had two different diets to contend with: I was a pescatarian, whereas Isaac ate meat.

I was totally winging it when it came to planning meals and cooking, which resulted in multiple trips to the grocery store, eating the same things for dinner night after night, wasting groceries that I bought with no plan to use, or coming home from work starving and snacking all evening instead of making a healthy meal for dinner.

"What's for Dinner?"

Whether you're planning meals for yourself or a family, this is a question that we all face daily, and without a plan you're always having to use mental space to come up with the answer. Then, after a long day of work, you have to go to the store because you don't have what you need at home *or* you end up throwing together something at home that doesn't taste great *or* you take the easy route and order takeout, which derails your health goals (and your budget goals, too). Been there, done that!

I get it, meal prep (and just the idea of eating healthier) can feel daunting! When I first learned about meal planning and prep, it was through fitness trainers that I followed online, so I thought that meal prep meant spending hours in the kitchen cooking full meals and portioning out my unseasoned protein, steamed greens, and rice into seven uniform little containers.

That version of meal prep felt very restrictive to me. Plus, eating the same thing day after day is pretty unsatisfying, and not sustainable in the long term. Through trial and error, I finally learned that healthy

eating doesn't need to be so prescriptive, and that there are many different ways to meal prep. I found a way that I actually enjoy, and I know you will, too!

Once I realized that there are different ways to meal prep, I started experimenting. One weekend I began small by just planning out our dinners for the week. I wrote out dinner ideas for each night, filling in a couple easy recipes I knew like the back of my hand, and then picked two brand-new recipes from cookbooks I'd been wanting to try.

Focusing only on dinner and picking just a couple new recipes made the process feel totally doable. That week I was amazed by how organized and prepared I felt. It was like a weight was lifted off my shoulders because the inevitable daily question of what we were going to have for dinner was already answered, and I had a little meal plan posted on the fridge to prove it.

Once I felt confident with meal planning and prepping dinner recipes, I started to include breakfast and lunch recipes as well. This was particularly useful when Isaac and I both worked outside our home and needed meals we could bring with us.

Lately, my meal prep strategy has changed a bit. There are weeks when I prep the majority of our meals, but most of the time I simply plan all the meals, buy the items I need, and fully prep only a few things like breakfast and snacks. I'm not saying my way is the only way to meal plan and prep, but it's a process that has worked for me over the years... through early adulthood and into parenthood. It not only keeps me feeling organized, but helps ensure my whole family is eating a wide variety of healthy, nutrient-rich foods. It's also been a key factor in being able to maintain my weight over the years, while still enjoying foods that I love day after day.

I've provided the framework here for you to see what doing a full prep looks like, but feel free to make it your own and find some hybrid between prepping everything and only the essentials that works for you. The beauty of meal prep is how flexible it is and how easy it can be adapted to your life.

"Healthy Eating" Defined

With so much research and so many different theories out there—not to mention loads of information coming from unqualified sources on the internet—it can be hard to answer the question of what exactly "healthy eating" is, but my definition is simple: 80 to 90 percent of the time you want to be eating whole, real foods that come from nature. And by that I mean foods with a single ingredient. There's a time and place for processed foods, but they shouldn't be foods you rely on regularly.

Foods that I recommend limiting include the following: processed foods, especially those with lots of preservatives or chemicals; canned items with added sugar and preservatives; foods containing artificial ingredients; processed meats; and even some meat substitutes. I'll share more on that in a bit.

When building meals, "mostly veggies" is my mantra, hence the name of this cookbook! Incorporating more vegetables into your meals will not only enrich your diet with more nutrients (think vitamins, minerals, antioxidants), but you'll be filling up on high-fiber foods that take longer to digest, keeping you feeling full longer and your digestive system working properly.

You want to load up a good portion of your plate, about half, with vegetables. I recommend starting with nonstarchy veggies, such as leafy greens, broccoli, cauliflower, tomatoes, and zucchini, because they're nutrient dense, low calorie, fiber rich, and low in carbohydrates. They'll really fill you up and make meals more satisfying. Starchy vegetables, such as potatoes, winter squash, peas, and corn, are also rich in nutrients and packed with fiber, but they tend to be higher in calories and carbohydrates. Just something to be mindful of.

Next, add a serving of protein to fill a quarter of your plate. Not only is protein the building block for every cell in the body, it helps repair and build tissue as well. It also promotes satiety after eating and can help stabilize blood sugar levels. There are plenty of plant-based sources of protein, so it's relatively easy to meet your daily protein needs while eating plant-focused meals.

One important thing to note is that many plant-based proteins are complete proteins, meaning they contain all nine essential aminos acids. These include quinoa, tofu, tempeh, edamame, buckwheat, hemp seeds, chia seeds, and nutritional yeast. Incomplete protein sources (like beans or rice) are still excellent options; they just need to be eaten as part of a varied diet that has complementary protein sources.

For the remaining quarter of your plate, you want to focus on complex carbohydrates. This includes whole grains (think bread, oats, brown rice, quinoa, and millet) or carb-rich foods like fruit and starchy vegetables. These foods will add fiber to your meals as well as a host of nutrients depending on what type of carbohydrate you choose. It's important to remember that while legumes do provide protein, they're a good source of carbohydrates as well.

Of course, we can't forget healthy fats! These can be toppings added to your plate, like avocado, dairy products, nuts, seeds, dressings, and so on. In addition, fat can be used to cook your protein and vegetables for added flavor.

Overall, healthy eating (and living) isn't about dieting or restriction but rather about balance. There are no "good" and "bad" foods...just healthier choices. And meal prep, in turn, is all about making those healthier choices so easy they become second nature.

I've included nutrition facts for every recipe in the book because having a general idea of calorie and macronutrient content can be important information to many people (including myself), and I want this book to be as comprehensive a resource as possible.

Why Plant-Forward?

While I personally don't feel the need to give my diet a specific label, plant-forward (or flexitarian) is pretty spot on. You'll find many definitions of plant-forward, but here's mine: Plant-forward is a way of eating and cooking that emphasizes plant-based foods such as vegetables, fruits, whole grains, legumes, nuts, and seeds. Dairy products, eggs, seafood, lean meat, and poultry aren't the focus, but they aren't excluded and can be part of a balanced diet.

While my blog, Eating Bird Food, contains recipes that fit an array of diets and dietary preferences, for the purpose of this cookbook I focused on providing healthy, attainable plant-forward meals that are easy to prepare in advance and are filled with my favorite food group: vegetables. All of the recipes are vegetarian and many are dairy-free, egg-free, and/or gluten-free as well. That said, you can easily swap the protein in many of the recipes if you do want to incorporate lean meat, poultry, or seafood into your diet. Whether you're strictly plant-based or just looking for more plant-forward meals, I want this cookbook to work for you!

As you'll notice when looking through, there are only a few recipes that call for packaged meat substitutes. This is because I don't recommend heavily relying on these foods for everyday meals. Yes, there are some "fake meat" products on the market that are made with less processed ingredients (like quinoa or pea protein), but many (ahem...most) are made with highly processed soy products, cheap inflammatory oils, flavorings, and preservatives. Some even contain a similar amount of saturated fat as meat products—and more sodium! In general, it's always important to check the label of packaged foods and make sure the ingredients match your health goals.

Thinking about making the switch to a plant-forward approach? Here are some benefits:

1. Eating more plants ensures that you're naturally eating more nutrient-rich foods in terms of vitamins, minerals, antioxidants, and fiber.

2. Despite stereotypes of expensive green juices and pricey cheese substitutes, buying plant-based foods can actually be much more cost-effective than relying on animal proteins. Legumes, grains, and plant-based proteins are some of the least expensive food items you can buy, especially if you're purchasing dry legumes from the bulk bins, but even cooked and canned legumes are very inexpensive. Think about it this way: a 1-pound steak costs around five times more than a 1-pound block of tofu, and a package of organic chicken breasts costs about three times more than a can of chickpeas!

3. Many veggie-forward dishes are easy to prepare because they can be made in one pot or pan. And that means there are fewer dishes to wash, which is always a win in my book.

4. Eating a plant-forward diet can be more convenient since many plant-based foods like legumes, grains, and nuts are shelf-stable, so you can keep them on hand for easy meals, whereas meat has a short shelf life. Plus, no more forgetting to take chicken or fish out of the freezer to thaw!

5. Last, but certainly not least, plant-forward eating is better for the environment. Less water is needed and less greenhouse gas is created.

How to Use
This Cookbook

For each recipe in this cookbook you'll find the basic instructions for how to complete the recipe in two ways: one option allows for serving the recipe right away and the other instructs you how to meal prep it for later.

Mostly Veggies is all about saving you time and being adaptable to your needs and individual dietary restrictions. See the key on the right for how this information is laid out easily for you throughout the book.

Dietary Labels

DF = DAIRY-FREE

GF = GLUTEN-FREE

EF = EGG-FREE

* = OPTION

Prep-Ahead Items

All items that can be prepped ahead are **bolded and highlighted.**

bananas
romaine lettuce
brussels sprouts
cauliflower
poblano pepper
red onion
avocado
tofu
edamame
white beans
chickpeas
black beans
rolled oats
chia seeds
salsa
tahini

The EBF Meal Prep Method

My 4-Step Method

Plan

If you read my blog, Eating Bird Food (EBF), you already know that I like cooking mostly because I *love* eating...not because I actually enjoy being in the kitchen all day. I'm all about taking shortcuts and making meal prep and cooking as easy as possible, while still being able to enjoy healthy food that tastes good. Yes, it's possible!

Over the years I developed an easy 4-step meal prep method that truly works. It doesn't involve spending all weekend in the kitchen cooking every single thing you're going to eat for the week. Nor will you be eating all of your meals straight from Tupperware.

My meal planning and prep process involves pulling out your calendar, planning out meal ideas for the week ahead, selecting recipes, writing a grocery list, getting the groceries you need, and doing a little prep to help save time throughout the week ahead. It's as simple as that!

Planning is key. I can't stress this enough! If you don't plan ahead and pick out recipes in advance, you'll be doing it on the fly all week.

Planning ahead keeps you organized and gives you structure. The first step is to break out your calendar and think about the week ahead so you can see what events you have, what days you might have to work late, what nights you already have dinner plans, and so on. Be as specific as possible.

Once you have your week mapped out, start filling in recipe ideas for each meal. You can keep this super simple when you're first getting the hang of meal prep. Here are some tips:

- Start with just one type of meal (like dinner) if planning every meal seems too overwhelming.

- Remember that you don't have to plan 21+ different recipes for the week. That would feel overwhelming to even the most advanced meal prep guru.

- Feel free to duplicate recipes and eat leftovers. I'm a huge fan of leftovers!

- Repeat breakfast and snack recipes. Often it's nice to stick with the same breakfast and snacks throughout the week to keep things simple, and then add a bit of variety with lunch and dinner options.

Create Your Shopping List, Take Inventory, and Shop

Once you have your recipes picked out, create a shopping list of the ingredients you need. Be sure to take inventory of what you already have in your fridge and pantry so you don't accidentally buy duplicates. Pro tip: Sometimes it can be helpful to look at what's in the fridge and the pantry *before* choosing recipes so you can use up things you already have on hand!

Then it's time to head to the grocery store to grab what you need. If you're following one of the meal plans and shopping lists I've provided (starting on page 32), just skim through the shopping list and jot down the items you need to purchase.

Or, if you have a lot going on, consider ordering your groceries online, for either delivery or curbside pickup. This saves me a ton of time. Plus, I find it prevents me from making impulse purchases because I'm hungry or I see some new kombucha flavor that I just *have* to try, thereby saving me money, too.

Here are some things to look for when grocery shopping:

- **Pre-chopped veggies:** Buy things that are already prepped to save time. They are more expensive and usually come with additional packaging, but sometimes it's worth the convenience factor. This includes pre-washed salad greens and pre-chopped veggies.

- **Canned beans:** You are more than welcome to cook dried beans from scratch, but this usually involves soaking and long cook times. For that reason, I'm a big fan of using canned beans for easy meals.

- **Frozen rice and quinoa:** These days you can buy frozen rice and quinoa at most grocery stores: I've seen white, brown, jasmine, basmati, and cauliflower rice at my local stores. Usually I'll make rice in my rice cooker, but frozen rice packets come in handy when you need a quick base for a meal.

- **Ready-to-go garlic and ginger:** Garlic and ginger are staples in my cooking, and sometimes it's really nice to buy these two things already prepped. Some options include jars of peeled and/or minced garlic, frozen garlic cubes, and frozen ginger cubes.

- **Staples:** It's always a great idea to pick up a few freezer and pantry staples, particularly when you see these items on sale! This includes things like canned beans, pasta, no-sugar-added pasta sauce, frozen stir-fry veggies, frozen cauliflower rice, and so on. In a pinch you can use these items to throw together a quick meal.

Get Your Meal Prep On!

Set aside about 3 hours, either all at once or spread across the week.

Plan out when you're going to do the basic meal prep for the recipes you picked. I usually do most of my meal prep on Sunday so I'm ready for the week ahead, and then a little more on Wednesday night or throughout the week while I'm already cooking dinner, but feel free to pick a day of the week that works for you.

There are three basic ways to prep:

- Prep individual food items, such as batch-cook quinoa, rice, roasted veggies, spaghetti squash noodles, and so on.

- Prep and assemble things to be cooked later; this includes chopping veggies and making any sauces you want to have on hand.

Prep and fully cook meals, such as salads, casseroles, curries, soups, and other meals that you can reheat throughout the week.

Look at your recipes for the week and decide which things you want to batch-cook, which items can be prepped ahead of time, and which meals can be fully cooked.

I like to fully cook most of my breakfast, lunch, and snack options, because I want those to be ready to eat on the fly throughout the week. Prepping and assembling is my preferred method for dinner recipes because it's nice to eat those things fresh the first night.

Prepping and assembling tends to require less time than fully cooking meals on my meal prep day, and then I don't mind spending 15 to 30 minutes pulling together the things I prepped to make an easy dinner. That said, if I have a busy week and know that I won't have the extra time to pull the meals together for dinner, I would opt for a freezer meal, a slow cooker option, or something else that I can fully cook and reheat when needed.

Here are some prep tasks that I find helpful:

- Batch-cook protein for quick meals: hard-boiled eggs, lentils, tofu, or tempeh.

- Batch-cook carb options: white rice, brown rice, quinoa, farro, or potatoes. This can be done on the stove or in a slow cooker or pressure cooker.

- Chop veggies for recipes (and snacking). You can also cook them as part of your meal prep by steaming, roasting, or grilling. My go-to snack is sliced veggies with hummus and, in order to make eating veggies easier, I buy them ready for snacking (think chopped carrots and jicama sticks) or I slice up a bunch at the beginning of the week and place them front and center in the fridge so they're the first thing I see when I open it looking for a snack.

- Batch-cook sauces and dressings on the weekend to save time when you're trying to get dinner on the table later in the week. I love making homemade dressings or marinades, but

you can also find healthy prepared sauces dressings at the grocery store for fast prep. Ke in mind that sauces are an easy way to change the flavor of a meal. Say you're prepping tofu and cauliflower rice. You can use teriyaki sauce and make tofu fried "rice" one night, or buy salsa, fajita seasoning, and cilantro and turn those same ingredients into a taco bowl another night.

STEP 4

Assemble, Cook (or Reheat), and Enjoy!

This is where you get to enjoy all of the prep work you did earlier in the week. It will depend on which recipes you chose and how much prep work you did in advance, but this step will involve some assembly, cooking (or reheating), and the best part: eating!

...tch-
...g Basics

Here are some simple batch-cooking recipes that I use weekly.

QUINOA

1 cup dried = 3 cups cooked

1. Rinse and drain the quinoa. Combine 1 cup quinoa and 2 cups water or broth in a medium saucepan.

2. Bring to a boil over medium-high heat. Reduce the heat to low, cover, and simmer until all the water is absorbed, about 15 minutes.

3. Remove from the heat and fluff the quinoa with a fork. Let cool, then store in an airtight container in the refrigerator.

Cooked quinoa will last for up to 5 days. Eat cold or reheat in the microwave with 1 to 2 tablespoons water to keep it from drying out.

FARRO

1 cup dried = 3 cups cooked

1. Rinse and drain the pearled farro. Combine 1 cup farro, 2½ cups water, and a pinch of salt in a medium saucepan.

2. Bring to a boil over medium-high heat. Reduce the heat to low, cover, and simmer for 20 to 30 minutes or until farro reaches the desired texture.

3. Remove from the heat and drain water if needed. Let cool, then store in an airtight container in the refrigerator.

Cooked farro will keep for up to 5 days. Eat cold or reheat in the microwave with 1 to 2 tablespoons water to keep it from drying out.

GREEN/BROWN LENTILS

1 cup dried = 2½ cups cooked

1. Rinse and drain the lentils, discarding any stones or debris. Combine 1 cup lentils, 2 cups water, and a pinch of salt in a medium saucepan.

2. Bring to a boil over medium-high heat. Reduce the heat to low, partially cover, and simmer until tender, 20 to 25 minutes.

3. Drain through a fine-mesh strainer to remove any excess water and rinse with cold water to cool. Store in an airtight container in the refrigerator.

Cooked lentils will keep for up to 5 days. Eat cold or reheat in the microwave with 1 to 2 tablespoons water to keep them from drying out.

BOILED EGGS

1. Place several eggs in a pot and cover with cold water, making sure the water is at least 1 inch above the eggs.

2. Bring to a boil over high heat.

3. Once boiling, cover, and remove from the heat.

4. Let the eggs sit, covered, for 5 to 6 minutes for soft-boiled eggs or up to 10 to 12 minutes for fully hard-boiled eggs. I've found 8 to 10 minutes to be the sweet spot for the way I like them.

5. Transfer the eggs to a bowl of ice water. Once cool, drain and store in the refrigerator.

Unpeeled boiled eggs will keep for up to 1 week.

WHITE RICE

1 cup dried = 3 cups cooked

1. Combine 1 cup white rice, 2 cups water, and a pinch of salt in a medium saucepan.

2. Bring to a boil over medium-high heat. Reduce the heat to low, cover, and simmer until all the water is absorbed, 15 to 20 minutes.

3. Remove from the heat and fluff the rice with a fork. Let cool, then store in an airtight container in the refrigerator.

Cooked white rice will keep for up to 4 days. Reheat in the microwave with 1 to 2 tablespoons water to keep it from drying out.

BROWN RICE

1 cup dried = 3 cups cooked

1. Combine 1 cup brown rice, 2½ cups water, and a pinch of salt in a medium saucepan.

2. Bring to a boil over medium-high heat. Reduce the heat to low, cover, and simmer until all the water is absorbed, 25 to 40 minutes.

3. Remove from the heat and fluff the rice with a fork. Let cool, then store in an airtight container in the refrigerator.

Cooked brown rice will keep for up to 4 days. Reheat in the microwave until piping hot with 1 to 2 tablespoons water to keep it from drying out.

Don't Forget to Include Indulgences

Remember that meal planning and prepping isn't about sticking to a restrictive diet; it's simply a lifestyle habit that will keep you cooking at home more and help you stay consistent with healthy eating.

When you're planning and prepping your meals, you want to focus on nutrient-rich, whole foods, but be sure to include the foods that you enjoy and incorporate a few treats and indulgences so you don't feel deprived.

For example, I love making healthy homemade treats like Coconut Protein Balls (page 225), Chocolate–Peanut Butter Shake (page 95), Crunch Factor Granola (page 61), and more that I can stash in the freezer and grab when a sugar craving hits! Just figure out which treats you can't live without and work those into your weekly meal plan.

Ready to Get Started?

So now that you've seen my meal prep system, it's time to get started! Once you get into a routine with meal prep, it will become second nature and feel easy. And, luckily for you, the meal plans and recipes in this book take care of most of the steps for you! All you have to do is choose a meal plan (or pick out which recipes you want to make), get your groceries, do your prep, and then enjoy all those delicious meals.

Plus, you'll get to take advantage of these amazing benefits:

- **Have more energy:** You'll be eating whole, real foods and feel fueled, avoiding that 3pm crash every day.

- **Look and feel your best:** Meal planning and prepping is what helps me stay consistent with healthy eating, and if you're not currently doing it, it's definitely going to help you eat healthier and maybe even shed unwanted weight.

- **Feel confident:** Once you get this process down, it will become second nature, and you'll start to feel more confident in and out of the kitchen.

- **Save time:** You'll save time in so many ways...on deciding what to eat, buying groceries, prepping and cooking each day, and even on waiting for food while eating out or picking up takeout.

- **Save money:** You can save thousands of dollars a year that would have gone to fast food, dining out, and wasted groceries.

Best Kitchen Tools for Meal Prep

When it comes to meal prep, you really don't need a ton of fancy kitchen gadgets, but there are a few tools to have on hand that will make your meal prep faster and more efficient. Here are my must-have items:

Glass storage containers: You can use any container you have on hand to store your prepped food, but I love glass containers because they don't leach harmful chemicals into your food like some plastics do, and you can easily reheat your food in the microwave or in the oven without dirtying an extra plate or bowl. I recommend getting a glass storage set so everything matches and they're easy to store—otherwise you'll end up with a cabinet full of mismatched storage containers that come toppling out every time you open the cabinet (I speak from experience, if you can't tell).

Mason jars: Mason jars are great storage containers because they're relatively inexpensive and can store pretty much anything! I love wide-mouth Ball mason jars for salads and pantry items, and smaller pint or half-pint jars for smaller portions of overnight oats, chia pudding, dressings, and sauces. I recommend purchasing some plastic lids for your mason jars because the metal lids that come with them are harder to clean and tend to rust.

Knives: Treat yourself to a set of good knives. Trust me, it's worth it! Chopping is so much easier and more effective when you have good knives. I love our Shun knives, but just look for a couple of high-quality knives in a price range you can afford. I recommend the following: a chef's knife, a paring knife, and a serrated bread knife.

Cutting boards: You'll want a few cutting boards in a variety of sizes to go along with your knives. If you eat meat, it's nice to have a cutting board specifically for meat and ones for fruits, veggies, and other foods.

Nonstick pots and pans: Like a good set of knives, a nice set of pans is an investment but will make your life in the kitchen much more enjoyable. I prefer to use nonstick pans so I don't have to add oil when cooking. Some of my favorite brands include Caraway, Our Place, and Scanpan.

Dutch oven: This doesn't need to be fancy or expensive, but a heavy-duty enameled Dutch oven with a lid is ideal for soups and stews.

Vegetable peeler: A good-quality vegetable peeler is key for easily removing the skin from fruits and vegetables.

Lemon/lime juicer: This inexpensive kitchen gadget makes a big difference because you're able to get so much more juice from your lemons and limes than you could if you just squeeze them by hand. Some even have a convenient storage compartment with measurements.

Large rimmed baking sheets: A few baking sheets are a great investment, and I've found that the extra-large or mega rimmed baking sheets are best for meal prep since you can fit more on the tray and roast veggies without them getting overcrowded or falling off the edge. Look for one that is 21 x 15 inches instead of the typical 10 x 15.

Parchment paper: Parchment is great for nonstick baking and makes for easy cleanup with roasted veggies and sheet pan meals.

Food wrap: Foil, plastic wrap, and more sustainable options like beeswax wrap are all options to have on hand for food storage when you've run out of storage containers or have a small item like half of a lemon or avocado to save for later.

Stasher bags: These reusable silicone bags are awesome for fridge and freezer food storage and a great replacement for single-use plastic bags. I recommend getting a variety of sizes for different uses. Of course, plastic storage bags also work if that's what you have on hand.

- **Salad spinner:** I love my salad spinner for drying off greens and herbs. There's nothing worse than a watered-down salad because your greens retained too much water after washing.

- **Food processor:** Food processors have many uses—I use mine for shredding veggies, making cauliflower rice, sauces, and so much more.

- **High-powered blender:** A high-quality blender is definitely an investment, but if it's in your budget, it's totally worth it! Not only does my Vitamix make the best smoothies, but I use it to make nut butters, dressings, and sauces and even to blend soups.

- **Muffin tin:** Muffin tins are really versatile and great for perfectly portioned meal prep recipes.

- **Silicone muffin liners:** This goes hand in hand with the muffin tin, but I swear by using silicone muffin liners. You don't need extra oil to keep things from sticking, and they make it so easy to get muffins, egg cups, and other items out of the tin.

- **9 x 13-inch, 9 x 11-inch, and 8 x 8-inch baking dishes:** I highly recommend all three of these sizes when it comes to baking dishes. The 9 x 13-inch and 9 x 11-inch dishes are great for casseroles and one-pan meals, and I frequently use my 8-inch square pan for baking.

- **Dry measuring cups and spoons:** These are necessary kitchen utensils. It can even be nice to have a couple sets!

- **Liquid measuring cups:** It's important to note that you need both dry measuring cups and glass or clear plastic liquid measuring cups. If you try to measure dry ingredients in a liquid measuring cup or vice versa, your measurements will likely be off.

- **Slow cooker:** I love my slow cooker! It's so convenient to throw ingredients in the slow cooker in the morning and have a delicious, healthy meal ready to eat at the end of the day.

- **Rice cooker:** This isn't absolutely necessary, but it does make the process of making rice really hands-off, and you get perfectly cooked, fluffy rice every time. Plus, no more boiled-water stains on the stovetop!

- **Air fryer:** This is another kitchen appliance that you don't need, but it can come in handy! I love using our air fryer for "roasting" vegetables, and it's fantastic for reheating leftovers.

EBF Pantry, Fridge, and Freezer Essentials

The following lists contain all of my favorite healthy eating essentials that you'll need for making the recipes in this cookbook.

Pantry Staples

- ⬭ grains: quinoa, white rice, brown rice, farro, old-fashioned rolled oats
- ⬭ chickpea or lentil pasta
- ⬭ jarred marinara sauce without added sugar (I like Rao's Homemade)
- ⬭ jarred pizza sauce without added sugar (I like Rao's Homemade)
- ⬭ shelf-stable natural sweeteners: honey, stevia, coconut sugar
- ⬭ nut butters: almond butter, peanut butter, cashew butter, walnut butter, coconut butter
- ⬭ nuts: almonds, cashews, walnuts, pecans, pistachios
- ⬭ seeds: chia, flax, hemp, pumpkin (pepitas), sunflower
- ⬭ oils: olive oil, coconut oil, avocado oil
- ⬭ cooking spray: avocado or olive oil for cooking, coconut oil for baking
- ⬭ extracts: vanilla and almond
- ⬭ reduced-sodium tamari, reduced-sodium soy sauce, and/or coconut aminos
- ⬭ vinegar: apple cider, red wine, balsamic, white balsamic
- ⬭ seasonings: fine sea salt (I use Redmond), ground black pepper, ground cinnamon, ground cumin, dried oregano, dried basil, garlic powder, onion powder, chili powder, paprika, crushed red pepper, cayenne pepper
- ⬭ pantry vegetables: garlic, yellow onion, sweet potato, spaghetti squash, butternut squash
- ⬭ plant-based protein powder with minimal ingredients and sugar (I like Nuzest and Sunwarrior)

- ⬭ canned coconut milk
- ⬭ nutritional yeast
- ⬭ baking supplies: whole-wheat pastry flour, oat flour, almond flour, coconut flour, unsweetened cocoa powder, baking powder, baking soda

Fridge Staples

- ⬭ veggies for meals
- ⬭ sliced veggies for snacking (carrots, cucumbers, celery, broccoli)
- ⬭ baby greens, like spinach and arugula
- ⬭ tofu and tempeh
- ⬭ eggs (look for pasture-raised)
- ⬭ plant-based milk: almond milk, oat milk, cashew milk, coconut milk, flax milk
- ⬭ cooked lentils
- ⬭ yogurt: plain Greek or coconut milk yogurt
- ⬭ cottage cheese
- ⬭ shredded cheese (plant-based if desired)
- ⬭ Dijon mustard
- ⬭ hummus
- ⬭ hot sauce
- ⬭ pure maple syrup (not pancake syrup)

Freezer Staples

- ⬭ veggies: broccoli, cauliflower, green beans, Brussels sprouts, corn, roasted plantains
- ⬭ stir-fry veggies
- ⬭ edamame
- ⬭ cauliflower rice
- ⬭ brown or white rice
- ⬭ quinoa
- ⬭ sprouted and/or whole grain bread

Storage and Reheating Tips

When it comes to the make-ahead meals and meal prep recipes, it's important to keep in mind food safety guidelines and proper reheating methods so you can fully enjoy everything you've prepared. I give suggestions for how to properly store every recipe in the book and references for how long they should last (for safety, I've noted conservative estimates).

Basic Food Storage Tips

- Don't overstuff your refrigerator. You want to leave plenty of room for the air to circulate. If airflow is blocked, the fridge will need to work harder to keep items at a safe temperature. It can also cause some items to get too cold and freeze.

- When meal prepping, hot foods should be allowed to cool for a bit, and then placed in the refrigerator within an hour or so of cooking; smaller portions are best because they'll cool faster.

- Store fresh cilantro, parsley, mint, and basil like a bouquet of flowers. Fill a glass or mason jar with about 1 inch of cold water, trim the ends of the herb stems, and place them in the jar. After a couple days the water will likely turn murky. Replace the water and trim the ends of the remaining herbs.

- Once you open a package of dry food (like oats, flour, sugar, cereal, pasta, and rice) it's best to transfer it to an airtight container to help prevent it from going stale.

- When freezing foods, be sure to label them so you remember what items are in the storage container and when you made them.

- It's important to package foods properly when freezing to prevent freezer burn. Foods with freezer burn are generally still safe to eat, but the quality of the food is diminished and it may not taste as good.

- Sometimes you'll need to use your best judgment when it comes to deciding if a food is still safe to eat. If something has visible signs of mold, seems slimy, or smells off, you'll want to toss the food. "When in doubt, throw it out!"

Produce Storage Tips

There's nothing worse than buying a ton of fresh produce and having it wilt or mold before you get a chance to use it! All fruits and vegetables go through different ripening processes. During these processes, natural ethylene gas is emitted from some types of produce and can spread to other fruits and vegetables, so storage methods are really important. Read over these tips so you can store your foods properly and reduce the chances of quick spoiling and/or flavor transfer. Unless otherwise specified, all of these guidelines refer to whole, uncut fruits and vegetables; always store cut produce in a closed container in the refrigerator.

Apples
- Store on a cool counter or in the refrigerator, away from strong-scented foods as they absorb flavors easily.

Avocados
- Store at room temperature until ripe.

- To speed up the ripening process, store in a paper bag with bananas or apples, or somewhere slightly above room temperature.

- Once ripe, transfer to the refrigerator.

- Refrigerate avocado halves with the pit still intact to prevent discoloration.

Bananas

- Store at room temperature out of direct sunlight.

- To speed up the ripening process, store in a paper bag with already ripe bananas or apples.

Berries (blackberries, blueberries, raspberries, strawberries)

- Submerge in a vinegar bath (3 parts water, 1 part white vinegar), then rinse with cold water in a colander and gently pat dry or use a salad spinner lined with paper towels.

- Immediately transfer to a paper towel–lined container or berry basket and store in the refrigerator for up to 5 days.

Broccoli

- Wrap in a damp cloth and store in the refrigerator.

- Refresh in ice water to maintain color.

Cabbage

- Store in the refrigerator for up to 3 weeks.

Cauliflower

- Store stem-side up in the refrigerator crisper drawer.

Carrots

- Store loose or in a sealed bag in the refrigerator crisper drawer for up to 4 weeks.

Celery

- Store in a closed container or wrapped in a damp cloth in the refrigerator for up to 2 weeks.

Corn

- Refrigerate unhusked, preferably for just 1 day but will keep up to 3 days.

Garlic

- Store whole bulbs at room temperature out of direct sunlight for up to 4 weeks. Individual, unpeeled cloves can be stored the same way for about 10 days. Once peeled, store the cloves in a sealed container in the refrigerator for up to 5 days.

Grapes

- Remove spoiled grapes or ones with broken skins and store, unwashed, in a bowl in the refrigerator.

Green beans

- Store in a paper bag in the refrigerator crisper drawer for up to 5 days.

Greens (chard, collards, kale)

- Store in a closed container or wrapped in a damp cloth in the refrigerator crisper drawer for up to 5 days.

Lemons and limes

- Store at room temperature for up to a week or in the refrigerator for up to 3–4 weeks.

Lettuce

- Store heads of lettuce in a plastic bag or wrapped in a damp cloth in the refrigerator crisper drawer for up to 3 weeks.

- Do not store with melons, apples, pears, or other ethylene gas–emitting fruits.

Mango

- Store at room temperature until ripe.

- Once ripe, transfer to the refrigerator and store for up to 3 days.

Melon

- Store in the refrigerator or at room temperature for up to 3 days.

Onions

- Store in a dry, dark, well-ventilated area.

Oranges

- Store on a cool counter for up to 1 week or in the refrigerator for up to 3 weeks.

Pears

- Store at room temperature until ripe.
- To speed up the ripening process, store with ripe bananas.
- Press the neck of the pear, right near the stem rather than the body of the pear, to check for ripeness.
- Once ripe, transfer to the refrigerator.

Peppers (bell peppers, chiles)

- Store in the refrigerator for up to 1 week.

Potatoes

- Store in a dry, dark, well-ventilated area.

Spinach

- Store, unwashed, in a closed container in the refrigerator crisper drawer.
- For pre-washed spinach sold in plastic bags or clamshell packaging, place a paper towel in with the spinach to absorb any moisture.

Summer squash (crookneck, zucchini)

- Store in the refrigerator crisper drawer for up to 5 days.

Tomatoes

- Store, stem side down, at room temperature.

Winter squash (butternut, kabocha, spaghetti squash)

- Store in a dry, dark, well-ventilated area for up to 1 month.

Reheating Tips

- My golden rule for reheating leftovers is to reheat the food in the same way it was originally cooked.

- I reheat most things on the stovetop or in the toaster oven or air fryer. The toaster oven and air fryer preheat faster than a regular oven and give foods a crisp texture, which you lose when reheating in the microwave. Both the toaster oven and air fryer work great for tofu, tempeh, sandwiches, bread, and even baked goods. If you're worried about the food drying out, simply wrap it in aluminum foil.

- Of course, there are times when you may want to use a microwave—or may have to, such as to reheat lunch at work. The microwave is best for foods that don't need to be crisp, like oatmeal, soups, stews, stir-fries, casseroles, and grains.

- For the best microwave results, spread your food out in an even layer, cover with a damp paper towel to help create some steam while the food is heating so it doesn't dry out (or splatter), and stir every so often for even heating.

- For roasted items, like sheet pan meals, I like to reheat them in the oven (or toaster oven). For one-pot meals or soups, I use a saucepan or skillet to reheat them.

EBF Meal Plans

These meal plans are meant as a guide to make your life easier, with the recipes all plotted out, complete with shopping lists and prep tasks. The grocery shopping and bulk of the meal prep are slated to be done on Sunday, but you don't have to follow the plan from Monday through Sunday if that doesn't work for your schedule. Each meal plan is meant to serve two people; you may need to adjust according to how many people you're planning for.

Spring

	MONDAY	TUESDAY	WEDNESDAY	THURSDAY	FRIDAY	SATURDAY	SUNDAY
BREAKFAST	Cinnamon Roll Baked Oatmeal	Banana Chia Pudding	Banana Chia Pudding	Banana Chia Pudding	Cinnamon Roll Baked Oatmeal	Cinnamon Roll Baked Oatmeal	Avocado Toast (2 pieces toast + ½ avocado + every-thing bagel seasoning)
LUNCH	Nourishing Grain Bowls with Creamy Tahini Sauce	Black Bean and Sweet Potato Jar Salad	Nourishing Grain Bowls with Creamy Tahini Sauce	Black Bean and Sweet Potato Jar Salad	Slow Cooker Chili Mac	Black Bean and Sweet Potato Jar Salad	Slow Cooker Chili Mac leftovers
DINNER	Spicy Chipotle Tofu Burrito Bowls	Spicy Chipotle Tofu Burrito Bowls	Add-the-Veggies Fried Rice	Slow Cooker Chili Mac	Add-the-Veggies Fried Rice	Dinner out!	Add-the-Veggies Fried Rice
SNACK	Edamame Hummus + veggies	Coconut Protein Balls	Edamame Hummus + veggies	Coconut Protein Balls	Edamame Hummus + veggies	Coconut Protein Balls	Edamame Hummus + veggies

SUNDAY

● Batch-cook about 10 cups brown rice for Nourishing Grain Bowls, Spicy Chipotle Tofu Burrito Bowls, and Add-the-Veggies Fried Rice. Follow the instructions in the EBF Batch-Cooking Basics section (page 21), using 3½ cups brown rice and 8¾ cups water.

● Fully make Cinnamon Roll Baked Oatmeal (page 74).

● Fully make a double batch of Banana Chia Pudding (page 42).

● Fully make Nourishing Grain

Bowls with Creamy Tahini Sauce (page 142) or prep as much as possible.

● Fully make Black Bean and Sweet Potato Jar Salads (page 120).

● Fully make Spicy Chipotle Tofu Burrito Bowls (page 134) or prep as much as possible.

● Fully make Edamame Hummus (page 221) and cut up veggies.

● Fully make Coconut Protein Balls (page 225).

WEDNESDAY

● Fully make a double batch of Add-the-Veggies Fried Rice (page 199).

THURSDAY

● Fully make Slow Cooker Chili Mac (page 207).

SPRING SHOPPING LIST

PRODUCE

- 3 heads romaine lettuce (20 cups shredded or chopped)
- 3 cups fresh cauliflower rice
- 1 pound Brussels sprouts
- 1 head cauliflower
- 2 cups broccoli florets
- 3 medium yellow onions
- 3 medium red onions
- 1 bunch green onions
- 1 shallot
- 2 heads garlic (13 cloves)
- 2-inch knob fresh ginger
- 2 red or orange bell peppers
- 1 medium poblano pepper
- 1 pint cherry tomatoes (2 cups chopped)
- 4 medium sweet potatoes
- 10 carrots (2 cups grated or shredded + 2 cups diced)
- 1 bunch fresh cilantro
- 1 bunch fresh parsley
- Veggies to cut up for dipping in hummus
- 2 avocados
- 4 limes
- 4 lemons
- 4 bananas

FROZEN

- 2 cups frozen peas
- 1 (12-ounce) bag frozen shelled edamame
- 2 (12-ounce) bags frozen corn kernels (about 5 cups; use fresh, if you like)

PROTEIN AND DAIRY

- 7 large eggs
- 1 (14- to 16-ounce) package extra-firm tofu
- 1½ cups shredded cheddar cheese
- 2 cups unsweetened vanilla almond milk

GRAINS

- 3½ cups old-fashioned rolled oats
- 3½ cups brown rice
- Whole-grain bread

CANNED AND PACKAGED ITEMS

- 2 (13.5-ounce) cans light coconut milk
- 3 (15-ounce) cans black beans
- 1 (15-ounce) can white beans
- 1 (15-ounce) can pinto beans
- 1 (15-ounce) can red kidney beans
- 1 (28-ounce) can diced tomatoes
- 1 (4.5-ounce) tube or (6-ounce) can tomato paste
- 1 (7-ounce) can chipotle peppers in adobo sauce
- 1 (8-ounce) box chickpea elbow pasta
- Salsa
- Tahini
- Cashew butter
- Coconut Butter (page 242)
- Almond butter
- Avocado oil
- Coconut oil
- Olive oil
- Apple cider vinegar

- Vegetable broth (2 cups)
- Reduced-sodium tamari, reduced-sodium soy sauce, or coconut aminos
- Sriracha (optional)
- Toasted sesame oil
- Chia seeds
- Vanilla plant-based protein powder
- Unsweetened shredded coconut
- Mini chocolate chips (I like Lily's)
- Baking powder
- Organic sugar or coconut sugar
- Powdered sugar
- Chopped pecans (optional)
- Vanilla extract

SEASONINGS

- Fine sea salt
- Ground black pepper
- Ground allspice
- Ground cinnamon
- Ground coriander
- Ground cumin
- Onion powder
- Chili powder
- Dried oregano
- Everything bagel seasoning

Summary

	MONDAY	TUESDAY	WEDNESDAY	THURSDAY	FRIDAY	SATURDAY	SUNDAY
BREAKFAST	Zucchini Bread Breakfast Cookies + hard-boiled egg	Chive, Potato, and Feta Egg Cups with fruit	Zucchini Bread Breakfast Cookies + hard-boiled egg	Zucchini Bread Breakfast Cookies + hard-boiled egg	Chive, Potato, and Feta Egg Cups with fruit	Chive, Potato, and Feta Egg Cups with fruit	Zucchini Bread Breakfast Cookies + hard-boiled egg
LUNCH	Mediterranean Farro Mason Jar Salad	BBQ Jackfruit Bowls leftovers	Mediterranean Farro Mason Jar Salad	Quinoa Black Bean Burgers	Quinoa Black Bean Burgers and/or Thai-Inspired Squash Noodles with Peanut Sauce	Mediterranean Farro Mason Jar Salad	Brunch out!
DINNER	BBQ Jackfruit Bowls	Quinoa Black Bean Burgers	Thai-Inspired Spaghetti Squash Noodles with Peanut Sauce	Taco-Stuffed Zucchini Boats	Dinner out!	Taco-Stuffed Zucchini Boats	Pesto Veggie and Cauliflower Gnocchi
SNACK	Tamari Roasted Almonds	Trail Mix Cookies	Tamari Roasted Almonds	Trail Mix Cookies	Tamari Roasted Almonds	Trail Mix Cookies	Tamari Roasted Almonds or Trail Mix Cookies

SUNDAY

⬤ Batch-cook about 4½ cups quinoa for BBQ Jackfruit Bowls, Quinoa Black Bean Burgers, and Taco-Stuffed Zucchini Boats. Follow the instructions in the EBF Batch-Cooking Basics section (page 20), using 1½ cups quinoa and 3 cups vegetable broth.

⬤ Hard-boil 8 eggs (page 20).

⬤ Fully make Zucchini Bread Breakfast Cookies (page 62).

⬤ Fully make Chive, Potato, and Feta Egg Cups (page 65).

⬤ Fully make Mediterranean Farro Mason Jar Salads (page 108).

⬤ Fully make BBQ Jackfruit Bowls (page 145) or prep as much as possible.

⬤ Fully make Quinoa Black Bean Burgers (page 204).

⬤ Fully make Thai-Inspired Spaghetti Squash Noodles with Peanut Sauce (page 192) or prep as much as possible.

⬤ Fully make Tamari Roasted Almonds (page 226).

⬤ Fully make Trail Mix Cookies (page 238).

WEDNESDAY

⬤ Prep the veggies for Taco-Stuffed Zucchini Boats (page 191).

⬤ Prep the veggies for Pesto Veggie and Cauliflower Gnocchi (page 166).

SUMMER SHOPPING LIST

PRODUCE

- 2 bunches kale or 1 (12-ounce) package (4 cups)
- 4 (5-ounce) packages baby arugula (12 cups)
- 1 (12-ounce) package coleslaw mix
- 1 large spaghetti squash
- 4 medium yellow onions
- 1 medium-large red onion
- 1 bunch green onions
- 1 head garlic (10 cloves)
- 2-inch knob fresh ginger
- 4 red bell peppers
- 1 pint cherry or grape tomatoes (1½ cups chopped)
- 1½ cups red potatoes
- 1 small sweet potato
- 6 medium-large zucchini
- 2 carrots (1 cup matchsticks)
- 1 cup button mushrooms
- 1 bunch fresh cilantro
- 1 bunch fresh chives
- 2 lemons
- 3 limes
- Mixed fruit, for breakfast

FROZEN

- 1 (12-ounce) package frozen corn kernels (1 cup)
- 2 (12-ounce) packages frozen cauliflower gnocchi

PROTEIN AND DAIRY

- 17 large eggs
- 1 (14- to 16-ounce) package extra-firm tofu
- 1 (5-ounce) container plain full-fat Greek yogurt
- ½ cup crumbled feta
- 1½ cups mini pearl mozzarella balls
- 1 cup shredded Mexican cheese blend
- Grated Parmesan cheese (optional)
- Oat milk

GRAINS

- 1½ cups old-fashioned rolled oats
- 1 cup quick oats
- 1½ cups quinoa
- ½ cup farro
- 1¼ cups white whole-wheat flour or whole-wheat pastry flour
- ¾ cup oat flour
- Burger buns

CANNED AND PACKAGED ITEMS

- 2 (15-ounce) cans chickpeas
- 2 (15-ounce) can black beans
- 1 (14-ounce) jar marinated artichoke hearts
- 1 (4.5-ounce) tube or (6-ounce) can tomato paste
- ⅓ cup dry-packed sun-dried tomatoes
- 1 (14-ounce) can green/unripe jackfruit packed in water
- Salsa
- Pesto
- Hot sauce
- Sambal oelek (optional)
- Creamy peanut butter
- BBQ sauce
- Avocado oil mayonnaise
- Coconut oil
- Olive oil
- Apple cider vinegar
- Red wine vinegar
- Dijon mustard
- Vegetable broth (2 cups)
- Reduced-sodium tamari, reduced-sodium soy sauce, or coconut aminos
- Ground flaxseed
- Baking soda
- Applesauce
- Raisins or dried cranberries
- Chopped salted peanuts (optional)
- Chopped walnuts
- Raw whole almonds
- Coconut sugar
- Brown sugar
- Pure maple syrup
- Chocolate chips
- Vanilla extract

SEASONINGS

- Fine sea salt
- Ground black pepper
- Ground cinnamon
- Ground cumin
- Paprika
- Chili powder
- Onion powder
- Garlic powder
- Dried oregano
- Italian seasoning
- Taco seasoning
- Crushed red pepper

Fall

	MONDAY	TUESDAY	WEDNESDAY	THURSDAY	FRIDAY	SATURDAY	SUNDAY
BREAKFAST	Sweet Potato Pancakes	Sweet Potato Pancakes	Chai-Spiced Overnight Oats	Chai-Spiced Overnight Oats	Berry Oat Smoothie	Berry Oat Smoothie	Berry Oat Smoothie
LUNCH	Curried Tofu Salad	Buffalo Tofu Mason Jar Salads	Curried Tofu Salad	Buffalo Tofu Mason Jar Salads	Curried Tofu Salad	Slow Cooker Tuscan White Bean Soup	Spaghetti Squash Pizza Bake
DINNER	Sheet Pan Kale and Eggs Hash	Cauliflower Tikka Masala	Tikka Masala leftovers	Slow Cooker Tuscan White Bean Soup	Dinner out!	Spaghetti Squash Pizza Bake	Slow Cooker Tuscan White Bean Soup
SNACK	Bird Food Granola Bars	Brownie Hummus	Bird Food Granola Bars	Brownie Hummus	Bird Food Granola Bars	Brownie Hummus	Bird Food Granola Bars or Brownie Hummus

SUNDAY

● Batch-cook about 5 cups brown rice for Buffalo Tofu Mason Jar Salads and Cauliflower Tikka Masala. Follow the instructions in the EBF Batch-Cooking Basics section (page 21), using 1⅔ cups brown rice and 4 cups water.

● Fully make a double batch of Sweet Potato Pancakes (page 58).

● Fully make 4 servings of Chai-Spiced Overnight Oats (page 48).

● Fully make Curried Tofu Salad (page 100).

● Fully make Buffalo Tofu Mason Jar Salads (page 116).

● Fully make Sheet Pan Kale and Eggs Hash (page 161) or prep as much as possible.

● Fully make Bird Food Granola Bars (page 222).

● Fully make Brownie Hummus (page 237).

WEDNESDAY

● Fully make Slow Cooker Tuscan White Bean Soup (page 203).

● Make 6 smoothie packs for Berry Oat Smoothie (page 91).

FALL SHOPPING LIST

PRODUCE

- 1 head romaine lettuce (8 cups chopped)
- 1 bunch curly kale
- 1 bunch lacinato kale
- 4 (5-ounce) bags baby spinach (7 cups)
- Lettuce or collard wrap, if desired for curried tofu salad
- 1 medium-large spaghetti squash
- 2 medium heads cauliflower
- 3 medium yellow onions
- 1 red onion
- 1 head garlic (10 cloves)
- 2-inch knob fresh ginger
- 3 red potatoes
- 2 medium sweet potatoes
- 2 red bell peppers
- 1 serrano pepper
- 1 pint cherry tomatoes (1 cup chopped)
- 2 carrots (1 cup grated or shredded)
- 3 large celery stalks (1½ cups chopped)
- 1 cup button mushrooms
- 2 bunches fresh cilantro
- 1 bunch fresh basil
- 3 medium bananas
- 1 lemon
- 2 apples, for serving with hummus
- ½ cup grapes

FROZEN

- 1 (10-ounce) bag frozen strawberries (3 cups)
- 1 (10-ounce) bag frozen blueberries (3 cups)
- 1 (10-ounce) bag frozen raspberries (3 cups)

PROTEIN AND DAIRY

- 11 large eggs
- 2 (14- to 16-ounce) packages extra-firm tofu
- 1 (5-ounce) container plain full-fat Greek yogurt
- ½ cup whole-milk ricotta cheese
- 2 cups shredded mozzarella
- 1 cup shredded sharp or white cheddar cheese
- Grated Parmesan cheese
- Unsweetened almond milk

GRAINS

- 7 cups old-fashioned rolled oats
- 1⅔ cups brown rice
- ½ cup quinoa
- Whole wheat wrap, pita pocket, bread, or crackers if desired for curried tofu salad

CANNED AND PACKAGED ITEMS

- Pure maple syrup or honey
- 1 cup pizza sauce
- 2 (15-ounce) cans white cannellini beans
- 1 (15-ounce) can chickpeas
- 1 (28-ounce) can crushed tomatoes
- 1 (4.5-ounce) tube or (6-ounce) can tomato paste
- 2 (13.5-ounce) cans full-fat coconut milk
- 1 (2.25-ounce) can sliced black olives
- Almond butter
- Cashew butter
- Avocado oil mayonnaise
- Avocado oil cooking spray
- Avocado oil
- Olive oil
- Coconut oil

- Apple cider vinegar
- Buffalo sauce
- Vegetable broth (4 cups)
- 1 (7-ounce) jar oil-packed sun-dried tomatoes
- 2 cups raisins
- 1 cup chocolate chips
- 1 (12-ounce) package Medjool dates (about 15 dates)
- Hot sauce
- Sliced almonds
- Chopped walnuts
- Roasted cashews
- Raw pepitas
- Raw sunflower seeds
- Chia seeds
- Hemp seeds
- Cocoa powder
- Unsweetened shredded coconut
- Vanilla extract

SEASONINGS

- Fine sea salt
- Ground black pepper
- Ground cardamom
- Ground cinnamon
- Ground cloves
- Ground ginger
- Dried basil
- Dried dill
- Dried parsley
- Garlic powder
- Onion powder
- Yellow curry powder
- Garam masala
- Paprika
- Italian seasoning
- Crushed red pepper (optional)

Winter

	MONDAY	TUESDAY	WEDNESDAY	THURSDAY	FRIDAY	SATURDAY	SUNDAY
BREAKFAST	Freezer Breakfast Sandwiches	Instant Oatmeal Packet— Apple Cinnamon	Instant Oatmeal Packet— Brown Sugar Walnut	Freezer Breakfast Sandwiches	Instant Oatmeal Packet— Brown Sugar Walnut	Freezer Breakfast Sandwiches	Instant Oatmeal Packet— Apple Cinnamon
LUNCH	Kale Edamame Salad with Zesty Almond Dressing	Kale Edamame Salad with Zesty Almond Dressing	20-Minute Veggie Lo Mein Bowls	Red Lentil and Sweet Potato Curry leftovers	Red Lentil and Sweet Potato Curry	Creamy "No Cream" Broccoli Cheese Soup	Creamy "No Cream" Broccoli Cheese Soup
DINNER	Veggie Sausage with Potatoes, Peppers, and Onions	20-Minute Veggie Lo Mein Bowls	Red Lentil and Sweet Potato Curry	Tofu Shakshuka	Creamy "No Cream" Broccoli Cheese Soup	Dinner out!	Tofu Shakshuka
SNACK	Pizza Trail Mix	Chocolate Chip Cookie Dough Bites	Pizza Trail Mix	Chocolate Chip Cookie Dough Bites	Pizza Trail Mix	Chocolate Chip Cookie Dough Bites	Pizza Trail Mix or Chocolate Chip Cookie Dough Bites

SUNDAY

- Batch-cook 6 cups brown rice for Red Lentil and Sweet Potato Curry and Tofu Shakshuka. Follow the instructions in the EBF Batch-Cooking Basics section (page 21). You'll need 2 cups brown rice and 5 cups water.

- Fully make Instant Oatmeal Packets (page 57).

- Fully make Freezer Breakfast Sandwiches (page 69).

- Fully make Kale Edamame Salad with Zesty Almond Dressing (page 119).

- Fully make Veggie Sausage with Potatoes, Peppers, and Onions (page 162) or prep as much as possible.

- Fully make 20-Minute Veggie Lo Mein Bowls (page 129) or prep as much as possible.

- Fully make Red Lentil and Sweet Potato Curry (page 188) or prep as much as possible.

- Fully make Pizza Trail Mix (page 217).

- Fully make Chocolate Chip Cookie Dough Bites (page 230).

WEDNESDAY

- Fully make Tofu Shakshuka (page 180) or prep as much as possible.

- Fully make Creamy "No Cream" Broccoli Cheese Soup (page 195) or prep as much as possible.

WINTER SHOPPING LIST

PRODUCE

- 1 bunch curly kale
- 2 cups baby spinach
- 1 (3.5-ounce) package shiitake mushrooms
- 1 head cauliflower
- 8 cups broccoli florets (about 2 heads)
- 1 cup snow peas
- 6 large carrots
- 4 medium yellow onions
- 1 red onion
- 1 bunch green onions
- 3 heads garlic (19 cloves)
- 2-inch piece fresh ginger
- 3 red bell peppers
- 1 green bell pepper
- 1 orange bell pepper
- 3 medium red potatoes
- 2 medium sweet potatoes
- 1 bunch fresh cilantro
- 1 bunch fresh parsley
- 1 lemon
- 1 lime

FROZEN

- 1 (12-ounce) bag frozen shelled edamame

PROTEIN AND DAIRY

- 12 large eggs
- 1 (14- to 16-ounce) package extra-firm tofu
- 1 (14-ounce) package plant-based Italian sausage links (I like Beyond Meat hot Italian sausages)
- 12 slices sliced pepper Jack or cheddar cheese
- 12 cups shredded cheddar cheese
- ½ cup crumbled feta cheese
- Unsweetened oat or almond milk

GRAINS

- 5¾ cups old-fashioned rolled oats
- Almond flour
- 1 (8-ounce) package whole-wheat spaghetti
- ⅓ cup quinoa
- 2 cups brown rice
- 12 English muffins
- Toasted sourdough bread, pita, or naan (optional)

CANNED AND PACKAGED ITEMS

- 1 (28-ounce) can diced tomatoes
- 1 (14-ounce) can diced tomatoes
- 1 (4.5-ounce) tube or (6-ounce) can tomato paste
- 1 (13.5-ounce) can light coconut milk
- Creamy almond butter
- Dry-packed sun-dried tomatoes
- Reduced-sodium tamari, reduced-sodium soy sauce, or coconut aminos
- Pure maple syrup
- Coconut oil
- Toasted sesame oil
- Olive oil
- Avocado oil
- Sriracha
- Honey
- Vegetable broth (6 cups)
- Nutritional yeast
- Unsweetened shredded coconut

- 1 cup dried red lentils
- Dried apples
- Chopped walnuts
- Dry-roasted and salted almonds
- Raw cashews
- Raw almonds
- Raw walnuts
- Brown sugar
- Mini chocolate chips

SEASONINGS

- Fine sea salt
- Ground black pepper
- Ground cinnamon
- Ground cumin
- Ground nutmeg
- Ground turmeric
- Cayenne pepper
- Chili powder
- Garam masala
- Onion powder
- Garlic powder
- Yellow curry powder
- Paprika
- Dried basil
- Dried oregano
- Dried thyme
- Italian seasoning

Breakfast

42 Chia Pudding (3 Ways)

47 Overnight Oats (4 Ways)

50 Butternut Squash Baked
    Oatmeal Cups

53 Kale Breakfast Quesadillas

54 PB&J Yogurt Jars

57 Instant Oatmeal Packets (4 Ways)

58 Sweet Potato Pancakes

61 Crunch Factor Granola

62 Zucchini Bread Breakfast Cookies

65 Chive, Potato, and Feta Egg Cups

66 Veggie Quiche with Sweet
    Potato Crust

69 Freezer Breakfast Sandwiches

70 Cottage Cheese Parfaits with
    Blueberry Compote

73 Savory Baked Oatmeal

74 Cinnamon Roll Baked Oatmeal

77 Roasted Veggie Breakfast Salad

Chia Pudding (3 Ways)

Basic chia pudding is one of the most popular recipes on my website and for good reason! Not only are chia seeds loaded with omega-3 fatty acids, fiber, and plant-based protein, but they've also been shown to control blood sugar levels, help with weight loss, and improve digestion. After the seeds soak in liquid (I recommend a plant-based milk), they expand and turn into a creamy and delicious breakfast or snack that's super filling. Chia seeds don't have any flavor of their own, but as you'll see with the following chia pudding recipes, there are many ways to add flavor with mix-ins and toppings.

With the banana pudding and sweet potato pie flavors, I recommend using light canned coconut milk for rich flavor and a thick consistency, but you are welcome to use your favorite plant-based milk, if desired. If your chia pudding is too thick after setting in the fridge, you can thin it out with a little water or plant-based milk. If it's too thin, you can add more chia seeds. **Serves 3**

BANANA CHIA PUDDING

1 (13.5-ounce) can light coconut milk

6 tablespoons chia seeds

1 tablespoon pure maple syrup

½ teaspoon vanilla extract

2 bananas, peeled and mashed

1 tablespoon almond butter

In a medium bowl, stir together the coconut milk, chia seeds, maple syrup, and vanilla. Let sit for 5 minutes, then stir the mixture again to dissolve any clumps that may have formed. Stir in the mashed banana and almond butter. Cover and place in the fridge to set for at least 30 minutes.

NUTRITION FACTS

Per serving: 1 jar | Calories: 321 | Carbohydrates: 38g | Protein: 6g | Fat: 19g | Fiber: 10g | Sugar: 17g

SWEET POTATO PIE CHIA PUDDING

1 (13.5-ounce) can light coconut milk

½ cup water

6 tablespoons chia seeds

2 tablespoons pure maple syrup

2 teaspoons pumpkin pie spice

1 teaspoon vanilla extract

½ cup mashed cooked sweet potato

1 tablespoon almond butter

1 tablespoon chopped pecans (toasted, if desired), for topping

In a medium bowl, stir together the coconut milk, ½ cup water, chia seeds, maple syrup, pumpkin pie spice, and vanilla. Let sit for 5 minutes, then stir the mixture again to dissolve any clumps that may have formed. Stir in the sweet potato and almond butter. Cover and place pudding in the fridge to set for at least 30 minutes. Top with the pecans when ready to eat.

NUTRITION FACTS

Per serving: 1 jar | Calories: 311 | Carbohydrates: 27g | Protein: 6g | Fat: 21g | Fiber: 8g | Sugar: 4g

NO-SUGAR TRIPLE BERRY CHIA PUDDING

2 cups unsweetened almond milk

6 tablespoons chia seeds

3 or 4 drops liquid stevia

½ teaspoon vanilla extract

½ cup mixed blueberries, raspberries, and chopped strawberries

1 tablespoon sliced toasted almonds, for topping

In a medium bowl, stir together the almond milk, chia seeds, stevia, and vanilla. Let sit for 5 minutes, then stir the mixture again to dissolve any clumps that may have formed. Cover and place in the fridge to set for at least 30 minutes. Top with berries and almonds when ready to eat.

NUTRITION FACTS

Per serving: 1 jar | Calories: 187 | Carbohydrates: 16g | Protein: 6g | Fat: 12g | Fiber: 11g | Sugar: 2g

BRITTANY'S TIP

If you want the texture to be smooth like traditional pudding, you can combine all the ingredients (besides the toppings) in a blender, then refrigerate to set.

Serve Immediately: Once set, stir and add additional milk if the pudding seems too thick. Sprinkle on any toppings and enjoy.

Meal Prep: Divide the pudding into three small glass jars and seal tightly. When ready to serve, stir and add additional milk if the pudding seems too thick. Sprinkle on any toppings and enjoy.

Store: In the refrigerator for up to 5 days.

Overnight Oats (4 Ways)

If you love oatmeal but can't stand the thought of ha[...] of oats on a hot summer day, this recipe is for you! C[...] combination of fiber-rich rolled oats with liquid and [...] overnight in the fridge. They're meant to be eaten c[...] them an easy no-cook recipe and the perfect way t[...] during the warm summer months. This grab-and-[...] is super customizable, and while I'm giving you four delicious [...] variations to start with here, I'm also sharing the base recipe so that you can experiment by adding your favorite mix-ins and toppings to create the overnight oats of your dreams. **Serves 1**

BASIC OVERNIGHT OATS

½ cup old-fashioned rolled oats

½ cup plant-based milk of choice

1 to 2 teaspoons chia seeds

1 teaspoon pure maple syrup (optional)

Toppings of choice

1. Combine the oats, milk, chia seeds, and maple syrup in a bowl or jar and stir to fully combine.

2. Cover and place in the fridge overnight to soak. (In a pinch, you can shorten the soak time to 2 hours.)

NUTRITION FACTS

Per serving: 1 jar | Calories: 259 | Carbohydrates: 38g | Protein: 9g | Fat: 7g | Fiber: 8g | Sugar: 5g

TIRAMISU OVERNIGHT OATS

½ cup old-fashioned rolled oats

¼ cup cold brew coffee

¼ cup unsweetened almond milk or oat milk

¼ cup coconut yogurt or coconut cream

1 tablespoon pure maple syrup

1 teaspoon chia seeds

½ teaspoon vanilla extract

1 teaspoon unsweetened cocoa powder, plus more for dusting

1 teaspoon instant espresso powder

1. Combine the oats, cold brew, milk, yogurt, maple syrup, chia seeds, vanilla, cocoa powder, and espresso powder in a bowl or jar and stir to fully combine. Sprinkle on a bit more cocoa powder.

2. Cover and place in the fridge overnight to soak. (If you're in a rush, you can shorten the soak time to 2 hours.)

NUTRITION FACTS

Per serving: 1 jar | Calories: 349 | Carbohydrates: 55g | Protein: 12g | Fat: 8g | Fiber: 7g | Sugar: 18g

...I-SPICED OVERNIGHT OATS

½ cup old-fashioned rolled oats

½ cup unsweetened almond milk or oat milk

¼ cup mashed banana

1 teaspoon pure maple syrup

1 teaspoon chia seeds

½ teaspoon vanilla extract

¼ teaspoon ground cinnamon

¼ teaspoon ground ginger

⅛ teaspoon ground cardamom

⅛ teaspoon ground cloves

1. Combine the oats, milk, banana, maple syrup, chia seeds, vanilla, and spices in a bowl or jar and stir to fully combine.

2. Cover and place in the fridge overnight to soak. (If you're in a rush, you can shorten the soak time to 2 hours.)

NUTRITION FACTS

Per serving: 1 jar | | Calories: 300 | Carbohydrates: 52g | Protein: 9g | Fat: 6g | Fiber: 8g | Sugar: 13g

PEANUT BUTTER PROTEIN OVERNIGHT OATS

½ cup old-fashioned rolled oats

¾ cup unsweetened almond milk or oat milk

1 scoop (25 grams) vanilla protein powder

2 tablespoons natural peanut butter, reserve ½ tablespoon for drizzling on top

1 teaspoon chia seeds

½ teaspoon vanilla extract

1. Combine the oats, milk, protein powder, 1½ tablespoons of the peanut butter, chia seeds, and vanilla in a bowl or jar and stir to fully combine.

2. Cover and place in the fridge overnight to soak. (If you're in a rush, you can shorten the soak time to 2 hours.)

NUTRITION FACTS

Per serving: 1 jar | Calories: 526 | Carbohydrates: 45g | Protein: 34g | Fat: 23g | Fiber: 11g | Sugar: 4g

DARK CHOCOLATE OVERNIGHT OATS

½ cup old-fashioned rolled oats

¾ cup unsweetened almond milk or oat milk

1 tablespoon unsweetened cocoa powder

2 teaspoons pure maple syrup

2 teaspoons dark chocolate chips or cacao nibs, plus more for topping

1 teaspoon chia seeds

½ teaspoon vanilla extract

1. Combine the oats, milk, cocoa powder, maple syrup, chocolate chips, chia seeds, and vanilla in a bowl or jar and stir to fully combine.

2. Cover and place in the fridge overnight to soak. (If you're in a rush, you can shorten the soak time to 2 hours.)

NUTRITION FACTS

Per serving: 1 jar | Calories: 296 | Carbohydrates: 46g | Protein: 10g | Fat: 7g | Fiber: 8g | Sugar: 10g

BRITTANY'S TIPS

● I add maple syrup for a little sweetness to most of my overnight oats recipes, but you can also use honey or a sugar substitute such as liquid stevia or monk fruit if you want to lower the sugar content.

● Overnight oats are meant to be eaten cold, but if you can't stand the thought of cold oatmeal, you can warm them up. After the oats have soaked overnight, transfer them to a microwave-safe bowl and heat until warm, 30 to 60 seconds, or transfer them to a saucepan and heat over medium heat, stirring, until warm. You may want to add some additional milk while heating if oats are too thick.

Serve Immediately: After soaking, remove the lid and stir. If the oats seems too thick, you can add a little more milk. Add toppings of choice and enjoy.

Store: In the refrigerator for up to 5 days.

Meal Prep: When ready to enjoy, remove the lid and stir. If the oats seems too thick, you can add a little more milk. Add toppings of choice and enjoy.

Butternut Squash Baked Oatmeal Cups

3 cups old-fashioned rolled oats

1½ cups unsweetened almond or oat milk

1 cup canned butternut squash puree or mashed cooked butternut squash

⅓ cup pure maple syrup

2 large eggs, whisked, or 2 flax eggs (see tip)

1 tablespoon coconut oil, melted

1 teaspoon vanilla extract

1 teaspoon baking powder

1 teaspoon ground cinnamon

1 teaspoon pumpkin pie spice

½ teaspoon fine sea salt

⅓ cup chopped pecans

¼ to ½ cup chocolate chips, divided (dairy-free, if needed)

Nut butter, for topping (optional)

These oatmeal cups have all the comfort of a nutrient-dense bowl of oatmeal, but with the portability and convenience of a muffin. While butternut squash tastes similar to pumpkin, it has double the fiber and iron and a bit more vitamin A and C. That said, you're welcome to use canned pumpkin if that's what you have on hand. These cups are relatively low in calories, so I recommend having two and/or pairing them with yogurt, eggs, fruit, or a smoothie for a more substantial breakfast. **Serves 12**

1. Preheat the oven to 350°F. Line a 12-cup muffin tin with silicone liners.

2. In a large bowl, mix together the oats, milk, butternut squash, maple syrup, eggs, coconut oil, vanilla, baking powder, cinnamon, pumpkin pie spice, and salt.

3. Stir in the chopped pecans and chocolate chips.

4. Scoop the mixture evenly into the lined muffin cups.

5. Bake for 30 to 35 minutes, until the center of each baked oatmeal cup is set and a toothpick comes out clean.

Serve Immediately: Enjoy warm. They're tasty plain, but absolutely delicious with a dollop of nut butter spread on top.

Meal Prep: Allow the cups to cool, then transfer to an airtight container. When ready to serve, follow the reheat instructions. They're tasty plain, but absolutely delicious with a dollop of nut butter spread on top.

Store: In the refrigerator for up to 5 days or in the freezer for up to 3 months.

Reheat: From the refrigerator, wrap one oatmeal cup in a paper towel and microwave until warm throughout, 30 to 60 seconds. Another option is to cut the cup in half and reheat in the toaster oven.

From the freezer, thaw a frozen cup by transferring it from the freezer to the refrigerator the night before, or defrost the cup in the microwave directly from frozen. Just wrap the frozen cup in a paper towel and heat in 30-second increments until warm throughout, about 1 minute. Once the cup is thawed, you can cut the cup in half and pop it in the toaster oven to crisp up a bit.

NUTRITION FACTS

Per serving: 1 cup | Calories: 192 | Carbohydrates: 27g | Protein: 6g | Fat: 7g | Fiber: 4g | Sugar: 7g

Kale Breakfast Quesadillas

5 large eggs

1 tablespoon unsweetened almond milk

1 tablespoon taco seasoning

1 teaspoon garlic powder

1 teaspoon fine sea salt

½ teaspoon ground black pepper

1½ teaspoons olive or avocado oil

½ cup diced yellow onion

2 cups (loosely packed) finely chopped kale

1 (15-ounce) can black beans, drained and rinsed

¼ cup chopped fresh cilantro

6 corn-and-flour tortillas (preferably whole-wheat flour)

1½ cups shredded pepper Jack cheese (or plant-based shredded cheese)

Guacamole and salsa, for serving

I'm calling these breakfast quesadillas because they have scrambled eggs in them, but you can eat them any time of the day. They're really easy to make and freeze well, so they're perfect for keeping your freezer stocked with a quick breakfast. If you're in a rush, they are great without toppings, but I love serving them with a side of guacamole and fresh salsa. **Serves 6**

1. In a large bowl, whisk together the eggs, milk, taco seasoning, garlic powder, salt, and pepper. Set aside.

2. Heat the oil in a large nonstick skillet over medium heat. Add the onion and sauté until translucent, 4 to 5 minutes. Add the kale and cook, stirring often, until it begins to wilt, about 1 minute. Reduce the heat to medium-low, add the black beans, and carefully pour in the egg mixture. Add the cilantro.

3. Cook the eggs low and slow, using a spatula to move the eggs around the pan often. Continue cooking until the eggs are scrambled and just set, about 5 minutes. Taste and season with additional salt or pepper, if needed. Remove from the heat. (If freezing the quesadillas, let the filling cool completely before proceeding.)

4. To assemble the quesadillas, sprinkle each tortilla with ¼ cup shredded cheese, leaving a small border all the way around the edge. Divide the egg mixture evenly on top, then fold the tortilla in half.

Serve Immediately: Carefully wipe out the skillet you used to cook the eggs (it may still be hot). Increase the heat to medium and lightly coat the skillet with nonstick cooking spray. Cook the assembled quesadillas on both sides until golden and the cheese is melted, 5 to 6 minutes total. Cut into wedges and serve warm with salsa and guacamole.

Store: In the freezer for up to 2 months.

Reheat: To cook from frozen, remove the plastic wrap and warm the quesadilla in the microwave until heated through, 2 to 3 minutes. Alternatively, you can let them thaw overnight in the refrigerator and cook in a skillet. I prefer to cook them in the skillet so the tortilla gets a little golden and crisp.

Meal Prep: To freeze, wrap each assembled quesadilla individually in plastic wrap. Arrange the quesadillas in a single layer on a baking sheet and freeze until the quesadillas are firm, then transfer them to a freezer bag or airtight container. When ready to serve, follow the reheat instructions. If possible, serve with salsa and guacamole.

NUTRITION FACTS

Per serving: 1 quesadilla | Calories: 305 | Carbohydrates: 22g | Protein: 20g | Fat: 16g | Fiber: 4g | Sugar: 1g

PB&J Yogurt Jars

Raspberry Chia Jam

1 cup fresh or frozen raspberries

1 tablespoon chia seeds

1½ teaspoons fresh lemon juice

1 teaspoon pure maple syrup or honey, plus more to taste (optional)

Yogurt Jars

3 cups plain full-fat Greek yogurt or coconut milk yogurt

¼ cup natural creamy or crunchy peanut butter

½ cup Crunch Factor Granola (page 61) or granola of choice, for topping

Remember when fruit-on-the-bottom yogurt cups were all the rage? I may be dating myself, but I loved those fruity cups and even thought they were healthy until I read the ingredient list one day and realized they used high-fructose corn syrup as a sweetener! With this recipe we use a low-sugar raspberry chia jam to line the bottom of the jar (and sweeten the protein-rich Greek yogurt a touch) and then top each with a little natural peanut butter for a delicious, classic combo that never gets old. You can add some texture with a granola topping (try my Crunch Factor Granola, page 61), but I recommend storing the granola separately and adding it right before serving, otherwise the granola will soften. **Serves 4**

1. To make the jam, put the raspberries in a small saucepan and cook over medium-high heat until the berries start to break down and the mixture is bubbling, 8 to 10 minutes. Use the back of a spoon or potato masher to mash the berries to your desired consistency.

2. Stir in the chia seeds and lemon juice. Carefully taste (the jam will be warm) and add sweetener, if desired. If your berries are sweet, you might not need to add any sweetener at all.

3. Remove the saucepan from the heat and set aside to cool and thicken, 5 to 10 minutes.

Serve Immediately: Spoon 2 to 3 tablespoons chia jam into each bowl, then top with ¾ cup yogurt and 1 tablespoon peanut butter. Use a spoon to swirl the peanut butter and chia jam into the yogurt. Sprinkle 2 tablespoons granola on top and enjoy.

Meal Prep: Spoon 2 to 3 tablespoons chia jam into 4 small jars, top each with ¾ cup yogurt and 1 tablespoon peanut butter. Cover the jars. Store the granola in a separate container at room temperature. When ready to serve, sprinkle on 2 tablespoons granola and enjoy.

Store: In the refrigerator for up to 1 week.

BRITTANY'S TIPS

These jars are super customizable in terms of the type of yogurt and nut butter you use. I recommend plain full-fat Greek yogurt for a protein-packed, low-sugar option and I love the flavor of peanut butter, but almond butter or cashew butter would be great as well.

The leftover jam can be used the same way you'd use regular jam—stirred into oatmeal, on toast, in a sandwich, or even as a filling for thumbprint cookies.

NUTRITION FACTS

Per serving: 1 jar | Calories: 399 | Carbohydrates: 23g | Protein: 22g | Fat: 21g | Fiber: 5g | Sugar: 16g

Instant Oatmeal Packets (4 Ways)

Time to upgrade those instant oatmeal packets you used to love as a kid (or still enjoy from time to time) with convenient homemade mixes. Making your own is less expensive, and you get to decide what goes into each packet, including how much sugar to add, if any, making them a healthier option as well. Using a blend of rolled oats and oat flour makes for quick and easy "instant" oatmeal that can be soaked in hot water or microwaved for an easy breakfast that's ready in less than 5 minutes. I've come up with four flavor options to get you started. Choose your favorite flavor and make a dozen packets, or make a few of each for a little variety. **Serves 12**

5¾ cups old-fashioned rolled oats, divided

Apple Cinnamon

1 tablespoon dried apples, chopped

¼ teaspoon ground cinnamon

Pinch fine sea salt

Blueberry Almond

1½ tablespoons dried or freeze-dried blueberries

1 tablespoon slivered almonds, chopped

Pinch fine sea salt

Brown Sugar Walnut

1 tablespoon chopped walnuts

2 teaspoons brown sugar or coconut sugar

Pinch fine sea salt

Super Seed

1 teaspoon ground flaxseed

1 teaspoon chia seeds

1 teaspoon hemp seeds

Pinch fine sea salt

1. Put 1¾ cups of the oats in a high-powered blender and blend into a fine flour.

Serve Immediately: Line up a bowl for each serving. Fill each with ⅓ cup whole rolled oats and 2 tablespoons oat flour. Add the appropriate mix-ins to each, depending on which flavor(s) you prefer. Cover the bowl with a plate to prevent the steam from escaping and let sit for 5 minutes. Remove the plate, stir the oats, and add any additional toppings or sweetener, if desired.

Alternatively, you can add ¾ cup water to a microwave-safe bowl, cover with a paper towel, and microwave for 2 minutes. Watch carefully near the end of the cooking time to make sure the oatmeal doesn't overflow. Stir the oats and add any additional toppings or sweetener, if desired.

Store: In the pantry for up to 1 month.

Meal Prep: Line up 12 small silicone or plastic bags or glass jars and fill each one with ⅓ cup whole rolled oats and 2 tablespoons oat flour. Add the appropriate mix-ins to each depending on which flavor(s) you prefer. When ready to enjoy, empty contents into a bowl (microwave-safe if necessary) and follow the serve-immediately instructions to heat.

NUTRITION FACTS

Per serving: 1 packet without mix-ins | Calories: 182 | Carbohydrates: 31g | Protein: 7g | Fat: 3g | Fiber: 5g | Sugar: 1g

Sweet Potato Pancakes

1⅓ cups old-fashioned rolled oats

2 large eggs, whisked, or 2 flax eggs (see tip)

½ cup mashed baked sweet potato

½ cup unsweetened almond milk

1 tablespoon pure maple syrup, plus more for topping

½ teaspoon vanilla extract

1 teaspoon baking powder

1 teaspoon ground cinnamon

¼ teaspoon fine sea salt

Pure maple syrup, for topping

Nut butter, for topping (optional)

Pancakes aren't just for weekend brunch anymore! When they're loaded with nutrient-dense ingredients (like whole-grain oats and sweet potato), you can feel good about eating them any day of the week, and they're surprisingly easy to prep. When my daughter was little, she was obsessed with pancakes and would ask for them almost every morning. Since I didn't have time to make them every day, I started making a big batch on Sunday to have on hand for a few days. The version I made for her was a simple blend of oats, mashed banana, and egg, which inspired this recipe for blender sweet potato pancakes. While these pancakes are a bit more elevated, they're still kid-friendly and great for when you have a leftover baked sweet potato that needs to be used up: 1 sweet potato will usually result in ½ cup mashed sweet potato. If you know you want to make these sweet potato pancakes as part of your meal prep, just be sure to pop an extra potato in the oven at dinner so you'll have your mashed sweet potato ready to go! **Serves 2**

1. Combine the oats, eggs, sweet potato, almond milk, maple syrup, vanilla, baking powder, cinnamon, and salt in a blender and blend until the batter is smooth. It's okay if there's a bit of texture from the oats.

2. Heat a large skillet or griddle over medium-low heat and spray with cooking spray, if necessary.

3. Scoop about ¼ cup batter for each pancake into the skillet.

4. Cook until little bubbles form and the edges of the pancakes are solid enough to put a spatula underneath, 4 to 5 minutes. Flip the pancakes and cook the other side for 1 for 2 minutes. Transfer the pancakes to a plate and continue with the remaining batter until you've used it all.

Serve Immediately: Place 4 pancakes on each plate, drizzle with maple syrup and/or nut butter, and enjoy.

Meal Prep: Allow the pancakes to cool and place in a storage container. To freeze, place on a parchment-lined baking sheet and freeze until firm, about 1 hour. Transfer the pancakes to a freezer bag. You can separate each pancake with parchment paper to prevent sticking, if desired. When ready to serve, follow the reheat instructions. Drizzle with maple syrup and/or nut butter and enjoy.

Store: In the refrigerator for up to 3 days or in the freezer for up to 3 months.

BRITTANY'S TIPS

🔘 To make 2 flax eggs, whisk together 2 tablespoons ground flaxseed and 6 tablespoons water. Let the mixture sit for 5 minutes to thicken and then use in place of the eggs.

🔘 You can also use this recipe to make waffles. Simply grease a waffle iron, pour on half of the batter, close the waffle iron, and cook until waffle is cooked through and golden. Repeat with the remaining batter.

Reheat: From the fridge, place 4 pancakes on a plate in a single layer and heat in the microwave until warm, 20 to 30 seconds.

From the freezer, place 4 pancakes on a plate in a single layer and microwave for 30 to 60 seconds. Alternatively, heat in a 375°F oven or toaster oven for 7 to 10 minutes.

NUTRITION FACTS

Per serving: 4 pancakes without toppings | Calories: 428 | Carbohydrates: 66g | Protein: 17g | Fat: 10g | Fiber: 10g | Sugar: 13g

Crunch Factor Granola

  EF

3 cups old-fashioned rolled oats

½ cup raw sunflower seeds

¼ cup ground flaxseed

¼ cup coconut oil, melted

¼ cup pure maple syrup

¼ cup coconut sugar

3 tablespoons water

1 teaspoon ground cinnamon

½ teaspoon fine sea salt

As a granola lover, I've been on a mission to create an amazing homemade granola with big, crunchy clusters, and this recipe totally fits the bill! The crunch factor is spot-on—and maybe even more important, the granola holds together well, which means you end up with a ton of huge clusters after breaking it apart. There are a few things that help this granola stick together: ground flaxseed, hot water, and not stirring the granola halfway through cooking. That's it! No need for egg whites. As an added bonus, this granola is nut-free, which means it's school-safe and perfect for those with nut allergies. I also have to mention that it smells so dang good while it's baking. I wish I could bottle it up and make a granola-scented candle. **Serves 14**

1. Preheat the oven to 300°F. Line a rimmed baking sheet with parchment paper.

2. Combine all the ingredients in a large bowl and toss to combine.

3. Spread the granola mixture out on the prepared baking sheet, pressing the mixture down with a spatula.

4. Bake for 45 minutes without stirring. Let the granola cool completely on the pan, then break it apart into clusters.

Serve Immediately: Use as a topping for yogurt or oatmeal, or eat it by the handful as a snack.

Meal Prep: Transfer all the granola to an airtight container, or divide it into individual portions. Use as a topping for yogurt or oatmeal, or eat it by the handful as a snack.

Store: In the pantry for up to 3 weeks or in the freezer for up to 3 months.

BRITTANY'S TIPS

Feel free to add dried fruit or other mix-ins to the granola after it cools. It is amazing with dried blueberries, raisins, or even chocolate chips.

This granola keeps wonderfully at room temperature, but I love storing my granola in the freezer to keep it extra crisp.

NUTRITION FACTS

Per serving: ¼ cup | Calories: 186 | Carbohydrates: 23g | Protein: 4g | Fat: 9g | Fiber: 3g | Sugar: 8g

Zucchini Bread Breakfast Cookies

1¼ cups white whole-wheat flour or whole-wheat pastry flour

1 cup old-fashioned rolled oats

1 teaspoon ground cinnamon

½ teaspoon baking soda

¼ teaspoon fine sea salt

1 cup shredded zucchini (squeeze out all excess moisture with a paper towel or cheesecloth before measuring)

½ cup pure maple syrup

1 large egg or flax egg (see tip)

¼ cup unsweetened applesauce

¼ cup coconut oil, melted

1 teaspoon vanilla extract

¼ cup chopped walnuts

¼ cup chocolate chips

BRITTANY'S TIPS

You can use 1:1 gluten-free flour or all-purpose flour as a sub for the whole-wheat flour. If you want the cookies to be gluten-free, be sure your oats are certified gluten-free as well.

To make a flax egg, whisk together 1 tablespoon ground flaxseed and 3 tablespoons water. Let the mixture sit for 5 minutes to thicken, then use in place of the egg.

Feel free to swap the chocolate chips for raisins or dried cranberries, if preferred.

Cookies for breakfast? Yup, and they're mama approved! These cookies are made with whole-wheat flour, rolled oats, a minimal amount of pure maple syrup for sweetness, and loads of zucchini. While zucchini is technically a fruit and not a veggie (who knew?), it is still an amazing addition to these cookies. It keeps them moist and adds a ton of nutrients, including a good amount of vitamin A, which is beneficial for immune and eye health. I recommend pairing these cookies with a good source of protein for breakfast. I typically have two cookies along with a hard-boiled egg or a simple protein shake, and my daughter has one cookie as breakfast "dessert" after she's eaten a little yogurt with fruit or scrambled eggs.

When making these cookies, freeze any leftover zucchini for the Chocolate Peanut Butter Shake (page 95)! **Serves 16**

1. Preheat the oven to 350°F. Line a rimmed baking sheet with parchment paper.

2. In a medium bowl, whisk together the flour, oats, cinnamon, baking soda, and salt.

3. In a large bowl, mix together the shredded zucchini, maple syrup, egg, applesauce, coconut oil, and vanilla until well combined.

4. Add the dry ingredients to the wet ingredients and mix until just combined. Gently fold in the walnuts and chocolate chips.

5. Using a medium cookie scoop, scoop the dough onto the prepared baking sheet, leaving 1 to 2 inches of space around each one. Use the palm of your hand to gently flatten each cookie.

6. Bake for 14 to 16 minutes, until the cookies are golden and firm around the edges.

7. Cool the cookies on the baking sheet for 10 minutes, then carefully transfer the cookies to a rack to cool completely (otherwise, the bottoms can brown too much).

Serve Immediately: Let the cookies cool and enjoy.

Meal Prep: Place the cooled cookies in an airtight container until ready to enjoy.

Store: In the pantry for up to 2 days, in the refrigerator for up to 5 days, or in the freezer for up to 3 months.

NUTRITION FACTS

Per serving: 1 cookie | Calories: 129 | Carbohydrates: 17g | Protein: 3g | Fat: 5g | Fiber: 2g | Sugar: 6g

Chive, Potato, and Feta Egg Cups

1 tablespoon olive or avocado oil

1½ cups ¼-inch diced red potatoes

1 cup diced yellow onion

1 cup diced button mushrooms

½ teaspoon fine sea salt, divided

8 large eggs

½ cup oat milk

½ cup crumbled feta cheese

½ teaspoon ground black pepper

⅓ cup chopped fresh chives

Hot sauce, for serving (optional)

Egg cups (aka egg muffins) are like mini frittatas. I love
super easy to make and already pre-portioned so you
from the fridge, reheat, and enjoy. Sometimes I find t
super filling on their own for breakfast, but because
potatoes and extra veggies they're a bit heartier and
feeling full for longer. Plus, the combo of potato, chive,
delicious and satisfying. Pairing two of these cups with a side of fruit,
yogurt, or even a slice of avocado toast is a great way to start the day!
I usually serve them with a drizzle of hot sauce for a little heat. **Serves 6**

1. Preheat the oven to 325°F. Line a 12-cup muffin tin with silicone
liners or coat with nonstick cooking spray.

2. Heat the oil in a large skillet over medium heat. Add the potatoes,
onion, mushrooms, and ¼ teaspoon of the salt and cook, stirring
frequently, until the potatoes are just cooked through, about 15
minutes. Remove from the heat and let cool for 5 minutes.

3. In a large bowl, whisk together the eggs, milk, feta cheese,
pepper, and remaining ¼ teaspoon salt. Stir in the chives and the
cooled potato mixture. Divide the egg mixture among the prepared
muffin cups.

4. Bake for about 25 minutes, until the egg cups are firm to the
touch. Let stand for 5 minutes before removing from the muffin tin.

Serve Immediately: Enjoy
warm with a sprinkle of hot
sauce, if desired.

Meal Prep: Let the egg cups
cool, then place in a storage
container. When ready to serve,
follow the reheat instructions
and sprinkle on hot sauce, if
desired.

Store: In the refrigerator for up to 5 days or in the freezer for up to
3 months.

Reheat: From the fridge, wrap one or two egg cups in a paper
towel and microwave until warm throughout, about 30 seconds.
Alternatively, you can reheat the egg cups in a 375°F oven or toaster
oven for 5 to 7 minutes, until warm throughout. I prefer to bake the
egg cups to keep them from getting rubbery and to crisp up the
outer edges a bit, too.

From the freezer, thaw overnight and then follow the fridge
instructions, or wrap the frozen egg cup(s) in a paper towel and
microwave until warm throughout, 40 to 60 seconds.

BRITTANY'S TIPS

To make these dairy-free,
simply use a vegan feta. I
recommend Violife.

Swap the red skinned
potatoes for sweet potatoes
for a different spin on these
egg cups.

NUTRITION FACTS

Per serving: 2 egg cups | Calories: 234 | Carbohydrates: 14g | Protein: 13g |
Fat: 14g | Fiber: 2g | Sugar: 3g

Veggie Quiche
with Sweet Potato Crust

I used to make quiche with a store-bought crust, or I would just skip the crust. Until, that is, I discovered how delicious quiche is with a sweet potato crust—I don't think I'll ever go back! It adds just the right amount of starchiness, a little crunch, and a bit of sweetness. As an added bonus, sweet potato is naturally gluten-free and low in calories, and provides 4 grams of fiber per serving, plus vitamins A and C. For the filling on this quiche, I add even more veggies with a combination of onion, bell pepper, and spinach. Most quiches tend to be weighed down with a ton of cheese, but I kept this one dairy-free and instead used nutritional yeast, which adds the perfect amount of cheesy flavor. I promise you won't miss it! **Serves 4**

1 medium sweet potato, scrubbed or peeled

½ teaspoon olive or avocado oil

2 cloves garlic, minced

1 yellow onion, chopped

1 red, orange, or yellow bell pepper, seeded and chopped

1 teaspoon fine sea salt

¼ teaspoon ground black pepper

2½ cups (loosely packed) baby spinach

6 large eggs

⅔ cup unsweetened oat milk or other plant-based milk

2 tablespoons nutritional yeast

2 teaspoons dried Italian seasoning

1. Preheat the oven to 350°F. Spray an 8-inch pie plate with avocado oil cooking spray.

2. Slice the sweet potato into thin rounds using a mandoline slicer or a very sharp knife. You want the slices to be only about ⅛ inch thick.

3. Layer the sweet potatoes in the bottom of the prepared pie plate, overlapping them a bit to avoid gaps in the crust. Use smaller pieces to line the sides. If your sweet potato was particularly large, you may need to slice the rounds in half so there's no gap between the base and the side. Spray the sweet potatoes with more cooking spray.

4. Bake the crust for 15 to 20 minutes, until the sweet potato slices are bright in color and fork-tender. Remove from the oven and set aside while preparing the filling. Increase the oven temperature to 375°F.

5. While the crust is baking, heat the oil in a medium skillet over medium heat. Sauté the garlic, onion, and bell pepper until fragrant and softened, 5 to 7 minutes. Season with the salt and pepper. Add the spinach and cook until wilted, 1 to 2 minutes. Remove from the heat.

6. In a large bowl, whisk together the eggs, milk, nutritional yeast, and Italian seasoning. Stir in the sautéed veggies.

7. Pour the egg and veggie mixture into the sweet potato crust. Bake for 25 to 35 minutes, until the eggs have set. Let cool, then cut into 4 pieces.

Serve Immediately: Serve warm. Pair with sides of your choice. I recommend sliced avocado, a side salad, and/or mixed fruit.

Meal Prep: Place the cooled quiche in a storage container, either all together or in individual portions. When ready to serve, follow the reheat instructions and pair with sides of your choice. I recommend sliced avocado, a side salad, and/or mixed fruit.

Store: In the refrigerator for up to 4 days. I don't recommend freezing this quiche because the sweet potatoes will get soggy.

Reheat: Bake individual portions in a 350°F oven for 5 to 10 minutes, until heated through. Alternatively, you can microwave the quiche for about 1 minute.

NUTRITION FACTS

Per serving: ¼ quiche | Calories: 176 | Carbohydrates: 19g | Protein: 13g | Fat: 5g | Fiber: 5g | Sugar: 6g

Freezer Breakfast Sandwiches

 DF*

12 large eggs

½ cup unsweetened almond milk or other plant-based milk

½ teaspoon fine sea salt

¼ teaspoon ground black pepper

¼ cup dry packed sun-dried tomatoes, finely chopped

2 cups (loosely packed) baby spinach, finely chopped

12 whole-grain English muffins, split

12 slices pepper Jack or cheddar cheese or plant-based sliced cheese

Skip the morning drive-thru and stock your freezer with these veggie-packed egg and cheese sandwiches. We're starting with whole-grain English muffins (I really like the Dave's Killer Bread brand) and adding veggies to the egg mixture in the form of baby spinach and sun-dried tomatoes. When picking out sun-dried tomatoes at the store, look for ones that are dry-packed in a bag rather than in a jar with oil. They're less messy to chop and a bit healthier, too. For the cheese I recommend a flavorful cheese like pepper Jack, but cheddar works as well if you prefer it. Personally, I like to add a thin layer of jam to the English muffin when I make one of these sandwiches for myself. The sweet and savory combo is just so good! Try it with Raspberry Chia Jam (page 54). **Serves 12**

1. Preheat the oven to 350°F. Spray a 9 x 13-inch baking dish with nonstick cooking spray.

2. In a medium bowl, whisk together the eggs, milk, salt, and pepper. Stir in the sun-dried tomatoes and spinach. Pour the mixture into the prepared baking dish.

3. Bake for 20 to 25 minutes, until the eggs are set. Once cool enough to handle, cut into 12 squares.

4. To assemble, place 1 slice of cheese and 1 square of baked egg on the bottom half of each English muffin. Top with the other half to make a sandwich.

Serve Immediately: Heat in a 350°F oven or toaster oven for 5 to 6 minutes, until the cheese is melted and the English muffin is a bit crisp.

Store: In the freezer for up to 3 months.

Meal Prep: Wrap each sandwich in aluminum foil and place in a large freezer bag. When ready to serve, follow the reheat instructions and enjoy.

Reheat: To thaw, let the frozen sandwich defrost in the fridge overnight. Or, remove the foil, wrap the sandwich in a paper towel, and microwave on the defrost setting for 2 to 4 minutes, flipping the sandwich over halfway. Then reheat in a 350°F oven or toaster oven for 5 to 6 minutes, until warm throughout and the English muffin is a bit crisp. Alternately, you can microwave the thawed sandwich on high, 1½ to 2 minutes longer.

BRITTANY'S TIPS

⬤ If you don't want the eggs hanging over the edge of the English muffins, you can use a large biscuit cutter or wide-mouth mason jar to cut the eggs into perfect rounds. If you decide to do this, just snack on the leftover scraps.

⬤ If avoiding dairy, use your favorite plant-based sliced cheese, and double-check your English muffin ingredients, as many of them have milk products in them.

NUTRITION FACTS

Per serving: 1 sandwich | Calories: 268 | Carbohydrates: 29g | Protein: 15g | Fat: 10g | Fiber: 3g | Sugar: 3g

Cottage Cheese Parfaits
with Blueberry Compote

Sometimes the simplest breakfast recipes are the best, especially when you've got limited time in the morning. These cottage cheese parfaits make for a protein-packed breakfast and taste amazing with the blueberry compote, crunchy granola, and hemp seeds sprinkled on top. They're basically my version of those fruit-on-the-side cottage cheese packs you can find at the grocery store, but a bit more elevated with a delicious blueberry compote sweetened with coconut sugar. The compote is really easy to make with frozen blueberries, but you can use fresh berries if you happen to have a good amount on hand. You can also use different berries if you prefer; raspberries or strawberries would make for a tasty variation. **Serves 4**

Blueberry Compote

1 (12-ounce bag) frozen blueberries (about 2½ cups)

¼ cup coconut sugar

2 tablespoons water, plus more if needed

2 teaspoons fresh lemon juice

1 teaspoon cornstarch or arrowroot powder

Cottage Cheese Parfaits

2 cups full-fat or 2% cottage cheese

1 cup Crunch Factor Granola (page 61)

¼ cup hemp seeds

1. In a small saucepan, combine the blueberries, coconut sugar, water, and lemon juice. Bring to a low boil over medium heat and cook until the blueberries start to break down, 6 to 8 minutes. You can use the back of a spoon or spatula to mash them a bit as well.

2. Lower the heat to medium-low and continue to cook for 10 to 15 minutes, stirring frequently to prevent the blueberries from burning or sticking to the pan. If this starts to happen, lower the heat again and add a small amount of water.

3. Once the mixture has thickened up a bit, add the cornstarch and cook for an additional minute, letting the mixture thicken even more. Set aside to cool.

Serve Immediately: Spoon ¼ cup blueberry compote into each bowl. Top with ½ cup cottage cheese, ¼ cup granola, and 1 tablespoon hemp seeds.

Meal Prep: Spoon ¼ cup blueberry compote into 4 small jars, then add ½ cup cottage cheese, ¼ cup granola, and 1 tablespoon hemp seeds. Store in the fridge until ready to enjoy.

Store: In the refrigerator for up to 4 days.

NUTRITION FACTS

Per serving: 1 parfait | Calories: 369 | Carbohydrates: 52g | Protein: 15g | Fat: 12g | Fiber: 6g | Sugar: 33g

BRITTANY'S TIPS

● The pieces of granola that are touching the cottage cheese will get a bit soft. I don't mind this, but if you'd like to keep your granola extra crunchy, you can store it separately and add it to the cottage cheese parfait just before serving, along with the hemp seeds.

● Any extra blueberry compote can be stored in an airtight container in the refrigerator for up to 1 week. Use it as a topping for toast, pancakes, waffles, or even desserts like cheesecake and ice cream. Yum!

● Greek yogurt can easily be swapped in for the cottage cheese if you're not a fan.

Savory Baked Oatmeal

I'm such a creature of habit when it comes to oatmeal and typically gravitate toward sweet oats, but years ago I finally persuaded myself to try savory oatmeal and now it's one of my favorite things to eat for breakfast. This baked version packs in lots of veggies, including onions, mushrooms, and spinach, as well as an egg and fresh herbs for plenty of flavor. The Parmesan cheese really takes it to the next level and makes it feel like something you'd order at a fancy brunch spot. **Serves 6**

1½ teaspoons olive or avocado oil

1 cup chopped yellow onion

2 cups chopped mushrooms (any variety)

3 cups (loosely packed) baby spinach or baby kale

2 cups old-fashioned rolled oats

1 teaspoon baking powder

1½ teaspoons Italian seasoning or herbes de Provence

½ teaspoon fine sea salt

½ teaspoon ground black pepper

2 cups unsweetened almond milk or oat milk

1 large egg, whisked, or 1 flax egg (see tip)

¼ cup grated or shredded Parmesan cheese, plus more for serving (optional)

Chopped fresh herbs, for garnish (optional)

1. Preheat the oven to 375°F. Coat an 8-inch square baking dish with nonstick cooking spray.

2. In a medium skillet, heat the oil over medium heat. Add the onion and mushrooms and sauté until the onion is translucent and the mushrooms are soft, 5 to 10 minutes. Add the spinach and let wilt for 1 to 2 minutes. Remove the skillet from the heat.

3. In a large bowl, whisk together the oats, baking powder, Italian seasoning, salt, and pepper. Add the milk, egg, cooked vegetables, and Parmesan and mix well.

4. Pour the mixture into the prepared baking dish.

5. Bake for about 45 minutes, until the center is set and the top of the oatmeal is golden brown. Let rest for 5 minutes, then cut into 6 portions.

Serve Immediately: Serve warm with fresh herbs for garnish and a sprinkle of Parmesan cheese, if desired.

Meal Prep: Transfer the baked oatmeal to a storage container, all together or in individual portions. To freeze, wrap individual portions in plastic wrap and place in a freezer bag. When ready to serve, follow the reheat instructions and serve warm with fresh herbs for garnish and a sprinkle of Parmesan cheese, if desired.

Store: In the refrigerator for up to 4 days or in the freezer for up to 3 months.

Reheat: From the fridge, bake individual portions in a 350°F oven or toaster oven for 5 to 10 minutes, until warm, or microwave for 1 minute. From the freezer, thaw overnight in the refrigerator and then reheat as instructed above, or reheat from frozen in the microwave for 1 to 2 minutes.

BRITTANY'S TIPS

To make this dairy-free, use a plant-based Parmesan cheese or nutritional yeast.

To make a flax egg, whisk together 1 tablespoon ground flaxseed and 3 tablespoons water. Let the mixture sit for 5 minutes to thicken, then use in place of the egg.

NUTRITION FACTS

Per serving: 1 portion | Calories: 210 | Carbohydrates: 27g | Protein: 11g | Fat: 7g | Fiber: 5g | Sugar: 2g

Cinnamon Roll Baked Oatmeal

I am a self-proclaimed baked oatmeal fanatic, to the point where, for one year straight, I made a new baked oatmeal recipe every month to share on Eating Bird Food. I love the fact that it's so customizable, with never-ending flavor ideas and inspiration! I now have over 20 baked oatmeal recipes on my website, and I'm sure there are more to come. This version is inspired by cinnamon rolls and has all the flavor you'd expect from the breakfast treat, but with less effort and time (no kneading or rising involved, thank goodness). Of course, the ingredients used for this baked oatmeal are more nutrient-rich than traditional cinnamon roll ingredients as well. I've added pecans as a mix-in because I like the texture they add, but they're certainly not essential. The icing is a fun addition and really gives this baked oatmeal a cinnamon roll vibe, but it's optional as well. **Serves 6**

Oatmeal

2 cups old-fashioned rolled oats

1 teaspoon ground cinnamon

1 teaspoon baking powder

½ teaspoon fine sea salt

2 cups unsweetened vanilla almond milk

½ cup mashed banana or unsweetened applesauce

¼ cup pure maple syrup

1 large egg or flax egg (see tip)

1 tablespoon coconut oil, melted

1 teaspoon vanilla extract

¼ cup chopped pecans (optional)

Icing

3 tablespoons powdered sugar

1 teaspoon unsweetened vanilla almond milk

1. Preheat the oven to 375°F. Spray an 8-inch square baking dish with nonstick cooking spray.

2. In a large bowl, mix together the oats, cinnamon, baking powder, salt, almond milk, banana, maple syrup, egg, coconut oil, and vanilla. Stir in the pecans (if using).

3. Pour the mixture into the prepared baking dish.

4. Bake for about 40 minutes, until the center has set and a toothpick inserted in the center comes out clean. Let cool for 5 minutes, then cut into 6 pieces.

5. While the baked oatmeal is cooling, make the icing. In a small bowl, whisk together the powdered sugar and almond milk until smooth. Transfer to a zip-top plastic bag, snip the corner, and pipe the icing over the baked oatmeal. Alternatively, you can simply drizzle the icing over the baked oatmeal using a spoon. You can also add the icing right before serving, if desired.

Serve Immediately: Serve warm with icing.

Meal Prep: Transfer the baked oatmeal (with or without icing) to a storage container, all together or in individual portions. To freeze, wrap individual portions in plastic wrap and then place in a freezer bag. When ready to serve, follow the reheat instructions and enjoy.

Store: In the refrigerator for up to 6 days or in the freezer for up to 3 months.

BRITTANY'S TIPS

To make a flax egg, whisk together 1 tablespoon ground flaxseed and 3 tablespoons of water. Let the mixture sit for 5 minutes to thicken, then use in place of the egg.

Want to bump up the protein? Add a scoop of unflavored protein powder. It won't affect the flavor at all, and you shouldn't need to add more liquid.

BRITTANY'S TIPS

● For a lower-sugar option, feel free to skip the powdered sugar icing and drizzle the baked oatmeal with Coconut Butter (page 242).

Reheat: From the fridge, bake in a 350°F oven or toaster oven for 5 to 10 minutes, until warm, or microwave for 1 minute. From the freezer, thaw overnight in the refrigerator and then reheat as instructed above, or reheat from frozen in the microwave for 1 to 2 minutes.

NUTRITION FACTS

Per serving: 1 portion with icing | Calories: 235 | Carbohydrates: 37g | Protein: 6g | Fat: 6g | Fiber: 4g | Sugar: 15g

Roasted Veggie Breakfast Salad

Some might call me crazy, but I love having a salad for breakfast! It feels so good to start my day by getting in at least one serving of vegetables before noon. This salad starts with a base of baby arugula and quinoa, topped with perfectly roasted veggies and two hard-boiled eggs. It's vibrant, full of different textures and flavors, and really satisfying. While it's delicious served cold, you can also heat the greens, quinoa, and veggies in a sauté pan or in the microwave for a minute or two for a warm breakfast salad. **Serves 4**

1 large sweet potato, scrubbed and diced

1 pound Brussels sprouts, halved

1 red onion, diced

3 tablespoons olive oil

1 teaspoon herbes de Provence

1 teaspoon fine sea salt, plus more to taste

½ teaspoon ground black pepper, plus more to taste

8 hard-boiled eggs (see page 20)

8 cups (loosely packed) baby arugula

2 cups cooked quinoa (see page 20; use ⅔ cup quinoa + 1⅓ cups water or vegetable broth)

1. Preheat the oven to 400°F.

2. In a large bowl, toss the sweet potato, Brussels sprouts, and onion with the olive oil, herbes de Provence, salt, and pepper. Spread out the veggies on a rimmed baking sheet and roast for 40 minutes, tossing after 20 minutes. Let cool for 10 minutes.

Serve Immediately: Peel the eggs and cut them in half. Put 2 cups arugula and ½ cup quinoa in each bowl. Divide the roasted veggie mixture evenly on top, then add the egg halves. Season with salt and pepper and enjoy.

Meal Prep: Peel the eggs (you can cut the eggs in half in advance or just before serving). Put 2 cups arugula and ½ cup quinoa in 4 meal prep containers. Divide the roasted veggie mixture evenly on top, then add 2 hard-boiled eggs. Season with salt and pepper.

Store: In the refrigerator for up to 4 days.

NUTRITION FACTS

Per serving: 1 bowl | Calories: 465 | Carbohydrates: 45g | Protein: 23g | Fat: 22g | Fiber: 5g | Sugar: 5g

BRITTANY'S TIP

I find this salad flavorful enough without a dressing, but feel free to top with a drizzle of olive oil and vinegar or your favorite salad dressing to amp up the flavor, or sprinkle a little hot sauce on the veggies.

Smoothies

80 Back-on-Track Green Smoothie

83 Coffee Date Smoothie

84 Antioxidant Boost Smoothie

87 Peaches and Greens Smoothie

88 24 Carrot Gold Smoothie

91 Berry Oat Smoothie

92 Red Velvet Cake Batter Protein Smoothie

95 Chocolate–Peanut Butter Shake

96 Avocado Mango Smoothie

Back-on-Track Green Smoothie

 DF GF EF

You know the feeling when you get back from an indulgent vacation and you're ready to nourish your body with healthy food? This is the smoothie to make! It's loaded with two types of greens, lots of hydrating fruit, creamy almond milk, and fresh ginger, which is anti-inflammatory and soothing to the digestive system. This smoothie can easily be prepped ahead to save time—even before you leave for vacation. **Serves 1**

1¼ cups unsweetened almond milk

1 banana, sliced and frozen

½ cup frozen mango chunks

½ cup frozen pineapple chunks

½ cup baby spinach

½ cup chopped kale

1-inch knob fresh ginger, peeled

Serve Immediately: Combine all the ingredients in a high-powered blender in the order listed and blend until smooth. Pour into a glass and enjoy.

Meal Prep: Put the banana, mango, pineapple, spinach, kale, and ginger in a small freezer bag. Squeeze out any excess air. When ready to serve, pour the almond milk into your blender and add the contents of the bag. Blend until smooth. Pour into a glass and enjoy.

Store: Smoothie packs in the freezer for up to 3 months.

BRITTANY'S TIP

Feel free to swap the almond milk for coconut water if you prefer.

NUTRITION FACTS

Per serving: 1 smoothie | Calories: 244 | Carbohydrates: 51g | Protein: 6g | Fat: 5g | Fiber: 6g | Sugar: 31g

Coffee Date Smoothie

Whether you love the convenience of combining your morning coffee and your protein shake (one less cup to wash!) or need a little energy boost around 3 p.m., this smoothie will save the day. It has a subtle coffee flavor from the cold brew and a nice sweetness from the frozen banana and dates. The vanilla protein powder helps ensure the smoothie is filling and satisfying, and the frozen cauliflower rice adds nutrients and volume while giving the smoothie a creamy texture. Trust me, you won't be able to taste the cauliflower, and it's a great way to sneak another veggie into your day. **Serves 1**

¾ cup cold brew coffee

¼ cup unsweetened almond or oat milk

1 banana, sliced and frozen

½ cup frozen cauliflower rice

1 scoop (25 grams) vanilla protein powder

1 pitted Medjool date

Serve Immediately: Combine all the ingredients in a high-powered blender in the order listed and blend until smooth. Pour into a glass and enjoy.

Meal Prep: Put the banana, cauliflower rice, protein powder, and date in a small freezer bag. Squeeze out any excess air. When ready to serve, pour the cold brew and almond milk into your blender and add the contents of the bag. Blend until smooth. Pour into a glass and enjoy.

Store: Smoothie packs in the freezer for up to 3 months.

NUTRITION FACTS

Per serving: 1 smoothie | Calories: 358 | Carbohydrates: 62g | Protein: 20g | Fat: 4g | Fiber: 8g | Sugar: 40g

BRITTANY'S TIPS

Try a mocha version of this smoothie by using chocolate protein powder instead of vanilla.

I prefer the smooth taste of cold brew, but in a pinch you can use leftover cold coffee for this smoothie.

Antioxidant Boost Smoothie

1 cup unsweetened oat milk or almond milk

½ cup frozen blueberries

½ banana, sliced and frozen

1 cup fresh baby spinach or frozen spinach

1½ teaspoons walnut or almond butter

1 tablespoon unsweetened cocoa powder or raw cacao powder

1 pitted Medjool date

We all know that antioxidants are good for us, but do you know why? Here's the quick and dirty: Antioxidants are important because they protect against free radicals, which are just atoms that contain an unpaired (odd) number of electrons. Free radicals are necessary for life as they are a by-product of cell metabolism, but when free radicals outnumber antioxidants in our body they create oxidative stress, which leads to a variety of diseases and signs of aging (yes, even wrinkles). The blueberries, bananas, spinach, and cocoa powder give this smoothie a hefty dose of antioxidants, and I include walnut butter as well because, of all the tree nuts, walnuts, pecans, and chestnuts have the highest amount of antioxidants. If you don't have walnut butter on hand, you can throw in 2 tablespoons raw walnuts or use almond butter instead. **Serves 1**

Serve Immediately: Combine all the ingredients in a high-powered blender in the order listed and blend until smooth. Pour into a glass and enjoy.

Meal Prep: Put the blueberries, banana, spinach, walnut butter, cocoa powder, and date in a small freezer bag. Squeeze out any excess air. When ready to serve, pour the milk into your blender and add the contents of the bag. Blend until smooth. Pour into a glass and enjoy.

Store: Smoothie packs in the freezer for up to 3 months.

NUTRITION FACTS

Per serving: 1 smoothie | Calories: 315 | Carbohydrates: 60g | Protein: 9g | Fat: 6g | Fiber: 9g | Sugar: 37g

Peaches and Greens Smoothie

Peaches are one of my favorite summer fruits, so I stock up on them whenever they're at our local farmers' market. Sometimes I go overboard and buy too many to eat in a week, so I'll slice and freeze some for smoothies. This creamy peach smoothie is one of my favorite ways to use up the frozen peaches: You can't taste the spinach at all, and the combo of peach and banana is reminiscent of sorbet—it's especially delightful with a little cinnamon. The Greek yogurt adds a nice boost of protein as well. **Serves 1**

¾ cup unsweetened vanilla almond milk

½ banana, sliced and frozen

1 cup frozen sliced peaches

1 cup fresh baby spinach or frozen spinach

¼ cup plain Greek yogurt

¼ teaspoon ground cinnamon

Serve Immediately: Combine all the ingredients in a high-powered blender in the order listed and blend until smooth. Pour into a glass and enjoy.

Meal Prep: Put the banana, peaches, spinach, and cinnamon in a small freezer bag. Squeeze out any excess air. When ready to serve, pour the milk and yogurt into your blender and add the contents of the bag. Blend until smooth. Pour into a glass and enjoy.

Store: Smoothie packs in the freezer for up to 3 months.

BRITTANY'S TIP

You can sub nondairy yogurt for the Greek yogurt if needed.

NUTRITION FACTS

Per serving: 1 smoothie | Calories: 222 | Carbohydrates: 35g | Protein: 9g | Fat: 5g | Fiber: 6g | Sugar: 25g

24 Carrot Gold Smoothie

Inspired by a smoothie delivery service, this combination tastes like sweet potato pie, minus the crust. The texture is nice and thick from the frozen banana, sweet potato, and chia seeds, so go ahead and eat this one with a spoon if you prefer. Be sure to cook your sweet potato before freezing it. Chop it into chunks and steam or bake it, then mash it and pop it in the freezer in ¼-cup portions. There's no need to peel before cooking, as the skin will blend up nicely and you'll get all those added health benefits, including fiber, antioxidants, and nutrients like potassium, manganese, and vitamins A, C, and E. **Serves 1**

1 cup unsweetened vanilla almond milk

½ banana, sliced and frozen

¼ cup grated or chopped carrots

¼ cup frozen cooked sweet potato (see headnote)

1 pitted Medjool date

2 tablespoons walnuts

1½ teaspoons chia seeds

½ teaspoon ground cinnamon

⅛ teaspoon ground ginger

Pinch ground nutmeg

Serve Immediately: Combine all the ingredients in a high-powered blender in the order listed and blend until smooth. Pour into a glass and enjoy.

Meal Prep: Put the banana, carrots, sweet potato, date, walnuts, chia seeds, cinnamon, ginger, and nutmeg in a small freezer bag. Squeeze out any excess air. When ready to serve, pour the milk into your blender and add the contents of the bag. Blend until smooth. Pour into a glass and enjoy.

Store: Smoothie packs in the freezer for up to 3 months.

NUTRITION FACTS ————————————

Per serving: 1 smoothie | Calories: 332 | Carbohydrates: 50g | Protein: 7g | Fat: 15g | Fiber: 10g | Sugar: 27g

Berry Oat Smoothie

I can't remember the first time I added rolled oats to a smoothie, but it was way before oat milk was something we could pick up at the grocery store! I remember the oats adding a bit of creaminess and giving the smoothie a little texture, which I loved. So even though we're using oat milk for this smoothie to make it extra creamy, I highly recommend adding the rolled oats too. An added bonus here is that the only fruit included is berries, so it's relatively low in sugar when compared to other smoothies! Once blended, this has all the fun flavors of a PB&J, with a hidden veggie boost from the spinach. **Serves 1**

1 cup unsweetened oat or almond milk

½ cup frozen strawberries

½ cup frozen blueberries

½ cup frozen raspberries

1 tablespoon old-fashioned rolled oats

1½ teaspoons chia seeds

1½ teaspoons hemp seeds

1 teaspoon almond butter

1 cup fresh baby spinach or frozen spinach

Serve Immediately: Combine all the ingredients in a high-powered blender in the order listed and blend until smooth. Pour into a glass and enjoy.

Meal Prep: Put the berries, oats, chia seeds, hemp seeds, almond butter, and spinach in a small freezer bag. Squeeze out any excess air. When ready to serve, pour the milk into your blender and add the contents of the bag. Blend until smooth. Pour into a glass and enjoy.

Store: Smoothie packs in the freezer for up to 3 months.

NUTRITION FACTS

Per serving: 1 smoothie | Calories: 338 | Carbohydrates: 47g | Protein: 10g | Fat: 13g | Fiber: 14g | Sugar: 22g

Red Velvet Cake Batter Protein Smoothie

1¼ cups unsweetened vanilla almond milk

2 bananas, sliced and frozen

¼ cup chopped beets

2 scoops (50 grams) chocolate protein powder

½ teaspoon almond extract

½ teaspoon butter flavoring

1 tablespoon Coconut Butter (page 242) or cashew butter

A protein smoothie that tastes like cake…need I say more? Whether you're an avid red velvet cake person or not, you're going to love this unique combo with banana, raw beet, chocolate protein powder, and coconut butter. It has the dreamiest texture and really does taste—and look!—like red velvet cake batter. It's also a great way to incorporate a less-common vegetable into your diet. **Serves 2**

Serve Immediately: Combine all the ingredients in a high-powered blender in the order listed and blend until smooth. Pour into two glasses and enjoy.

Meal Prep: Put the banana, beets, chocolate protein powder, almond extract, butter flavoring, and coconut butter in a freezer bag. Squeeze out any excess air. When ready to serve, pour the milk into your blender and add the contents of the container. Blend until smooth. Pour into two glasses and enjoy.

Store: Smoothie packs in the freezer for up to 3 months.

NUTRITION FACTS

Per serving: ½ recipe | Calories: 283 | Carbohydrates: 32g | Protein: 22g | Fat: 9g | Fiber: 5g | Sugar: 16g

Chocolate–Peanut Butter Shake

1 cup unsweetened almond or oat milk

½ **banana, sliced and frozen**

½ **cup frozen chopped or grated zucchini**

2 pitted Medjool dates

1 scoop (25 grams) chocolate protein powder

1 tablespoon peanut butter

1 tablespoon unsweetened cocoa powder

3 or 4 ice cubes

BRITTANY'S TIP

Add 1 teaspoon maca powder to this smoothie to make it taste like a chocolate malted milkshake.

Healthy, veggie-filled, and loaded with protein...not how you'd typically describe your average chocolate shake, but we're making it happen with this one. The frozen banana and zucchini give it the perfect, creamy texture, and the Medjool dates add a good amount of sweetness. I can't resist adding peanut butter to my chocolate shakes, but you can omit it if you're craving a more classic flavor. **Serves 1**

Serve Immediately: Combine all the ingredients in a high-powered blender in the order listed and blend until smooth. Pour into a glass and enjoy.

Meal Prep: Put the banana, zucchini, dates, protein powder, peanut butter, and cocoa powder in a small freezer bag. Squeeze out any excess air. When ready to serve, add the milk, ice cubes, and the contents of the bag into your blender. Blend until smooth. Pour into a glass and enjoy.

Store: Smoothie packs in the freezer for up to 3 months.

NUTRITION FACTS

Per serving: 1 smoothie | Calories: 460 | Carbohydrates: 62g | Protein: 29g | Fat: 13g | Fiber: 7g | Sugar: 43g

Avocado Mango Smoothie

1 cup cold water

1½ cups frozen mango chunks

½ medium avocado

2 tablespoons unsweetened shredded coconut, plus more for topping

1 teaspoon honey or 1 pitted Medjool date

1 teaspoon fresh lime juice

½ teaspoon vanilla extract

BRITTANY'S TIP

Frozen avocado is really convenient for this smoothie and easy to find at most grocery stores now. You can also freeze fresh avocados if you have one that's perfectly ripe and you're not ready to use it!

If you've never tried avocado in your smoothies, I'm so excited for you to learn what you've been missing. Avocado is not only loaded with healthy fats that make smoothies ultra-satisfying, but it provides the most amazing, creamy texture. The added combo of mango and coconut for this smoothie makes it taste like a frozen tropical cocktail. Feel free to use fresh or frozen avocado for this smoothie! **Serves 1**

Serve Immediately: Combine all the ingredients in a high-powered blender in the order listed and blend until smooth. Add more liquid if necessary and/or more honey to get the consistency and sweetness level you like. Pour into a glass, top with shredded coconut, and enjoy.

Meal Prep: Put the mango, avocado, and coconut in a small freezer bag. Squeeze out any excess air. When ready to serve, pour the water into your blender and add the contents of the bag along with the honey or date, lime juice, and vanilla. Blend until smooth. Pour into a glass and enjoy.

Store: Smoothie packs in the freezer for up to 3 months.

NUTRITION FACTS

Per serving: 1 smoothie | Calories: 396 | Carbohydrates: 49g | Protein: 4g | Fat: 23g | Fiber: 12g | Sugar: 36g

Meal-Size Salads

100   Curried Tofu Salad

103   White Bean Quinoa Salad

104   Seaside Chickpea Salad

107   Walnut Pesto Pasta Salad

108   Mediterranean Farro
      Mason Jar Salads

111   Cobb Salad with Coconut Bacon

112   Harvest Kale Salad with
      Balsamic Tempeh and Wild Rice

115   Lentil Taco Salad Bowls

116   Buffalo Tofu Mason Jar Salads

119   Kale Edamame Salad
      with Zesty Almond Dressing

120   Black Bean and Sweet Potato
      Jar Salads

123   Greek Couscous Salad

Curried Tofu Salad

*

1 (14- to 16-ounce) package extra-firm tofu, pressed, drained, and cut into ¼-inch cubes

1 teaspoon fine sea salt, plus more to taste

½ teaspoon ground black pepper, plus more to taste

1 cup finely chopped celery

½ cup finely chopped red onion

½ cup raisins

½ cup chopped red grapes

½ cup roasted cashews, chopped

⅓ cup avocado oil mayonnaise or plant-based mayonnaise

2 tablespoons apple cider vinegar

1 tablespoon pure maple syrup

1 tablespoon yellow curry powder

1½ teaspoons olive oil

Chopped fresh cilantro, for garnish (optional)

This tofu salad is bursting with curry flavor, packs in a ton of fresh veggies, and has a delightful hint of sweetness from the raisins and grapes. Protein-packed salads like this one are great for meal prep because you can serve them up in a variety of ways for quick lunches through the week—over a bed of greens ("salad on salad," as I like to call it), wrapped in a lettuce leaf, stuffed into a wrap, as a filling for a sandwich, or straight up from the container, which is what I usually end up doing! When purchasing curry powder for this recipe, look for yellow curry powder, which is a vibrant spice blend usually containing ground turmeric, cumin, coriander, ginger, fenugreek, as well as other spices, depending on the blend. **Serves 6**

1. Heat a large skillet over medium heat and spray with avocado oil spray. Add the tofu, season with a little salt and pepper, and sauté, tossing occasionally, until golden brown on all sides, about 10 minutes. Transfer to a large bowl and let cool.

2. Once the tofu is cool, add the celery, red onion, raisins, grapes, and cashews and toss to combine.

3. In a small bowl, whisk together the mayonnaise, vinegar, maple syrup, curry powder, olive oil, salt, and pepper. Pour the dressing over the tofu mixture and toss to combine. Taste and add more pepper, if desired.

Serve Immediately: Serve in a lettuce wrap, collard wrap, whole-wheat wrap, or pita pocket, or on bread, with crackers, or over a bed of greens. Garnish with cilantro, if desired.

Meal Prep: Transfer the tofu salad to a storage container, all together or in 6 individual portions. Serve in a lettuce wrap, collard wrap, whole-wheat wrap, or pita pocket, or on bread, with crackers, or over a bed of greens. Garnish with cilantro, if desired.

Store: In the refrigerator for up to 5 days.

NUTRITION FACTS

Per serving: ⅙ recipe | Calories: 228 | Carbohydrates: 23g | Protein: 10g | Fat: 11g | Fiber: 3g | Sugar: 14g

White Bean Quinoa Salad

We're packing a protein punch with this salad, as each ser[...] grams! Unlike many plant-based protein sources, quinoa is a[...] protein containing all 9 essential amino acids. Not to mention, [...] contains a good amount of fiber and a variety of vitamins and mi[...] as well. The best part about this salad is how quickly it comes toget[...] since you can prep all the other ingredients while the quinoa cooks. Serve this salad as an easy lunch on its own or as a side salad with a main course. While it works anytime of the year, I find it best during the warm summer months when cherry tomatoes and basil are at their peak! **Serves 4**

3 cups cooked quinoa (see page 20; use 1 cup quinoa + 2 cups water)

1½ cups cherry tomatoes, finely chopped

1 (15-ounce) can cannellini beans, drained and rinsed

¾ cup crumbled feta cheese or plant-based feta cheese

½ cup diced red onion

¼ cup fresh lemon juice

¼ cup olive oil

1 teaspoon fine sea salt

½ teaspoon ground black pepper

1 cup chopped fresh basil

2 avocados, peeled, pitted, and chopped

1. In a medium bowl, stir together the cooked and cooled quinoa, tomatoes, beans, feta, and onion.

2. In a small bowl, whisk together the lemon juice, oil, salt, and pepper. Pour the dressing over the quinoa mixture, add the basil, and toss to combine. Serve the salad right away (below) or cover and let the mixture chill in the fridge for a few hours.

Serve Immediately: Evenly divide the salad into 4 bowls, top each with chopped avocado, and enjoy.

Meal Prep: Divide the salad evenly into 4 meal prep containers. Top with the avocado if desired. (I prefer to add the avocado right before serving so it stays fresh and doesn't turn brown.)

Store: In the refrigerator for up to 5 days.

NUTRITION FACTS

Per serving: ¼ recipe | Calories: 502 | Carbohydrates: 62g | Protein: 16g | Fat: 24g | Fiber: 15g | Sugar: 2g

BRITTANY'S TIPS

Pack more veggies into this salad by adding 1 cup baby spinach at the same time you add the cherry tomatoes.

To add more flavor, you can cook the quinoa in vegetable broth instead of water.

This plant-based take on tuna salad uses mashed chickpeas as the base, crumbled nori flakes for a hint of the sea, and a combo of tahini and vegan mayonnaise to bind it all together. While it doesn't taste exactly the same as tuna salad, it has its own delicious flavor (thanks to the fresh dill) and a nice crunch from the onion and celery. Plus, it's just as versatile and plenty filling. You can make a batch and have it for lunch in different ways throughout the week...serve it up with crackers, stuff it into a pita pocket, or make a lettuce wrap or an open-faced sandwich. All of these options would be great paired with a side of mixed fruit salad. **Serves 4**

2 (15-ounce) cans chickpeas, drained and rinsed

½ cup diced red onion

½ cup dill pickle relish

½ cup diced celery

¼ cup chopped fresh dill

4 snack-size sheets nori, crumbled

¼ cup tahini

2 tablespoons avocado oil mayonnaise (or plant-based mayonnaise)

4 teaspoons Dijon mustard

1 teaspoon fine sea salt

1 teaspoon ground black pepper

1. Put the chickpeas in a medium bowl and mash with a fork or potato masher until all the chickpeas are broken down but still have some texture.

2. Add the remaining ingredients and toss to combine. Taste and season with additional salt and pepper, if desired.

Serve Immediately: Serve in a lettuce wrap, collard wrap, whole-wheat wrap, or pita pocket, or on toasted bread, with crackers, or over a bed of greens.

Meal Prep: Transfer the chickpea salad to a storage container, all together or in 4 individual portions. Alternatively, you can make wraps and store those.

Store: In the refrigerator for up to 5 days.

BRITTANY'S TIP

Make a tasty open-faced "tuna" melt by dividing a portion of the salad between slices of toasted bread or English muffin halves. Top with sliced or shredded cheese and bake in a 375°F oven or toaster oven for 7 to 10 minutes, until the cheese is melted.

NUTRITION FACTS

Per serving: ¾ cup salad | Calories: 335 | Carbohydrates: 44g | Protein: 16g | Fat: 12g | Fiber: 15g | Sugar: 3g

Walnut Pesto Pasta Salad

Most pasta salads lack in the veggies and protein depa[...] this one. Thanks to the chickpea pasta and a variety o[...] this salad checks both boxes! While you could certainly [...] for a cookout or potluck contribution, it's also a flavorf[...] meal to bring to work when you're stuck in a salad rut. T[...] pesto sauce is made with walnuts instead of the typical [...] a budget-friendly spin. Plus, walnuts are quite a powerhouse when it comes to nutrition: They contain a high amount of omega-3 fatty acids and antioxidants, and studies have shown that walnuts can help lower cholesterol as well! **Serves 6**

Pasta Salad

2 (8-ounce) boxes chickpea rotini pasta

1 cup frozen peas, thawed

1 cup chopped cherry tomatoes

1 cup baby arugula

1 (8-ounce) package feta cheese or plant-based feta cheese, crumbled

1 tablespoon extra-virgin olive oil

Fine sea salt and ground black pepper to taste

Walnut Pesto

1 cup (loosely packed) baby arugula

1 cup (loosely packed) fresh basil

⅓ cup extra-virgin olive oil

Juice of 1 lemon (about 3 tablespoons)

1 clove garlic, peeled

¼ teaspoon fine sea salt

½ cup lightly toasted walnuts

1. Cook the pasta until al dente according to the package instructions. Rinse with cool water and drain. Let the pasta cool for 5 to 10 minutes.

2. Meanwhile, to make the pesto, combine the arugula, basil, olive oil, lemon juice, garlic, and salt in a food processor and process until smooth. Add the walnuts and pulse until the walnuts are ground to the desired consistency.

3. Transfer the pasta to a large bowl and toss with the thawed peas, tomatoes, arugula, feta, and olive oil. Add ½ cup pesto and mix well, then taste and add more if you'd like; I like my noodles well coated so I use all of the pesto. Taste and season liberally with salt and pepper.

Serve Immediately: Evenly divide the pasta salad into 6 bowls or plates and serve cold or at room temperature.

Meal Prep: Transfer to a large storage container or divide among 6 meal prep containers.

Store: In the refrigerator for up to 4 days.

NUTRITION FACTS

Per serving: ⅙ recipe | Calories: 551 | Carbohydrates: 58g | Protein: 26g | Fat: 28g | Fiber: 9g | Sugar: 4g

BRITTANY'S TIP

I prefer to use legume-based pasta for the added nutrients, but you can definitely make this dish with a 1-pound box of regular pasta if desired.

Mediterranean Farro Mason Jar Salads

If you're not cooking with farro, you're missing out! It has a delicious, mildly nutty flavor and an irresistible chewy texture. It also has a host of health benefits, providing fiber, B vitamins, iron, zinc, and a good amount of protein in each serving. As with all mason jar salads, we start by adding the vinaigrette on the bottom. This ensures that the chickpeas and tomatoes have time to soak in the dressing so they're extra flavorful, while the greens stay nice and fresh at the top of the jar. If you're not a farro fan or are gluten-free, you could easily use brown rice or quinoa instead. I find the mini mozzarella pearls to be the best size for this salad, but if you aren't able to find them at the store you can buy larger mozzarella balls and chop them into ¼-inch pieces. **Serves 6**

Red Wine Vinaigrette

1 cup extra-virgin olive oil

⅔ cup red wine vinegar

¼ cup fresh lemon juice

2 tablespoons Dijon mustard

2 cloves garlic, minced

2 teaspoons pure maple syrup or honey

2 teaspoons dried oregano

1½ teaspoons fine sea salt

1 teaspoon ground black pepper

Farro Salad

2 (15-ounce) cans chickpeas, drained and rinsed

1½ cups chopped cherry or grape tomatoes

1½ cups mozzarella pearls

1½ cups marinated artichoke hearts, drained and chopped

1½ cups cooked farro (see page 20; use ½ cup farro + 1¼ cups water or vegetable broth)

12 cups baby arugula

⅓ cup chopped dry-packed sun-dried tomatoes

1. Whisk together all the ingredients for the red wine vinaigrette in a bowl or glass jar.

2. Although you can simply assemble these salads in a bowl as follows, I like serving them out of jars, even if I'll be eating them right away, to really get everything coated in the dressing. To assemble the jars, spoon 3 tablespoons vinaigrette into 6 wide-mouth quart-size mason jars. Layer the ingredients in this order: ½ cup chickpeas, ¼ cup tomatoes, ¼ cup mozzarella pearls, ¼ cup artichoke hearts, ¼ cup farro, 2 cups arugula, and 1 tablespoon sun-dried tomatoes.

Serve Immediately: Shake the jar to coat the salad with dressing and pour into a large salad bowl or plate. You can eat it straight from the jar if needed, but I find it much easier to transfer the salad to another container.

Meal Prep: When ready to serve, shake the jar to coat the salad with dressing and pour into a large salad bowl or plate. You can eat it straight from the jar if needed, but I find it much easier to transfer the salad to another container.

Store: In the refrigerator for up to 1 week.

NUTRITION FACTS

Per serving: ⅙ recipe | Calories: 659 | Carbohydrates: 48g | Protein: 22g | Fat: 44g | Fiber: 13g | Sugar: 5g

BRITTANY'S TIP

If you don't have large mason jars, you can make these salads in any airtight containers. Line the bottom of the container with the arugula and layer all the ingredients one by one on top of the greens. Store the dressing in a separate container.

Cobb Salad
with Coconut Bacon

If I had to pick one salad to eat every day it would most likely be a Cobb salad. They're always packed with a variety of toppings and leave you feeling really satisfied, which isn't the case with some other salads. Here, we're putting a veggie spin on the Cobb by loading it up with plant-based toppings, including savory and crunchy coconut bacon. If you've never had coconut bacon, you're in for a treat! It adds the perfect amount of texture to this salad. The creamy avocado green goddess dressing really brings this salad to life! **Serves 4**

Avocado Green Goddess Dressing

½ ripe medium avocado

1 clove garlic, peeled

Juice of ½ lemon (about 1½ tablespoons)

1 tablespoon (packed) fresh cilantro

1 tablespoon (packed) fresh dill

2 tablespoons Greek yogurt or plant-based sour cream

1 tablespoon olive oil

1 tablespoon apple cider vinegar

½ teaspoon pure maple syrup

¼ teaspoon fine sea salt

⅛ teaspoon ground black pepper

¼ to ½ cup water

Cobb Salad

12 cups chopped romaine lettuce (about 3 romaine hearts)

1 (15-ounce) can chickpeas, drained and rinsed

4 baby cucumbers, sliced or chopped (about 1⅓ cups)

1 cup cherry or grape tomatoes, halved

1 cup grated or shredded carrots

½ cup thawed frozen corn kernels

½ cup chopped red onion

4 hard-boiled eggs (see page 20), sliced (optional)

½ cup crumbled blue cheese, feta cheese, or plant-based cheese

¼ cup chopped fresh dill

½ cup Coconut Bacon (page 246)

Fine sea salt and cracked black pepper to taste

Combine all the dressing ingredients (starting with ¼ cup water) in a high-powered blender and blend until smooth, adding up to ¼ cup more water if needed.

Serve Immediately: Make a bed of 3 cups romaine in each shallow bowl or plate and top with ⅓ cup chickpeas, ⅓ cup cucumber, ¼ cup tomatoes, ¼ cup carrots, 2 tablespoons corn, 2 tablespoons onion, 1 sliced hard-boiled egg (if using), 2 tablespoons cheese, 1 tablespoon dill, and 2 tablespoons coconut bacon. Drizzle on some dressing, season with salt and pepper, and enjoy.

Meal Prep: Line the bottoms of 4 meal prep containers with 3 cups romaine and top with ⅓ cup chickpeas, ⅓ cup cucumber, ¼ cup tomatoes, ¼ cup carrots, 2 tablespoons corn, 2 tablespoons onion, 1 sliced hard-boiled egg (if using), 2 tablespoons cheese, 1 tablespoon dill, and 2 tablespoons coconut bacon. Season with salt and pepper. Pack the dressing in separate containers and drizzle on the salad before serving.

Store: In the refrigerator for up to 5 days.

NUTRITION FACTS

Per serving: 1 salad with egg and 2 tablespoons dressing | Calories: 638 | Carbohydrates: 83g | Protein: 30g | Fat: 24g | Fiber: 26g | Sugar: 21g

Harvest Kale Salad
with Balsamic Tempeh and Wild Rice

I absolutely adore Sweetgreen salads, particularly their Harvest Bowl, but unfortunately I don't have a Sweetgreen location nearby, so I created this version, which features flavorful balsamic tempeh, roasted sweet potatoes, wild rice, apple, and shredded kale. You might be surprised to learn that wild rice, despite its name, isn't actually rice at all: It's the seed of an aquatic grass, and it contains more protein than other rices, as well as the same amount of fiber as brown rice. I find wild rice a bit firm on its own, so for this recipe I recommend using a wild rice blend that combines wild rice with black, brown, and red rice. It's hearty, filling, and can be served cold or with warm components if you're craving something cozy on a cool day! **Serves 6**

Balsamic Tempeh

2 tablespoons pure maple syrup

2 tablespoons balsamic vinegar

1½ teaspoons reduced-sodium tamari, reduced-sodium soy sauce, or coconut aminos

2½ teaspoons avocado or olive oil, divided

1 clove garlic, minced

1 (8-ounce) package tempeh (gluten-free if needed), cut into ⅓-inch cubes

Salad Bowls

2 medium sweet potatoes, scrubbed and diced

2 teaspoons olive or avocado oil

2 bunches lacinato kale, chopped (about 8 cups)

3 cups cooked wild rice blend (follow the package instructions, using 1 cup wild rice blend and 1¾ cups water)

1 sweet apple, cored and chopped (I like Honeycrisp)

4 ounces goat cheese, crumbled

¼ cup slivered almonds, toasted

1. In a shallow dish, whisk together the maple syrup, balsamic vinegar, tamari, 1 teaspoon of the oil, and the garlic. Add the tempeh and toss to coat. Cover and let the tempeh marinate in the fridge for at least 1 hour or up to 24 hours. Stir the mixture a couple times while marinating.

2. Meanwhile, preheat the oven to 400°F. Spread out the sweet potato chunks on a rimmed baking sheet. Add the oil and toss well. Roast for 30 to 40 minutes, until tender. Let cool.

3. Combine all the dressing ingredients in a blender and blend until smooth. Set aside.

4. Heat the remaining 1½ teaspoons oil in a large skillet over medium-high heat. Add the tempeh (without pouring the marinade in) and cook until golden brown, 4 to 5 minutes per side. Pour in the marinade and simmer, tossing occasionally, until the sauce has reduced to a glaze on the tempeh, 5 to 7 minutes.

5. Remove from the heat.

Serve Immediately: Layer each salad bowl with a base of 1⅓ cups chopped kale, a scant ½ cup wild rice, and ½ cup roasted sweet potato. Evenly divide the tempeh on top, then add 2 tablespoons chopped apple, 1 tablespoon crumbled goat cheese, and 2 teaspoons toasted almonds. Serve warm, drizzled with the dressing.

Meal Prep: Layer 6 meal prep containers with a base of 1⅓ cups chopped kale, ½ cup wild rice, and ½ cup roasted sweet potato. Evenly divide the tempeh on top, then add 2 tablespoons chopped apple, 1 tablespoon crumbled goat cheese, and 2 teaspoons toasted almonds. Store the dressing separately and drizzle on when ready to serve. These bowls can be served cold or warm (see the reheat instructions). If you're planning to serve it warm, I recommend storing the tempeh, rice, and

Creamy Balsamic Dressing

½ cup balsamic vinegar

½ cup extra-virgin olive oil

2 tablespoons Greek yogurt or plant-based sour cream

1 tablespoon pure maple syrup

1 teaspoon Dijon mustard

1 clove garlic, minced

½ teaspoon fine sea salt

Pinch ground black pepper

sweet potatoes in separate containers so you can reheat those components before assembling your salad bowls.

Store: In the refrigerator for up to 1 week.

Reheat: Reheat the rice in a microwave until warm, 30 to 60 seconds. Reheat the tempeh and sweet potatoes in a 375°F oven or toaster oven for 5 to 7 minutes, until warm.

NUTRITION FACTS

Per serving: 1 salad with 2 tablespoons dressing | Calories: 805 | Carbohydrates: 83g | Protein: 30g | Fat: 40g | Fiber: 13g | Sugar: 24g

Lentil Taco Salad Bowls

Lentils may be small, but they are certainly not lacking when it comes to nutrition. They're a great source of plant-based protein, iron, potassium, and fiber. For salads, I prefer to use green or black lentils because they stay firmer and hold their shape better than brown or red. For this salad, the lentils are cooked and seasoned to make a simple lentil taco "meat." There are a lot of topping suggestions for this salad, so just pick whatever sounds good to you or use what you have on hand.
Serves 4

Lentil Taco "Meat"

½ cup green lentils, rinsed and drained

1 cup water

1½ teaspoons olive oil

1 cup chopped yellow onion

1 clove garlic, minced

2 tablespoons salsa

1½ tablespoons taco seasoning

Fine sea salt, to taste

Southwest Chipotle Dressing

½ cup plain Greek yogurt or plant-based sour cream

1 tablespoon fresh lime juice

1 tablespoon taco seasoning

1 tablespoon water

1½ teaspoons adobo sauce (from canned chipotles in adobo)

1 teaspoon pure maple syrup

⅛ teaspoon fine sea salt

Salad Bowls

8 cups chopped romaine lettuce (about 2 romaine hearts)

1⅓ cups diced cherry tomatoes

1⅓ cups frozen corn kernels, thawed

1 cup shredded Mexican cheese (optional)

½ cup chopped red onion

¼ cup chopped fresh cilantro

Topping suggestions: guacamole or sliced avocado, salsa, hot sauce, crumbled tortilla chips

1. Combine the lentils and water in a medium saucepan and bring to a boil over high heat. Reduce to a simmer, cover, and cook until the lentils are tender but not mushy, about 20 minutes. Drain any excess water.

2. Meanwhile, heat the oil in a medium skillet over medium heat. Add the onion and garlic and sauté until fragrant, 6 to 7 minutes. Add the salsa, taco seasoning, and lentils and stir to combine. Taste and add salt if needed.

3. Whisk together all the dressing ingredients until well combined.

Serve Immediately: Fill each bowl with 2 cups romaine lettuce, ½ cup lentil taco meat, ⅓ cup tomatoes, ⅓ cup corn, ¼ cup shredded cheese (if using), 2 tablespoons red onion, and 1 tablespoon cilantro. Drizzle on the dressing and add your toppings of choice.

Meal Prep: Fill 4 meal prep containers with 2 cups romaine lettuce, ½ cup lentil taco meat, ⅓ cup tomatoes, ⅓ cup corn, ¼ cup shredded cheese (if using), 2 tablespoons red onion, and 1 tablespoon cilantro. When ready to serve, drizzle on the dressing and add your toppings of choice.

Store: In the refrigerator for up to 1 week.

NUTRITION FACTS

Per serving: 1 salad with 2 tablespoons dressing | Calories: 332 | Carbohydrates: 37g | Protein: 15g | Fat: 15g | Fiber: 10g | Sugar: 9g

BRITTANY'S TIP

I love the creaminess of the Southwest Chipotle Dressing, but Cilantro Lime Dressing (page 120) is also delicious on this salad if you want to switch things up.

Buffalo Tofu Mason Jar Salads

Buffalo sauce isn't just for wings and game day appetizers! Here, its spicy flavor works beautifully as a sauce for sautéed tofu. This mason jar salad has a generous amount of crunchy fresh veggies and a creamy Greek yogurt ranch dressing to balance out the heat from the buffalo sauce. You can certainly make your own buffalo sauce, but I typically use store-bought out of convenience. When looking for buffalo sauce at the store, try to find one that is made with better oils (like avocado oil and olive oil) without gums or natural flavors added. I recommend Primal Kitchen or Tessemae's. Both are gluten-free, vegan, and very tasty. **Serves 4**

Buffalo Tofu

1 tablespoons olive or avocado oil

1 (14- to 16-ounce) package extra-firm tofu, pressed, drained, and cut into ⅓-inch cubes

½ cup buffalo sauce

Greek Yogurt Ranch Dressing

¼ cup plain full-fat Greek yogurt or plant-based sour cream

¼ cup avocado oil mayonnaise or plant-based mayonnaise

1 to 2 tablespoons water

1 teaspoon fresh lemon juice or white vinegar

1½ teaspoons dried parsley

¾ teaspoon garlic powder

½ teaspoon dried dill or 1 tablespoon chopped fresh dill

¼ teaspoon onion powder

⅛ teaspoon fine sea salt

Pinch ground black pepper

Mason Jars

¼ cup diced red onion

½ cup chopped celery

1 cup grated or shredded carrots

2 cups cooked brown rice (see page 21; use ⅔ cup rice + 1⅓ cups water)

1 cup chopped cherry tomatoes

8 cups chopped romaine lettuce (about 2 romaine hearts)

1. Heat the oil in a large skillet over medium-high heat. Add the tofu and cook, tossing occasionally, until golden on all sides, 7 to 10 minutes. You may want to do this in batches if your skillet isn't large enough and the tofu isn't able to fit in a single layer. Once the tofu is golden, turn off the heat and add the buffalo sauce. Toss to coat, then set aside.

2. Meanwhile, in a small bowl, whisk together all the ranch dressing ingredients, starting with 1 tablespoon water and adding more if needed to achieve the desired consistency.

3. Although you can simply assemble these salads in a bowl as follows, I like serving them out of jars, even if I'll be eating them right away, to really get everything coated in the dressing. To assemble the jars, spoon 3 to 4 tablespoons dressing into 4 wide-mouth quart-size jars. Layer in the salad ingredients in this order: 1 tablespoon red onion, 2 tablespoons celery, ¼ cup carrots, ½ cup rice, ¼ cup cherry tomatoes, 2 cups chopped romaine and a quarter of the buffalo tofu mixture.

Serve Immediately: Shake the jar to coat the salad with the dressing, then pour into a large salad bowl or plate. You can eat it straight from the jar if needed, but I find it much easier to transfer the salad to another dish.

Meal Prep: When ready to serve, shake the jar to coat the salad with the dressing, then pour into a large salad bowl or plate. You can eat it straight from the jar if needed, but I find it much easier to transfer the salad to another dish.

Store: In the refrigerator for up to 1 week.

NUTRITION FACTS

Per serving: 1 jar with 2 tablespoons dressing | Calories: 444 | Carbohydrates: 35g | Protein: 24g | Fat: 24g | Fiber: 5g | Sugar: 4g

The spice level of buffalo sauces varies. I use mild, but feel free to use medium or hot based on your preference.

Instead of brown rice, you can use farro (see page 20; use ⅔ cup farro + 1⅓ cups water) or quinoa (see page 20; use ⅔ cup quinoa + 1⅓ cups water).

Kale Edamame Salad with Zesty Almond Dressing

Some of my absolute favorite salads start with a base of thinly sliced kale, not only because it's a nutritional superstar (thanks to its high vitamin and mineral content), but because its heartiness allows it to hold up well in the fridge for a few days, even with dressing! This salad is vibrant in color, crunchy, and loaded with protein from the edamame. And the almond dressing is savory with a hint of sweetness that gives the salad a lovely umami flavor. I could eat this salad every week!

Serves 4

Zesty Almond Dressing

¼ cup natural creamy almond butter

Juice of 1 lime (2 tablespoons)

2 tablespoons reduced-sodium tamari, reduced-sodium soy sauce, or coconut aminos

2 tablespoons water

1 tablespoon pure maple syrup

1½ teaspoons toasted sesame oil

1 teaspoon sriracha, or more to taste

1 teaspoon grated fresh ginger

1 teaspoon minced garlic

Kale Edamame Salad

1 (12-ounce) bag frozen shelled edamame

1 bunch curly kale, stemmed and thinly sliced (3 to 4 cups)

1 cup diced red onion

1 cup thinly sliced red bell pepper

2 carrots, peeled and thinly sliced or shredded

1 cup cooked quinoa (see page 20; use ⅓ cup quinoa + ⅔ cup water)

2 tablespoons chopped fresh cilantro

½ cup dry-roasted salted almonds, coarsely chopped

1. Combine all the dressing ingredients in a blender and blend until smooth and creamy. Alternatively, combine all the ingredients in a glass jar, cover, and shake until smooth.

2. Cook the edamame according to the package directions. Drain and rinse with cold water to cool.

3. In a large bowl, toss the kale, onion, bell pepper, carrots, quinoa, and cilantro. Add the edamame and almonds and top with the dressing. Mix until all the ingredients are well coated.

Serve Immediately: Divide the salad evenly into 4 bowls and enjoy cold.

Meal Prep: Divide the salad evenly into 4 meal prep containers and enjoy cold.

Store: In the refrigerator for 4 days.

NUTRITION FACTS

Per serving: ¼ recipe | Calories: 449 | Carbohydrates: 50g | Protein: 23g | Fat: 20g | Fiber: 13g | Sugar: 13g

BRITTANY'S TIP

If you don't have edamame on hand, you can use a 15-ounce can black beans or chickpeas instead. Just drain, rinse, and add to the salad instead of the edamame.

Black Bean and Sweet Potato Jar Salads

A simple, layered black bean salad is where my love for mason jar salads started. The jars used to impress everyone at my office when I brought one for lunch. Not only were the colors beautiful, but the idea of being able to pack a salad without needing a separate container for dressing was such a novel concept. Although this updated version of my go-to jar salad still involves black beans, I added even more veggies to the mix with cauliflower rice and chili-roasted sweet potatoes. The cilantro-lime dressing steals the show with a zesty flavor that permeates and almost pickles the red onion and carrots. As an added bonus, cilantro is a good source of vitamins A, K, and C and offers additional health benefits, including blood sugar stabilization and anti-inflammatory properties.

Serves 6

Sweet Potatoes

4 medium sweet potatoes, scrubbed and cut into ½-inch pieces

2 teaspoons olive oil

1 teaspoon chili powder

1 teaspoon fine sea salt

Cilantro-Lime Dressing

1 cup extra-virgin olive oil

½ cup fresh lime juice

½ cup fresh cilantro

4 cloves garlic, peeled

4 teaspoons pure maple syrup

1 teaspoon ground coriander

1 teaspoon fine sea salt, plus more to taste

1 teaspoon ground black pepper, plus more to taste

Mason Jars

¾ cup diced red onion

2 cups grated or shredded carrots

2 (15-ounce) cans black beans, drained and rinsed

3 cups fresh cauliflower rice

2 cups fresh or thawed corn kernels

12 cups shredded or chopped romaine lettuce (about 3 romaine hearts)

2 cups chopped cherry or grape tomatoes

1. Preheat the oven to 400°F.

2. Put the sweet potatoes in a large bowl and toss with the oil, chili powder, and salt. Spread onto a rimmed baking sheet and bake for 20 to 30 minutes, until fork-tender.

3. Meanwhile, combine all the dressing ingredients in a blender and blend until combined. Taste and add more salt and pepper if needed.

4. Although you can simply assemble these salads in a bowl as follows, I like serving them out of jars, even if I'll be eating them right away, to really get everything coated in the dressing. To assemble the jars, spoon 3 to 4 tablespoons dressing into 6 wide-mouth quart-size jars or whichever containers you have on hand. Layer in the salad ingredients in this order: 2 tablespoons red onion, $^1/_3$ cup carrots, ½ cup black beans, ½ cup cauliflower rice, $^1/_3$ cup corn, $^2/_3$ cup roasted sweet potatoes, 2 cups romaine lettuce, and ½ cup tomatoes.

Serve Immediately: Shake the jar to coat the salad with dressing, then pour into a large salad bowl or plate. You can eat it straight from the jar if needed, but I find it much easier to transfer the salad to another dish.

Meal Prep: When ready to serve, shake the jar to coat the salad with dressing, then pour into a large salad bowl or plate. You can eat it straight from the jar if needed, but I find it much easier to transfer the salad to another dish.

Store: In the refrigerator for up to 1 week.

NUTRITION FACTS

Per serving: 1 jar | Calories: 476 | Carbohydrates: 65g | Protein: 16g | Fat: 17g | Fiber: 16g | Sugar: 14g

BRITTANY'S TIP

● Make this salad even more
flavorful by using grilled corn
or frozen fire-roasted corn that
has been thawed.

Greek Couscous Salad

 DF * EF

1 cup whole-wheat couscous

2 cups baby arugula or spinach, chopped

⅓ cup dry-packed sun-dried tomatoes, chopped

1 cup diced cucumber

10 Kalamata olives, pitted and chopped

½ cup canned cannellini beans

½ cup crumbled feta cheese or plant-based feta cheese

Cracked black pepper to taste (optional)

White Balsamic Dressing

¼ cup white balsamic vinegar

3 tablespoons extra-virgin olive oil

1½ tablespoons pure maple syrup

1 teaspoon Dijon mustard

1 clove garlic, minced

¾ teaspoon dried oregano

½ teaspoon fine sea salt

This healthy and hearty couscous salad is loaded with Mediterranean flavors like sun-dried tomatoes, olives, and feta. It can be made with Moroccan couscous or Israeli (also called pearl) couscous. Both are technically considered pasta, but I find Moroccan couscous is more grain-like, similar to the size and texture of quinoa. Both varieties cook up quickly and are similar in terms of nutrients as well. No matter which couscous you're using, I do recommend looking for whole-wheat couscous as it will have more fiber. For the dressing, I prefer using white balsamic vinegar as regular balsamic will give the salad a brown tint that isn't the prettiest. If you don't care what the salad looks like, you can certainly use regular balsamic vinegar, especially if that's all you have on hand. Regardless, this salad is always a crowd-pleaser! **Serves 4**

1. Cook the couscous according to package instructions. Fluff with a fork (or drain, if using pearl couscous) and transfer to a large bowl to cool.

2. While the couscous cools, make the dressing by whisking together all the ingredients in a small bowl or jar.

3. To the bowl with the couscous, add the arugula, sun-dried tomatoes, cucumber, olives, white beans, and feta.

4. Add the dressing and toss again. Taste and season with pepper, if desired.

Serve Immediately: Divide the salad into 4 bowls and enjoy, or chill in the fridge before serving.

Meal Prep: Divide the salad into 4 meal prep containers and enjoy cold.

Store: In the refrigerator for up to 5 days.

NUTRITION FACTS

Per serving: ¼ recipe | Calories: 447 | Carbohydrates: 61g | Protein: 15g | Fat: 16g | Fiber: 7g | Sugar: 12g

Bowl Meals

126   Stewed Chickpea Quinoa Bowls

129   20-Minute Veggie Lo Mein Bowls

130   Tofu Curry with Potatoes
       and Carrots

133   Cauliflower Rice Tex-Mex Casserole

134   Spicy Chipotle Tofu Burrito Bowls

137   Jerk Chickpeas with Roasted
       Plantains

138   Coco-Bacon Loaded Sweet
       Potatoes

141   Tofu Egg Roll in a Bowl

142   Nourishing Grain Bowls with Creamy
       Tahini Sauce

145   BBQ Jackfruit Bowls

146   Cauliflower Tikka Masala

149   EBF Power Bowl with Roasted Sweet
       Potatoes and Kale

150   Thai Lentil Meatballs with Coconut
       Curry Broth

Stewed Chickpea Quinoa Bowls

With this dish, chickpeas are simmered in a tomato stew with warming spices like ginger, cinnamon, and star anise to create a cozy and hearty meal-in-a-bowl. It's great for meal prep because it tastes even better after sitting in the fridge for a day or two. If you're unfamiliar with whole star anise, it's a seed pod from a plant that is native to China, and it adds a lovely depth of flavor to this stew. Any leftover pods can be used for making pho broth, a homemade chai spice mix, mulled wine, or poached pears. If you can't find it, use ½ teaspoon Chinese five-spice powder (star anise is one of the five spices) or ¼ teaspoon fennel seeds as a sub. **Serves 4**

1 tablespoon olive or avocado oil

1 medium yellow onion, finely chopped

2 cloves garlic, minced

2 teaspoons minced fresh ginger

2 tablespoons coconut sugar

4 bay leaves

2 cinnamon sticks

1 whole star anise

1 teaspoon ground coriander

¼ teaspoon ground cinnamon

2 tablespoons apple cider vinegar

1 cup water or vegetable broth

1 (28-ounce) can crushed tomatoes

2 (15-ounce) cans chickpeas, drained and rinsed

2 teaspoons fine sea salt

1 teaspoon ground black pepper

4 cups cooked quinoa (see page 20; use 1⅓ cups quinoa + 2⅔ cups water)

1.   Heat the oil in an extra large skillet or Dutch oven over medium-high heat. Add the onion, garlic, and ginger and sauté until fragrant, 5 to 7 minutes. Add the coconut sugar, bay leaves, cinnamon sticks, star anise, coriander, and cinnamon and cook for 1 minute. Add the apple cider vinegar to deglaze the pan, scraping up any browned bits from the bottom.

2.   Add the water or broth, crushed tomatoes, chickpeas, salt, and pepper. Bring the mixture to a boil, then reduce the heat and simmer for 40 minutes. Carefully remove the star anise pod, cinnamon sticks, and bay leaves before serving.

Serve Immediately: Scoop 1 cup cooked quinoa into each bowl, then evenly divide the stewed chickpeas on top. Serve warm.

Meal Prep: Let the stew and quinoa cool. Spoon 1 cup cooked quinoa into 4 meal prep containers, then evenly divide the stewed chickpeas on top. When ready to serve, follow the reheat instructions.

Store: In the refrigerator for up to 5 days. If you want to freeze this meal, I recommend freezing the stewed chickpeas without the quinoa. Let the chickpeas cool completely, then transfer to an airtight container and freeze for up to 3 months. You can freeze the cooked quinoa separately or make fresh quinoa for serving.

Reheat: From the refrigerator, reheat in the microwave for 1 to 2 minutes or on the stovetop until warm. From frozen, let the stewed chickpeas thaw in the refrigerator overnight. Once thawed, reheat in the microwave for 1 to 2 minutes or on the stovetop until warm. Serve with warm quinoa (either freshly made or reheated from frozen).

BRITTANY'S TIP

To add some greens to this dish, stir in 2 to 3 cups baby spinach or chopped Swiss chard when you have 5 to 10 minutes left of simmering.

NUTRITION FACTS

Per serving: ¼ recipe | Calories: 420 | Carbohydrates: 75g | Protein: 19g | Fat: 8g | Fiber: 19g | Sugar: 14g

20-Minute Veggie Lo Mein Bowl

Growing up, my go-to order from my local Chinese takeout restaurant was always lo mein, but I hadn't had it in years…until I began working on this recipe. Lo mein is a Chinese noodle dish that comes together quickly with vegetables, protein, and a sesame oil–based sauce. The noodles are fully cooked and tossed into a wok or skillet with stir-fried vegetables and sauce. Egg noodles are traditionally used, but we're using whole-wheat spaghetti noodles to boost the nutrition a bit. That said, the star of the show here is the plethora of vegetables. They bring an array of color, nutrition, and crunch to this dish. My favorite is the broccoli because the florets soak up a good amount of sauce and get so flavorful. **Serves 4**

Veggie Lo Mein

1 (8-ounce) package whole-wheat spaghetti

1 tablespoon olive or avocado oil

1 (3.5-ounce) package shiitake mushrooms, stemmed and thinly sliced

1 red bell pepper, seeded and thinly sliced

1 cup grated carrots

3 cloves garlic, minced

3 cups chopped broccoli florets

1 cup snow peas

¼ teaspoon fine sea salt, plus more to taste

Sliced green onions, for garnish

Lo Mein Sauce

⅓ cup reduced-sodium tamari, reduced-sodium soy sauce, or coconut aminos

1 tablespoon grated fresh ginger

1 tablespoon honey or pure maple syrup

1 tablespoon toasted sesame oil

2 teaspoons sriracha

1. Bring a large pot of salted water to a rapid boil. Cook the spaghetti until just shy of al dente, 8 to 12 minutes, then drain. You want the noodles to be a little undercooked.

2. While the spaghetti cooks, whisk together all the sauce ingredients in a bowl.

3. Heat the oil in a large skillet or wok over medium-high heat. Add the mushrooms, bell pepper, carrots, and garlic and cook, stirring frequently, until tender, 3 to 4 minutes. Add the broccoli and snow peas and toss to combine. Season the vegetables with the salt and cook for another 2 to 3 minutes.

4. Add the noodles and sauce to the skillet and toss to combine with the vegetable mixture. Taste and add more salt, if desired.

Serve Immediately: Divide the lo mein evenly into 4 bowls. Garnish with green onions and serve warm.

Meal Prep: Divide the lo mein evenly into 4 meal prep containers and garnish with green onions. When ready to serve, follow the reheat instructions.

Store: In the refrigerator for up to 5 days.

Reheat: Heat the lo mein in the microwave 1 to 2 minutes or on the stovetop until warm.

NUTRITION FACTS ———————————————

Per serving: ¼ recipe | Calories: 358 | Carbohydrates: 59g | Protein: 16g | Fat: 10g | Fiber: 12g | Sugar: 12g

Tofu Curry
with Potatoes and Carrots

Curries are one of my go-to comfort food meals to make at home because they're so quick and easy when using store-bought curry paste and ground spices. This version is my take on massaman curry, the dish I always order whenever we do takeout from our favorite Thai restaurant. Massaman curry is a red curry that traditionally uses dry whole spices and also features roasted peanuts. For this version I used red curry paste that's easy to find in stores, as well as many ground spices that you probably already have at home. While this curry is aromatic, it's relatively mild when it comes to the spice level and has a nice sweetness from the peas and carrots. **Serves 4**

2 tablespoons avocado oil, divided

1 (14- to 16-ounce) package extra-firm tofu, drained, pressed, and cut into ½-inch cubes

1 teaspoon fine sea salt, divided

½ teaspoon ground black pepper, plus more to taste

2 cloves garlic, minced

1 tablespoon grated fresh ginger

1 medium yellow onion, chopped

3 tablespoons red curry paste

2 teaspoons ground turmeric

1 teaspoon chili powder

1 (13.5-ounce) can coconut milk

1 cup vegetable broth

3 cups chopped Yukon Gold potatoes (about 1 pound)

3 carrots, chopped

1 cup frozen peas

Juice of ½ lime

4 cups cooked cauliflower rice

Fresh cilantro, for garnish

Chopped roasted salted peanuts, for garnish

1. Heat 1 tablespoon of the oil in a large skillet over medium-high heat. Add the tofu and cook, tossing occasionally, until golden on all sides, 7 to 10 minutes. You may want to do this in batches if your skillet isn't large enough and the tofu isn't able to fit in a single layer. Season the tofu with ½ teaspoon of the salt and the pepper while it cooks. Once the tofu is golden, transfer it to a bowl.

2. Add the remaining 1 tablespoon oil to the same skillet over medium heat. Add the garlic, ginger, and onion and sauté until fragrant, 4 to 5 minutes.

3. Add the curry paste, turmeric, chili powder, and remaining ½ teaspoon salt and cook for an additional 30 seconds. Add the coconut milk, veggie broth, potatoes, and carrots and stir.

4. Cover the pan and bring to a boil, then reduce the heat and let simmer for 15 minutes. Add the frozen peas, tofu, and lime juice and heat until just warm, about 5 minutes.

Serve Immediately: Scoop 1 cup cauliflower rice into 4 bowls, then evenly divide the curry on top. Garnish with cilantro and chopped peanuts.

Meal Prep: Scoop 1 cup cauliflower rice into 4 meal prep containers, then divide the curry evenly on top. When ready to serve, follow the reheat instructions and garnish with cilantro and chopped peanuts.

Store: In the refrigerator for up to 5 days

Reheat: Reheat in the microwave for 1 to 2 minutes or on the stovetop until warm.

BRITTANY'S TIPS

● To make the prep for this recipe really easy I recommend using "steam in the bag" cauliflower rice. Or of course you can always make and cook your own cauliflower rice!

● Feel free to use Thai jasmine white rice or brown rice instead of cauliflower rice, if desired.

NUTRITION FACTS

Per serving: ¼ recipe | Calories: 555 | Carbohydrates: 57g | Protein: 23g | Fat: 28g | Fiber: 14g | Sugar: 13g

Cauliflower Rice Tex-Mex Casserole

1 teaspoon olive oil

1 yellow onion, chopped

1 red or green bell pepper, seeded and chopped

½ jalapeño pepper, seeded and minced (optional)

1 tablespoon taco seasoning

¼ teaspoon fine sea salt

1 cup salsa

½ cup frozen sweet corn kernels, thawed

1 (15-ounce) can black beans, drained and rinsed

1 (12-ounce) package frozen cauliflower rice

¼ cup chopped fresh cilantro, plus more for garnish

1 cup shredded cheddar cheese

This dish is sure to be a family favorite! It's cheesy, flavorful, and made in one pan. With the combination of sweet corn and black beans, you'll hardly notice that cauliflower rice is being substituted for white rice. If you're making this to serve to little ones, just be mindful of the spice level of your taco seasoning and salsa as brands will vary, and you can always omit the jalapeños if desired! **Serves 3**

1. Heat the oil in a large skillet over medium-high heat. Add the onion, bell pepper, and jalapeño (if using) and sauté until fragrant and the onion is translucent, 5 to 6 minutes. Add the taco seasoning and salt and quickly toss to combine, then add the salsa.

2. Add the corn, black beans, frozen cauliflower rice, and cilantro and cook until the sauce has evaporated and the mixture has thickened, about 10 minutes. Stir in the cheese and cook until just melted.

Serve Immediately: Evenly divide the casserole into 3 bowls and top with fresh cilantro. Serve warm.

Meal Prep: Evenly divide the casserole into 3 meal prep containers. When ready to serve, follow the reheat instructions. Top with fresh cilantro and enjoy.

Store: In the refrigerator for up to 4 days.

Reheat: In the microwave for 1 to 2 minutes or on the stovetop until warm.

NUTRITION FACTS

Per serving: ⅓ recipe | Calories: 402 | Carbohydrates: 52g | Protein: 26g | Fat: 14g | Fiber: 16g | Sugar: 11g

BRITTANY'S TIP

You can use canned white beans in place of the black beans, if desired.

Spicy Chipotle Tofu Burrito Bowls

Love Chipotle burrito bowls? Me too, which is why I set out to remake my go-to order: the sofritas burrito bowl. Sofritas is essentially spicy braised tofu with a flavorful sauce made from a charred poblano pepper and canned chipotle peppers in adobo sauce. The upside of making burrito bowls at home is that you can add as much guacamole as you like, no extra charge! **Serves 4**

Chipotle Tofu

1 medium poblano pepper

1 large or two small canned chipotle peppers in adobo sauce, plus 2 tablespoons adobo sauce

¼ cup chopped yellow onion

3 cloves garlic, peeled

¼ to ½ cup water

2 tablespoons tomato paste

1 tablespoon reduced-sodium tamari, reduced-sodium soy sauce, or coconut aminos

1½ teaspoons apple cider vinegar

½ teaspoon organic sugar or coconut sugar

½ teaspoon fine sea salt

1 tablespoon olive oil

1 (14- to 16-ounce) package extra-firm tofu, drained, pressed, and cut into ¼-inch cubes

Burrito Bowls

8 cups shredded romaine lettuce (about 2 romaine hearts)

2 cups cooked white or brown rice (see page 21; use ⅔ cup white rice + 1⅓ cups water, or ⅔ cup brown rice + 1⅔ cups water)

1 cup canned black beans

½ cup fresh salsa

½ cup diced red onion

¼ cup chopped fresh cilantro

1 avocado, peeled, pitted, and sliced, or guacamole

1. Char the poblano pepper by holding it over the flame of a gas range until it's blistered all over, 2 to 3 minutes. Be sure to rotate the pepper using tongs so it gets charred on all sides. Alternatively, you can broil it in the oven: Rub a little olive oil over the outside of the pepper and broil, flipping every few minutes, for 15 to 20 minutes or until the pepper is blistered. Place charred pepper in a bowl and cover with a plate or plastic wrap for about 10 minutes. Once pepper is cool and the skin has loosened, remove the skin, stem, and seeds.

2. In a food processor or high-powered blender, combine the roasted poblano pepper, chipotle peppers and adobo sauce, onion, garlic, ¼ cup water, tomato paste, tamari, apple cider vinegar, sugar, and salt. Blend until smooth.

3. In a large skillet, heat the olive oil over medium-high heat. Add the tofu and cook, tossing occasionally, until golden on all sides, 7 to 10 minutes. You may want to do this in batches if your skillet isn't large enough and the tofu isn't able to fit in a single layer. Once golden, use your spatula to crumble the tofu into small pieces. You can leave some cubes larger for more texture.

4. Pour the sauce into the skillet with the tofu and simmer for about 10 minutes, adding up to ¼ cup more water if the sauce seems too thick or is starting to stick to the skillet.

Serve Immediately: Make a bed of 2 cups romaine lettuce in each bowl and divide the tofu mixture on top. Add ½ cup warm rice, ¼ cup black beans, 2 tablespoons salsa, 2 tablespoons red onion, 1 tablespoon cilantro, and avocado slices or a dollop of guacamole.

Meal Prep: Scoop ½ cup rice and one quarter of the tofu mixture into 4 meal prep containers. Store the other components of the bowls in separate containers. When ready to serve, follow the reheat instructions for the rice and tofu. Add 2 cups romaine lettuce to each bowl and top with the warm tofu and rice, ¼ cup black beans, 2 tablespoons salsa, 2 tablespoons red onion, 1 tablespoon cilantro, and avocado slices or a dollop of guacamole.

BRITTANY'S TIP

The topping options for burrito bowls are endless. For even more flavor, try adding thawed frozen corn and/or a little shredded cheese.

Reheat: Reheat the tofu and rice in the microwave for 1 to 2 minutes or on the stovetop until warm.

Store: In the refrigerator for up to 5 days.

NUTRITION FACTS

Per serving: 1 bowl | Calories: 424 | Carbohydrates: 52g | Protein: 19g | Fat: 16g | Fiber: 12g | Sugar: 6g

BRITTANY'S TIPS

If you're using fresh plantains, be sure to look for ones that are mostly brown or black. Unripe or green plantains aren't sweet and won't be as tasty in this recipe.

To save time, you can use frozen sliced plantains, available at many supermarkets. If using, roast the plantains according to package instructions.

Jerk Chickpeas
with Sweet Plantains

Jerk is a style of cooking that originated in Jamaica, where meat (traditionally pork or chicken) is either dry-rubbed or wet-marinated with a mixture of herbs and spices and slow-roasted over a fire or grill. Jerk seasoning blends usually include chiles, thyme, onion, garlic, and spices like cinnamon, ginger, allspice, and cloves. For this dish I used jerk seasoning as my inspiration to make a mild but still flavorful simmering sauce for chickpeas. To be honest, while I love the flavor of the jerk chickpeas, what I'm really here for are the roasted plantains! **Serves 4**

2 or 3 very ripe plantains, peeled and sliced diagonally into ½-inch pieces

1¼ teaspoons fine sea salt, divided

1 tablespoon olive oil

½ cup diced yellow onion

3 cloves garlic, minced

1 teaspoon minced fresh ginger

1½ teaspoons dried thyme

1½ teaspoons ground cinnamon

¾ teaspoon ground allspice

½ teaspoon ground cumin

¼ teaspoon ground black pepper

Pinch cayenne pepper

1 cup water

2 tablespoons tomato paste

½ teaspoon coconut sugar

2 (15-ounce) cans chickpeas, drained and rinsed

1 red, orange, or yellow bell pepper, seeded and chopped

¼ cup plant-based sour cream

2 tablespoons apple cider vinegar

3 cups cooked white rice (see page 21; use 1 cup rice + 2 cups water)

2 green onions, chopped

2 tablespoons chopped fresh cilantro

1. Preheat the oven to 400°F. Line a rimmed baking sheet with parchment paper and spray it with nonstick cooking spray.

2. Spread out the plantains on the prepared baking sheet and spray the tops with a good amount of cooking spray. Sprinkle with ¼ teaspoon of the salt and bake for 20 to 30 minutes, until golden, flipping the plantains about halfway through baking. If you're using frozen plantains, roast according to the package instructions.

3. Meanwhile, heat the olive oil in a large saucepan over medium heat. Add the onion, garlic, and ginger and sauté until fragrant, 2 to 3 minutes. Add the dried thyme, ground spices, remaining 1 teaspoon salt, black pepper, and cayenne pepper. Stir to combine and cook for 30 seconds more.

4. Add the water, tomato paste, and coconut sugar and simmer for 5 minutes to thicken.

5. Stir in the chickpeas and bell pepper. Simmer for another 10 minutes, stirring occasionally. Stir in the sour cream and apple cider vinegar and simmer for another 3 minutes.

Serve Immediately: Spoon ¾ cup rice into each bowl, then divide the jerk chickpeas and plantains evenly on top. Garnish with the green onions and cilantro and serve warm.

Meal Prep: Spoon ¾ cup rice into 4 meal prep containers, then divide the jerk chickpeas and plantains evenly on top. When ready to serve, follow the reheat instructions, garnish with the green onions and cilantro, and serve.

Store: In the refrigerator for up to 5 days.

Reheat: Heat the bowl in the microwave for 1 to 2 minutes, until warm throughout. You can also reheat the plantains separately in a 375°F oven or toaster oven for 5 to 6 minutes.

NUTRITION FACTS ————————————————

Per serving: ¼ recipe | Calories: 532 | Carbohydrates: 102g | Protein: 16g | Fat: 11g | Fiber: 13g | Sugar: 23g

Coco-Bacon Loaded Sweet Potatoes

Sweet potatoes are one of my favorite veggies, and I'm all about turning them into a meal whenever possible. For this bowl meal, the "bowl" is the baked sweet potato itself, and we're loading it with a variety of toppings to make a hearty and filling dish. When you think of loaded sweet potatoes your mind might drift to cheese, sour cream, scallions, and bacon, but with this version we're piling more veggies on top of the sweet potatoes and sprinkling on maple-sweetened coconut bacon. The dish reminds me of a colorful sweet potato hash with a bit of Mexican flair. If you want to make it feel even more like a hash (and add more protein), feel free to add a fried egg on top. **Serves 4**

4 medium sweet potatoes, scrubbed

1 teaspoon olive or avocado oil

½ cup chopped yellow onion

Fine sea salt and ground black pepper to taste

1 (15-ounce) can black beans, drained and rinsed

1 cup frozen corn kernels

1 cup chopped kale

1 avocado, peeled, pitted, and diced

2 green onions (green part only), sliced

½ cup Coconut Bacon (page 246)

¼ cup chopped fresh cilantro

1 recipe Southwest Chipotle Dressing (page 115)

1. Preheat the oven to 400°F.

2. Pierce the sweet potatoes with a fork several times and bake directly on the oven rack, with a pan on the rack beneath to catch any drippings, for about 1 hour, until tender.

3. When the potatoes have about 10 minutes left, heat the oil in a large skillet over medium-high heat. Add the onion and sauté until soft, 5 to 7 minutes. Season with salt and pepper. Add the black beans, corn, and kale, toss to combine, and cook until the kale wilts, about 5 minutes. Remove from the heat.

Serve Immediately: Cut the sweet potatoes open lengthwise and mash each side with a fork. Season with a little sea salt and pepper. Evenly divide the veggie and black bean mixture on top, then one-quarter of the avocado, 1 to 2 tablespoons green onions, 2 tablespoons coconut bacon, and 1 table-spoon cilantro. Drizzle on the dressing and serve warm.

Meal Prep: Store baked sweet potatoes and veggie and black bean mixture in separate airtight containers. When ready to serve, follow the reheat instructions. Cut the sweet potatoes open lengthwise and mash each side with a fork. Season with a little sea salt and pepper. Evenly divide the veggie and black bean mixture on top, then one-quarter of the avocado, 1 to 2 tablespoons green onions, 2 tablespoons coconut bacon, and 1 table-spoon cilantro. Drizzle on the dressing and serve warm.

Store: In the refrigerator for up to 4 days.

BRITTANY'S TIP

 If you're making this recipe and also want to prep breakfast, add an extra sweet potato to the oven so you can use it to make Sweet Potato Pie Chia Pudding (page 42).

Reheat: Remove a sweet potato from the refrigerator and let it come to room temperature. Bake in a 350°F oven for about 20 minutes, until warm throughout. Heat the veggie and black bean mixture in a skillet over medium heat until warm, 4 to 5 minutes. Alternatively, cut the baked sweet potato in half, mash, and top with the veggie and black bean mixture. Cover with a damp paper towel and microwave for 1 to 2 minutes.

NUTRITION FACTS

Per serving: 1 loaded sweet potato with 2 tablespoons dressing | Calories: 311 | Carbohydrates: 52g | Protein: 12g | Fat: 67 | Fiber: 14g | Sugar: 13g

BRITTANY'S TIP

● You can swap the packaged coleslaw mix for broccoli slaw if you like a little more crunch. I prefer a cabbage-based slaw, but broccoli slaw can be a fun way to switch up the veggies.

● You can use cauliflower rice or quinoa in place of the brown or white rice.

Tofu Egg Roll in a Bowl

Egg rolls are a classic Chinese-American appetizer that I grew up loving. Even back then I gravitated toward vegetables more than meat and would order vegetable spring rolls, which are typically made with shredded cabbage and carrots, green onion, soy sauce, and spices. With this recipe we're taking the ingredients and flavors you'd find in a vegetable egg roll and turning them into a main course. We're losing the fried wrapper and simply sautéing everything in one pan to make a light and flavorful vegetable-packed meal that has a good amount of protein from the tofu. To make things quick and easy, I like to use packaged coleslaw mix and shredded carrots as the base, but feel free to shred your own cabbage and carrots. I recommend serving the cabbage and tofu mixture over rice (or with rice on the side) to make this bowl a bit more filling. **Serves 4**

2 tablespoons toasted sesame oil

2 cloves garlic, minced

2 teaspoons minced fresh ginger

1 medium yellow onion, chopped

1 (14- to 16-ounce) package extra-firm tofu, pressed, drained, and crumbled into bite-size pieces

1 (3.5-ounce) package shiitake mushrooms, stemmed and chopped

½ teaspoon fine sea salt

½ teaspoon ground black pepper

¼ cup reduced-sodium tamari, reduced-sodium soy sauce, or coconut aminos, plus more to taste

1 tablespoon chili garlic sauce (such as sambal oelek), plus more to taste

1 tablespoon rice vinegar

½ teaspoon coconut sugar

1 (12-ounce) package coleslaw mix or 5 to 6 cups shredded green and red cabbage

1 cup matchstick or shredded carrots

4 cups cooked white or brown rice (see page 21; use 1⅓ cups white rice + 2⅔ cups water, or 1⅓ cups brown rice + 3⅓ cups water)

2 green onions, chopped, for serving

Fresh cilantro, for serving

Sriracha, for serving

1. Heat the sesame oil in a large skillet over medium heat. Add the garlic, ginger, and onion and cook until fragrant and the onion is translucent, 5 to 7 minutes.

2. Add the crumbled tofu and mushrooms and season with the salt and pepper. Cook for 3 minutes, then add the tamari, chili garlic sauce, rice vinegar, and sugar. Cook until the mushrooms have softened and the tofu is starting to get some golden brown spots, 3 to 4 minutes.

3. Add the coleslaw mix and carrots and cook, stirring occasionally, until the cabbage has softened just a bit, 3 to 4 minutes. Taste and add more tamari or chili garlic sauce, if needed.

Serve Immediately: Scoop 1 cup rice into 4 bowls, then evenly divide the egg roll mixture on top. Garnish with the green onions, cilantro, sriracha, and extra tamari, if desired.

Meal Prep: Scoop 1 cup rice into 4 meal prep containers, then divide the egg roll mixture evenly on top. Garnish with the green onions and cilantro. When ready to serve, follow the reheat instructions and serve with sriracha and extra tamari, if desired.

Store: In the refrigerator for up to 5 days.

Reheat: Reheat in the microwave 1 to 2 minutes or on the stovetop until warm.

NUTRITION FACTS

Per serving: ¼ recipe with white rice | Calories: 451 | Carbohydrates: 63g | Protein: 19g | Fat: 12g | Fiber: 7g | Sugar: 8g

Nourishing Grain Bowls
with Creamy Tahini Sauce

I love a good roasted veggie bowl, especially when cruciferous veggies like Brussels sprouts and cauliflower are involved. Cruciferous vegetables are not only high in fiber, they're rich in vitamins and minerals as well as phytonutrients called glucosinolates, which can help reduce the risk of cancer. Brussels sprouts in particular have the highest amount of vitamin E and vitamin B_1 when compared to all cruciferous veggies! These bowls start with a base of brown rice and are topped with the roasted vegetables and lemony white beans. Everything is drizzled with my Creamy Tahini Sauce for a deliciously hearty bowl that can be eaten at any temperature. **Serves 4**

1 pound Brussels sprouts, trimmed and halved

1 medium head cauliflower, chopped

1 medium red onion, cut into ½-inch-thick wedges

3 tablespoons avocado oil

1 tablespoon dried oregano

1 teaspoon fine sea salt

½ teaspoon ground allspice

½ teaspoon ground black pepper

2 cups cooked brown rice (see page 21; use ⅔ cup dry brown rice + 1⅓ cups water)

Creamy Tahini Sauce

¼ cup tahini

3 tablespoons fresh lemon juice

3 tablespoons olive oil

3 tablespoons water

2 cloves garlic, finely minced

¼ teaspoon fine sea salt

1 teaspoon pure maple syrup

Lemony White Beans

1 (15-ounce) can white beans, drained and rinsed

2 tablespoons fresh lemon juice

1 tablespoon olive oil

1 tablespoon chopped shallot

¼ cup chopped fresh parsley

Fine sea salt and ground black pepper to taste

1. Preheat the oven to 425°F.

2. Make the tahini sauce by whisking together all the ingredients until well combined. Add water to thin if the sauce is too thick to drizzle, starting with 1 teaspoon and adding more as needed.

3. In a large bowl, toss the Brussels sprouts, cauliflower, and onion with the oil, oregano, salt, allspice, and pepper.

4. Spread out the veggies in a single layer on a rimmed baking sheet. (You may need to use two baking sheets for this.)

5. Roast for 20 minutes, then toss the veggies and continue roasting for another 10 to 20 minutes, until tender and golden brown in some spots.

6. While the veggies are roasting, toss together all the ingredients for the lemony white beans in a medium bowl.

Serve Immediately: Scoop ½ cup warm brown rice into 4 bowls, then evenly divide the roasted veggies and white beans on top. Drizzle on the tahini sauce and enjoy.

Meal Prep: Scoop ½ cup brown rice into 4 meal prep containers and divide the roasted veggies and white beans evenly on top. Store the tahini sauce in a separate container.

Reheat: This bowl can be eaten cold or at room temperature, but if you prefer it warm, heat the ingredients in a skillet over medium-low heat until warm throughout, 4 to 5 minutes. Alternatively, you can microwave for 1 to 2 minutes.

NUTRITION FACTS ————

Per serving: ¼ recipe with 2 tablespoons sauce | Calories: 558 | Carbohydrates: 81g | Protein: 12g | Fat: 22g | Fiber: 14g | Sugar: 14g

BRITTANY'S TIPS

● This bowl would also be delicious with Avocado Green Goddess Dressing (page 111) drizzled on top for a different twist.

● This sauce will thicken up as it sits in the refrigerator. Give it a stir and add a little water to thin, if necessary.

BBQ Jackfruit Bowls

I love a good BBQ sandwich, but find it's less messy to eat when it's served in a bowl—and skipping the bun leaves more room to fill up on healthy vegetables instead of simple carbs! If you're new to jackfruit, it's a tropical fruit native to South India that is rich in vitamin C, vitamin A, B vitamins, and potassium. In comparison to other fruits, jackfruit provides more protein (about 3 grams per cup) while also providing 3 grams of fiber. While it can be eaten fresh and is used in both sweet and savory dishes, it's become really popular as a plant-based meat substitute because the texture resembles shredded meat, making it a perfect plant-based BBQ stand-in. As noted in the ingredient list, be sure to look for canned green/unripe jackfruit packed in water as ripe jackfruit is very sweet and typically packed in syrup. **Serves 4**

1 (14-ounce) can green/unripe jackfruit, packed in water, drained

1 teaspoons olive or avocado oil

2 cloves garlic, minced

1½ teaspoons brown sugar

1 teaspoon paprika

½ teaspoon chili powder

½ teaspoon onion powder

½ teaspoon garlic powder

¼ teaspoon fine sea salt

¼ to ½ cup barbecue sauce

2 cups cooked quinoa (see page 20; use ⅔ cup quinoa + 1⅓ cups vegetable broth), cooled

1 cup frozen sweet corn kernels, thawed

Cabbage Slaw

¼ cup plain full-fat Greek yogurt or plant-based yogurt

¼ cup avocado oil mayonnaise or plant-based mayonnaise

2 tablespoons pure maple syrup

2 tablespoons apple cider vinegar

2 teaspoons Dijon mustard

½ teaspoon fine sea salt

½ teaspoon ground black pepper

1 (12-ounce) package coleslaw mix (5 to 6 cups)

1. Break apart the jackfruit pieces by hand until they're shredded and resemble pulled meat.

2. Heat the oil in a large skillet over medium heat. Add the garlic and cook until fragrant, 1 to 2 minutes.

3. Add the shredded jackfruit, brown sugar, and seasonings and toss well to combine. Reduce the heat to low and cook for 1 minute, then add ¼ cup barbecue sauce. Coat the jackfruit in the sauce, adding up to ¼ cup more sauce if needed. Cook until the jackfruit is warm throughout, 3 to 4 minutes. Remove from the heat.

4. To make the slaw, whisk together the yogurt, mayonnaise, maple syrup, vinegar, mustard, salt, and pepper in a large bowl. Add the coleslaw mix and toss to coat with the dressing.

Serve Immediately: Scoop ½ cup quinoa into 4 bowls. Divide the jackfruit BBQ evenly on top of the quinoa, then divide the coleslaw evenly on top of the jackfruit. Add ¼ cup thawed corn. Serve at room temperature.

Meal Prep: Scoop ½ cup quinoa into 4 meal prep containers. Divide the jackfruit BBQ evenly on top of the quinoa, then divide the coleslaw evenly on top of the jackfruit. Add ¼ cup thawed corn.

Store: In the refrigerator for up to 4 days.

NUTRITION FACTS

Per serving: ¼ recipe | Calories: 427 | Carbohydrates: 65g | Protein: 9g | Fat: 17g | Fiber: 5g | Sugar: 33g

Cauliflower Tikka Masala

Tikka masala is a popular Indian dish traditionally made by grilling yogurt-marinated chicken and serving it with a tomato-cream sauce. Inspired by these same flavors, this cauliflower version skips the yogurt; instead, the cauliflower is roasted to perfection with garam masala and then served with a tomato sauce made creamy thanks to added coconut milk. If you don't have garam masala in your spice cabinet, be sure to pick up a jar. It's an aromatic spice blend with cinnamon, pepper, coriander, nutmeg (or mace), cumin, and cardamom, and it's essential for this recipe. **Serves 4**

Roasted Cauliflower

2 medium heads cauliflower, trimmed and cut into bite-size florets

1 tablespoon olive oil

2 teaspoons garam masala

½ teaspoon fine sea salt

Sauce

1 tablespoon olive oil

½ medium yellow onion, diced

2 cloves garlic, chopped

2 teaspoons minced fresh ginger

1 serrano chile, seeded and diced

1 tablespoon tomato paste

1 tablespoon garam masala

½ teaspoon fine sea salt

1 (28-ounce) can crushed tomatoes

1 cup canned coconut milk

3 cups cooked white rice or quinoa (see pages 20–21; use 1 cup white rice or quinoa + 2 cups water)

Chopped fresh cilantro, for garnish

1. Preheat the oven to 400°F.

2. In a large bowl, toss the cauliflower with the olive oil, garam masala, and salt. Spread out the seasoned cauliflower on a rimmed baking sheet and roast for 20 minutes. Toss the cauliflower, then continue roasting for another 20 to 25 minutes, until lightly browned.

3. After tossing the cauliflower at the 20-minute mark, make the sauce. Heat the oil in a medium skillet over medium heat. Add the onion, garlic, and ginger and cook until the onion is fragrant and soft, 5 to 7 minutes. Add the serrano, tomato paste, garam masala, and salt and cook for 1 minute.

4. Add the crushed tomatoes. Once simmering, reduce the heat to medium low, cover, and cook for 15 minutes. Add the coconut milk and roasted cauliflower and stir until combined and warm throughout.

Serve Immediately: Scoop ¾ cup rice or quinoa into each bowl, then evenly divide the cauliflower tikka masala on top. Garnish with cilantro and enjoy.

Meal Prep: Scoop ¾ cup rice or quinoa into 4 meal prep containers, then evenly divide the cauliflower tikka masala on top. When ready to serve, follow the reheat instructions. Garnish with cilantro and enjoy.

Store: In the refrigerator for up to 4 days.

Reheat: Heat the cauliflower tikka masala with the rice or quinoa in a saucepan over medium heat until warm, 4 to 5 minutes. Alternatively, you can reheat it in the microwave for 1 to 2 minutes.

BRITTANY'S TIP

Serrano chiles are smaller and hotter than jalapeños, but if you can't find serrano peppers, feel free to use a jalapeño instead. You can also omit it entirely if you don't like spicy food.

NUTRITION FACTS

Per serving: ¼ recipe | Calories: 456 | Carbohydrates: 68g | Protein: 13g | Fat: 17g | Fiber: 11g | Sugar: 8g

BRITTANY'S TIP

● Feel free to make the peanut sauce with a different nut butter. Almond butter, cashew butter, and sun butter all work great!

EBF Power Bowl
with Roasted Sweet Potatoes and Kale

2 sweet potatoes, peeled and cut into ¼-inch pieces

½ cup coarsely chopped red onion

3 tablespoons plus 2 teaspoons olive oil, divided

½ teaspoon plus a pinch fine sea salt, divided

¼ teaspoon plus a pinch ground black pepper, divided

¼ teaspoon ground cumin

2½ cups chopped curly kale

2 cups cooked brown rice or quinoa (see pages 20–21; use ⅔ cup brown rice or quinoa + 1⅓ cups water)

1 (15-ounce) can chickpeas, drained and rinsed

Peanut Sauce

½ cup no-sugar-added natural peanut butter

2 tablespoons fresh lime juice

1 tablespoon reduced-sodium tamari, reduced-sodium soy sauce, or coconut aminos

1-inch knob fresh ginger, peeled

2 cloves garlic, peeled

2 teaspoons pure maple syrup

1 teaspoon sambal oelek or crushed red pepper

1 to 4 tablespoons water

If you haven't noticed yet, sweet potatoes and kale have a tendency to make it into a lot of my recipes. They're two of my favorite veggies and I just can't stay away from them. For this bowl meal we're serving roasted sweet potatoes, onion, and kale over a bed of rice with chickpeas and the most delicious peanut sauce for drizzling. You'll want to lick the bowl on this one because the sauce is so dang good! **Serves 3**

1. Preheat the oven to 400°F.

2. On a rimmed baking sheet, toss the sweet potatoes and onion with 1 tablespoon olive oil, ½ teaspoon salt, ¼ teaspoon pepper, and the cumin. Spread out in an even layer and roast for 10 minutes. Use a spatula to flip over and push the sweet potatoes and onion to one side of the sheet. Add the kale to the empty side of the baking sheet and drizzle with 2 teaspoons olive oil and a pinch each of salt and pepper. Roast for about 10 minutes more, until the sweet potatoes are fork-tender.

3. Meanwhile, combine all the sauce ingredients (starting with 1 tablespoon water) in a blender and blend until smooth. Add up to 3 tablespoons more water, if needed, to reach the desired consistency. You want the sauce to be thick but still drizzle-able.

Serve Immediately: Put ⅔ cup brown rice or quinoa in each bowl. Evenly divide the roasted vegetables on top, then add ½ cup chickpeas. Drizzle with the peanut sauce and serve warm.

Meal Prep: Put ⅔ cup brown rice or quinoa in 3 meal prep containers. Evenly divide the roasted vegetables on top, then add ½ cup chickpeas. Store the peanut sauce in a separate container. When ready to serve, follow the reheat instructions, drizzle the peanut sauce on top, and enjoy.

Store: In the refrigerator for up to 5 days.

Reheat: Reheat the bowl ingredients in a skillet over medium-low heat until warm throughout, 4 to 5 minutes. Alternatively, you can microwave for 1 to 2 minutes.

NUTRITION FACTS

Per serving: ⅓ recipe with quinoa and 2 tablespoons sauce | Calories: 665 | Carbohydrates: 79g | Protein: 21g | Fat: 32g | Fiber: 15g | Sugar: 14g

Thai Lentil Meatballs
with Coconut Curry Broth

Readers couldn't get enough of the Eating Bird Food lentil meatloaf recipe, so I adapted it into the base for a meatball recipe, but with a Thai-inspired spin. The meatballs themselves are full of umami flavor from the tamari, miso, and curry paste. You can certainly enjoy them on their own, but, if you ask me, meatballs are always better with sauce, and the coconut curry broth here transforms them into a simple but complete meal. I like making a big batch of the meatballs to freeze so I can simply defrost them and whip up the coconut curry broth on the day I want to enjoy this dish. **Serves 4**

½ cup brown or green lentils, rinsed and drained

1⅓ cups water

1 bay leaf

½ cup chopped walnuts

1 tablespoon olive oil or avocado oil

½ large onion, chopped

3 cloves garlic, minced

1 celery stalk, chopped

1 carrot, peeled and chopped

1 cup old-fashioned rolled oats

3 tablespoons reduced-sodium tamari, reduced-sodium soy sauce, or coconut aminos

2 tablespoons ground flaxseed

2 tablespoons green curry paste

1 tablespoon miso paste

2 teaspoons pure maple syrup

1 teaspoon apple cider vinegar

1 teaspoon dried basil

¼ teaspoon fine sea salt

¼ teaspoon ground black pepper

1. Preheat the oven to 350°F. Line a rimmed baking sheet with parchment paper.

2. In a small saucepan, combine the lentils, water, and bay leaf. Bring to a boil over medium-high heat, then reduce the heat to low, cover, and simmer until all the liquid is absorbed and the lentils are tender, 15 to 20 minutes. Remove from the heat, discard the bay leaf, and set the lentils aside to cool.

3. While the lentils are cooking, spread out the walnuts on a rimmed baking sheet and bake for 8 to 10 minutes, until lightly toasted. Set aside to cool, but leave the oven on.

4. Heat the oil in a medium sauté pan over medium heat and cook the onion, garlic, celery, and carrot until they soften and become fragrant, 5 to 10 minutes. Set aside to cool.

5. Reserve ½ cup of the cooked lentils and put the rest in a food processor, along with the cooked veggies, toasted walnuts, oats, tamari, flaxseed, curry paste, miso paste, maple syrup, apple cider vinegar, dried basil, salt, and pepper. Pulse until just combined and the texture is to your liking. You want the mixture to stick together, without being completely pureed.

6. Stir in the reserved ½ cup lentils.

7. Scoop out 1½ tablespoons of the lentil mixture and shape into a meatball. Place on the prepared baking sheet. Repeat with the remaining mixture. You should get about 20 meatballs.

8. Bake the meatballs for 10 minutes, then flip and bake for another 10 minutes.

9. Meanwhile, to make curry broth, heat the oil in a large skillet over medium heat. Add the garlic, ginger, and onion and cook until fragrant, about 5 minutes. Stir in the bell pepper, coconut milk, vegetable broth, curry paste, and salt and bring to a low boil for about 5 minutes.

10. Remove the skillet from the heat and stir in the spinach and cilantro.

Coconut Curry Broth

2 teaspoons avocado oil

2 cloves garlic, minced

2 teaspoons grated fresh ginger

1 medium yellow onion, chopped

1 yellow bell pepper, seeded and chopped

1 (13.5-ounce) can coconut milk

1 cup vegetable broth

3 tablespoons green curry paste

¼ teaspoon fine sea salt

1 cup (loosely packed) baby spinach

¼ cup chopped fresh cilantro, plus more for garnish

3 cups cooked brown rice (see page 21; use 1 cup rice + 2 cups water)

¼ cup sliced green onions, for garnish

Serve Immediately: Scoop ¾ cup brown rice into each bowl, pour one quarter of the coconut curry broth over the rice, and top with 4 or 5 meatballs. Garnish each serving with more cilantro and a few green onions and serve.

Meal Prep: Store the meatballs, broth, and rice in separate storage containers. The meatballs can be frozen, but I don't recommend freezing the broth. When ready to serve, follow the reheat instructions. Scoop ¾ cup cooked brown rice into a bowl, pour one quarter of the coconut curry broth over the rice, and top with 4 or 5 meatballs. Garnish with more cilantro and a few green onions and serve.

Store: Meatballs, broth, and rice separately in the fridge for up to 5 days, or meatballs in the freezer for up to 1 month.

Reheat: To reheat the lentil meatballs from the refrigerator, warm in a skillet over medium heat for 5 to 10 minutes. Heat the broth in a saucepan over medium heat until warm and heat the rice in the microwave for 1 to 2 minutes. Thaw the frozen meatballs in the fridge overnight and then reheat from the refrigerator.

NUTRITION FACTS

Per serving: ¼ recipe | Calories: 721 | Carbohydrates: 81g | Protein: 19g | Fat: 38g | Fiber: 20g | Sugar: 18g

Sheet Pan Meals

154 Orange Tempeh and Broccoli

157 Lemony Fall Harvest Sheet Pan Meal

158 Portobello Mushroom Fajitas

161 Sheet Pan Kale and Eggs Hash

162 Veggie Sausage with Potatoes, Peppers, and Onions

165 Cauliflower and Chickpea Shawarma Pita Pockets

166 Pesto Veggie and Cauliflower Gnocchi

169 Black Bean and Cauliflower Burritos

170 Maple-Chipotle Veggies and Chickpeas

173 Eat the Rainbow Sheet Pan Meal

Orange Tempeh and Broccoli

1½ cups orange juice

⅓ cup reduced-sodium tamari, reduced-sodium soy sauce, or coconut aminos

2 tablespoons pure maple syrup

1 tablespoon minced fresh ginger

1 tablespoon minced garlic

2 tablespoons arrowroot powder or cornstarch

2 (8-ounce) packages tempeh, cut into ¼-inch cubes

2 heads broccoli, cut into florets (about 5 cups)

2 tablespoons olive oil

1 teaspoon fine sea salt

½ teaspoon ground black pepper

2 cups cooked brown or white rice (see page 21; use ⅔ cup brown rice + 1⅓ cups water, or ⅔ cup white rice + 1⅓ cups water)

Sriracha, for serving (optional)

BRITTANY'S TIPS

● Feel free to swap the tempeh for tofu, if desired. Use 1 (14- to 16-ounce) package extra-firm tofu, drained and pressed.

● You can serve the tempeh over cauliflower rice instead of brown or white rice, if you prefer.

I haven't always loved tempeh, but a lucky happenstance led me to a recipe with a sticky orange sauce that brought me around to this nutritional powerhouse, and I'm so glad it did. Tempeh is a complete source of plant-based protein (1 cup has 31 grams) and a great source of B vitamins, manganese, and isoflavones. This sheet pan tempeh is a spin on that original recipe I fell in love with, a tasty orange marinade that not only flavors the tempeh before it's baked but also doubles as a sauce for the entire dish. I recommend chopping the tempeh into small, bite-size pieces so that each bite can really soak up all the flavor while marinating. **Serves 4**

1. In a shallow dish, whisk together the orange juice, tamari, maple syrup, ginger, garlic, and arrowroot powder. Add the tempeh, cover, and let marinate in the refrigerator for least 2 hours or overnight. If possible, toss the tempeh once or twice to make sure all sides of the tempeh are getting coated with the marinade.

2. When ready to cook, preheat the oven to 400°F. Line a rimmed baking sheet with parchment paper.

3. In a large bowl, toss the broccoli florets with the olive oil, salt, and pepper.

4. Spread out the broccoli florets on the prepared baking sheet and use a slotted spoon to scoop the tempeh onto the baking sheet as well. Reserve the marinade. Roast the tempeh and broccoli for 15 minutes, toss, and roast for another 15 minutes or so, until the tempeh is golden brown and the broccoli is bright green with a few browned spots.

5. Meanwhile, heat the reserved marinade in a small saucepan over medium heat. Cook until it's thick enough to coat the back of a spoon, 5 to 10 minutes.

6. Once the tempeh and broccoli are done, pour the thickened sauce over the tempeh and broccoli and toss to coat.

Serve Immediately: Scoop ½ cup rice into each bowl, then evenly divide the tempeh and broccoli mixture on top. Serve warm, drizzled with sriracha, if desired.

Meal Prep: Scoop ½ cup rice into 4 meal prep containers, then evenly divide the tempeh and broccoli mixture on top. When ready to serve, follow the reheat instructions. Serve warm, drizzled with sriracha, if desired.

Store: In the refrigerator for up to 4 days.

Reheat: Microwave until warm throughout, 1 to 2 minutes.

NUTRITION FACTS

Per serving: ¼ recipe | Calories: 502 | Carbohydrates: 67g | Protein: 31g | Fat: 14g | Fiber: 12g | Sugar: 16g

Lemony Fall Harvest Sheet Pan Meal

3 cups ½-inch cubes butternut squash

1 pound Brussels sprouts, trimmed and halved

2 (15-ounce) cans chickpeas, drained and rinsed

½ medium yellow onion, chopped

¼ cup olive oil

3 tablespoons balsamic vinegar

1 tablespoon minced garlic

1 tablespoon pure maple syrup

2 teaspoons fine sea salt

1½ teaspoon ground black pepper

1 teaspoon fennel seeds

1 teaspoon paprika

1 teaspoon garlic powder

Pinch ground nutmeg

2 lemons, sliced

2 cups cooked brown rice, white rice, or quinoa (see pages 20–21; use ⅔ cup brown rice + 1⅓ cups water, or ⅔ cup white rice or quinoa + 1⅓ cups water)

Fresh parsley or cilantro, for garnish

Hot sauce, for serving (optional)

BRITTANY'S TIPS

- Add a little crunch by sprinkling pepitas on top when serving.

- You can use cauliflower rice instead of cooked rice or quinoa.

This fall-inspired sheet pan dish came about when I had leftover butternut squash and yellow onion after peeling and chopping the veggies for my Butternut Squash and Black Bean Enchiladas (page 200). If you ever find yourself with a surplus of chopped veggies, the quickest and easiest way to use them is often a sheet pan meal with a little rice, quinoa, or lettuce and whatever sauce or dressing you have in your fridge at the time. The chickpea, butternut squash, and Brussels sprout combo here is delicious on its own, but the balsamic sauce makes this dish really shine. Add the fresh lemon slices and you've got a delightfully bright yet warm dish that you'll want to make on a regular rotation. I recommend serving the chickpea and veggie mixture over your favorite grain or cauliflower rice. If you're looking for more protein, feel free to serve a fried or poached egg on top of the finished dish.

Serves 4

1. Preheat the oven to 375°F.

2. In a large bowl, toss the butternut squash, Brussels sprouts, chickpeas, and onion with the olive oil, balsamic vinegar, garlic, maple syrup, salt, pepper, fennel, paprika, garlic powder, and nutmeg.

3. Spread out the chickpea-veggie mixture on one or two rimmed baking sheets and scatter the lemon slices on top.

4. Roast for 30 minutes, toss, then continue roasting for another 20 to 30 minutes, until the chickpeas are crisp and the butternut squash is fork-tender. Remove from the oven and discard the lemon slices.

Serve Immediately: Scoop ½ cup rice into each bowl, then evenly divide the chickpea-veggie mixture on top. Serve warm, garnished with fresh herbs and hot sauce (if desired).

Meal Prep: Scoop ½ cup rice into 4 meal prep containers, then evenly divide the chickpea-veggie mixture on top. When ready to serve, follow the reheat instructions. Serve warm, garnished with fresh herbs and hot sauce (if desired).

Store: In the refrigerator for up to 1 week.

Reheat: Microwave until warm throughout, about 1 minute.

NUTRITION FACTS

Per serving: ¼ recipe with brown rice | Calories: 545 | Carbohydrates: 89g | Protein: 18g | Fat: 17g | Fiber: 22g | Sugar: 13g

Portobello Mushroom Fajitas

Turning fajitas into a sheet pan meal makes the prep and cleanup process so simple, and I love this veggie-packed version with portobello mushrooms. Portobellos are a good source of essential nutrients (including vitamin B, fiber, and a bit of plant-based protein) and their meaty texture and umami flavor make them the perfect meat replacement in fajitas. The healthy fats in the cashew queso add a cheesy, creamy component that makes them really satisfying. **Serves 4**

4 portobello mushrooms caps, cleaned and sliced

3 tri-color bell peppers, seeded and thinly sliced

1 yellow onion, thinly sliced

2 tablespoons olive or avocado oil

1 tablespoon chili powder

1 teaspoon garlic powder

1 teaspoon onion powder

1 teaspoon ground cumin

1 teaspoon paprika

1 teaspoon dried oregano

1 teaspoon fine sea salt

½ teaspoon ground black pepper

8 to 12 flour, corn, or grain-free tortillas

1 recipe Cashew Queso (page 245)

Toppings of choice: salsa, sour cream, shredded cheese, chopped romaine lettuce, sliced jalapeños, fresh cilantro, sliced avocado, and/or guacamole

1. Preheat the oven to 375°F.

2. In a large bowl, toss the mushrooms, bell peppers, and onion with the olive oil and seasonings.

3. Spread out the seasoned veggies on a parchment-lined rimmed baking sheet and roast for 30 minutes, tossing after 15 minutes.

Serve Immediately: Serve the veggies in warm tortillas, topped with cashew queso and other toppings of your choice.

Meal Prep: Store the veggies, cashew queso, and toppings in separate airtight containers. When ready to serve, follow the reheat instructions for the veggies. Serve the veggies in warm tortillas topped with cashew queso and other toppings of your choice.

Store: Fajita filling in the refrigerator for up to 4 days. Cashew queso in the refrigerator for up to 1 week.

Reheat: Heat the veggies in a skillet over medium heat until warm throughout or microwave for about 1 minute.

NUTRITION FACTS

Per serving: 2 filled tortillas with 2 tablespoons queso | Calories: 434 | Carbohydrates: 53g | Protein: 12g | Fat: 20g | Fiber: 6g | Sugar: 6g

BRITTANY'S TIPS

● Packaged portobello mushroom caps will likely already be clean and ready to use, but if desired you can use a damp paper towel or kitchen cloth to remove any remaining dirt. Some sources suggest that you should remove the gills of the mushroom caps, but I don't find it necessary for this recipe.

● This recipe would also work well on a grill. Preheat the grill to medium-high. In step 3, rather than putting the seasoned vegetables on a baking sheet, put them on a grill pan and grill for about 10 minutes, turning occasionally.

● The cashew queso will thicken up as it sits in the fridge. You can warm it up to thin it out a bit and/or add additional water, if needed.

Sheet Pan Kale and Eggs Hash

When I was growing up, every now and then my mom would say we could have breakfast for dinner, and those ended up being some of my favorite meals of all time. Even now, breakfast is my favorite meal of the day, so anytime I can bring breakfast foods into my dinner rotation, I'm all for it. This sheet pan hash was adapted from a recipe my brother and sister-in-law made for the group on a family beach trip—they made it for breakfast, but as soon as I tasted it I knew it would work perfectly as a breakfast-for-dinner recipe. It's hearty, flavorful, and a definite crowd pleaser. **Serves 3**

3 red potatoes, scrubbed and cut into ½-inch cubes

1 medium yellow onion, thinly sliced

1 red or orange bell pepper, seeded and sliced

2½ tablespoons olive oil, divided

1 teaspoon paprika

1 teaspoon garlic powder

¾ teaspoon fine sea salt, divided, plus more to taste

¼ teaspoon ground black pepper, divided, plus more to taste

1 bunch curly kale, chopped (3 to 4 cups packed)

1 cup shredded sharp or white cheddar cheese (optional)

6 large eggs

Hot sauce, for serving (optional)

1. Preheat the oven to 425°F.

2. In a large bowl, toss together the potatoes, onion, an ell pepper with 2 tablespoons of the oil, the paprika, garlic powd teaspoon of the salt, and ⅛ teaspoon of the pepper.

3. Spread out the vegetables on a parchment-lined ed baking sheet and bake for 20 minutes. Rem rom the oven, toss the veggies, and scatter the kale on top. Sprinkle the remaining ½ tablespoon oil, remaining ¼ teaspoon salt, and remaining ⅛ teaspoon pepper on the kale. Toss to combine, return the baking sheet to the oven, and roast for 8 to 10 minutes, until the kale is wilted.

4. Remove the baking sheet from the oven. Toss the veggies and top with the shredded cheese, if using. With a spatula, make 6 wells in the veggies, then crack 1 egg into each well. Season the eggs with a little salt and pepper.

5. Return the baking sheet to the oven and bake for 5 to 6 minutes, until the whites of the eggs are cooked through and the cheese is melted.

Serve Immediately: Evenly divide the hash mixture on 3 plates with 2 eggs to each. Serve with hot sauce, if desired.

Meal Prep: Evenly divide the hash mixture into 3 meal prep containers with 2 eggs each. When ready to serve, follow the reheat instructions. Serve with hot sauce, if desired.

Store: In the refrigerator for up to 4 days.

Reheat: Heat in the microwave until warm throughout, 1 to 2 minutes.

NUTRITION FACTS

Per serving: ⅓ hash with 2 eggs | Calories: 561 | Carbohydrates: 42g | Protein: 29g | Fat: 34g | Fiber: 5g | Sugar: 5g

Veggie Sausage
with Potatoes, Peppers, and Onions

As you've probably noticed, I don't use many meat substitutes in my recipes (learn more about why on page 14), but I really wanted to create a plant-based version of a popular chicken sausage sheet pan meal from my website, and I knew beans just wouldn't bring the texture and flavor I was going for. This recipe is especially delicious with Beyond Meat Italian sausages. They give the dish the same herby flavor you'd expect from traditional Italian sausage and they don't dry out while roasting like other brands of plant-based sausage I tested. If you love the combo of peppers, onions, and potatoes (and who doesn't?), this one is a must-try. Added bonus: It couldn't be easier to make. Simply combine everything in a bowl, dump it onto your baking sheet, bake, and enjoy! **Serves 4**

1 (14-ounce) package plant-based Italian sausage links (such as Beyond Meat), cut into 2-inch rounds

3 medium red potatoes, cut into 1-inch chunks

1 large green bell pepper, seeded and cut into large chunks

1 large red bell pepper, seeded and cut into large chunks

1 yellow onion, cut into wedges

3 tablespoons olive oil

3 cloves garlic, minced

1 tablespoon Italian seasoning

½ teaspoon fine sea salt

¼ teaspoon ground black pepper

1. Preheat the oven to 400ºF.

2. In a large bowl, toss the sausage, potatoes, bell peppers, and onion with the olive oil, garlic, Italian seasoning, salt, and pepper.

3. Spread out the sausage and vegetables on a parchment-lined rimmed baking sheet and bake for 20 minutes. Toss everything, then continue roasting for about 20 minutes more, until the potatoes are fork-tender and golden in spots.

Serve Immediately: Evenly divide the sausage and veggies into 4 bowls and enjoy.

Meal Prep: Evenly divide the sausage and veggies into 4 meal prep containers. When ready to serve, follow the reheat instructions and enjoy.

Store: In the refrigerator for up to 5 days.

Reheat: Heat in the microwave until warm throughout, 1 to 2 minutes.

BRITTANY'S TIP

I find this dish filling enough on its own, but you could always serve it over steamed rice or quinoa to bulk it up a bit.

NUTRITION FACTS

Per serving: ¼ recipe | Calories: 407 | Carbohydrates: 34g | Protein: 20g | Fat: 23g | Fiber: 7g | Sugar: 5g

Cauliflower and Chickpea Shawarma Pita Pockets

In this plant-based spin on chicken shawarma, cauliflower and chickpeas are seasoned and roasted with a Middle Eastern–inspired spice blend. To make this dish a full meal, I recommend serving it in pita pockets with shredded lettuce, tomato, cucumber, cilantro, and tahini sauce. Of course, you can always skip the pita pocket and turn this into a big salad as well. Simply add extra romaine lettuce for your base and maybe some additional tomatoes and cucumber. **Serves 4**

1 medium head cauliflower, cut into bite-size florets (about 4 cups)

1 (15-ounce) can chickpeas, drained, rinsed, and patted dry

½ medium red onion, coarsely chopped

2 tablespoons olive oil

2 tablespoons fresh lemon juice

2 cloves garlic, minced

1½ teaspoons ground coriander

1½ teaspoons ground cumin

1½ teaspoons paprika

1½ teaspoons fine sea salt

1 teaspoon ground black pepper

4 whole-grain pita pockets or other gluten-free wraps

1 cup shredded romaine lettuce

1 cup chopped cherry or grape tomatoes

1 cup diced cucumber

¼ cup chopped fresh cilantro

1 recipe Creamy Tahini Sauce (page 142)

1. Preheat the oven to 400°F.

2. In a large bowl, toss the cauliflower, chickpeas, and red onion with the olive oil, lemon juice, garlic, and seasonings until evenly coated.

3. Spread out the mixture in a single layer on one or two rimmed baking sheets. Roast for 30 to 40 minutes, tossing halfway, until the cauliflower is brown in some spots and fork-tender.

Serve Immediately: If planning to serve immediately, wrap the pita pockets in aluminum foil and heat them in the oven for the last 6 to 8 minutes. Evenly divide the cauliflower-chickpea mixture into 4 pita pockets. Top each with ¼ cup lettuce, 1 tablespoon tomatoes, ¼ cup cucumber, and 1 tablespoon cilantro. Drizzle with 1 to 2 tablespoons tahini sauce and enjoy.

Meal Prep: Store the cauliflower-chickpea mixture and the tahini sauce in separate containers until ready to serve, or fill the pita pockets with the cauliflower-chickpea mixture and toppings and place in 4 meal prep containers with a small container of 1 to 2 tablespoons tahini sauce on the side for each. When ready to serve, follow the reheat instructions, if desired. Drizzle with the tahini sauce and enjoy.

Store: In the refrigerator up to 4 days.

Reheat: These pita pockets can be eaten warm or cold, but I highly recommend heating up the pita pocket in the microwave by wrapping it in a wet paper towel and heating for 15 to 30 seconds. If you like, you can also heat up the cauliflower-chickpea mixture in a skillet over medium heat for about 5 minutes or in the microwave for 1 to 2 minutes.

NUTRITION FACTS ───────────

Per serving: ¼ recipe in 1 pita pocket with 2 tablespoons dressing | Calories: 434 | Carbohydrates: 49g | Protein: 16g | Fat: 22g | Fiber: 15g | Sugar: 10g

Pesto Veggie and Cauliflower Gnocchi

When cauliflower gnocchi first came out, it wasn't love at first bite for me because following the instructions on the package resulted in sticky, mushy gnocchi. However, if you roast cauliflower gnocchi, they get a golden, crisp exterior that's perfection. So that's how we're cooking them for this sheet pan meal! All the fresh veggies and pesto make this dish so colorful and flavorful. It's been an instant hit with everyone who's tried it, even kiddos who aren't usually drawn to veggies. **Serves 3**

2 red or orange bell peppers, seeded and cut into ½-inch pieces

4 cups (loosely packed) coarsely chopped kale

1 medium-large red onion, cut into ½-inch pieces

2 cloves garlic, minced

1 tablespoon plus 2 teaspoons olive oil, divided

1 teaspoon Italian seasoning

¾ teaspoon fine sea salt, divided

½ teaspoon ground black pepper, divided

2 (12-ounce) packages frozen cauliflower gnocchi (such as Trader Joe's)

¼ cup store-bought pesto or **Walnut Pesto (page 107)**

Grated Parmesan cheese, for garnish (optional)

1. Preheat the oven to 450°F. Line two rimmed baking sheets with parchment paper.

2. In a large bowl, toss the peppers, kale, and onion with the garlic, 1 tablespoon of the oil, the Italian seasoning, ½ teaspoon of the salt, and ¼ teaspoon of the pepper until evenly coated.

3. Spread out the veggies in a single layer on one of the lined baking sheets.

4. In the same bowl, toss the frozen gnocchi with the remaining 2 teaspoons olive oil, remaining ¼ teaspoon salt, and remaining ¼ teaspoon pepper.

5. Spread out the gnocchi in a single layer on the second lined baking sheet. Reserve the bowl.

6. Place the baking sheet with the gnocchi in the oven and roast for 25 minutes. Remove from the oven, toss, and continue roasting for another 15 to 20 minutes, until the edges are a bit golden. At the same time you add the gnocchi back into the oven, place the baking sheet with the veggies in the oven as well. Roast the veggies for about 15 minutes, until they are bright and tender.

7. Once everything is done roasting, combine the veggies and gnocchi in the reserved bowl. Top with the pesto and toss to coat.

Serve Immediately: Evenly divide the gnocchi and veggies into 3 bowls. Serve with grated Parmesan, if desired.

Meal Prep: Evenly divide the gnocchi and veggies into 3 meal prep containers. When ready to serve, follow the reheat instructions. Serve with grated Parmesan, if desired.

Store: In the refrigerator for up to 4 days.

Reheat: Heat in a skillet over medium heat until warm, about 5 minutes. Or microwave for 1 to 2 minutes.

BRITTANY'S TIP

Don't skip the parchment paper. It is the key for the gnocchi to get golden brown and to prevent it from sticking to the pan. It also makes for easy cleanup.

NUTRITION FACTS

Per serving: ⅓ recipe | Calories: 475 | Carbohydrates: 58g | Protein: 9g | Fat: 21g | Fiber: 15g | Sugar: 8g

Black Bean and Cauliflower Burritos

Doing a little prep work to have these burritos stashed in the freezer for a quick lunch or dinner is so worth it! The veggies and beans are coated in a variety of spices before roasting, which gives the burritos a ton of flavor. Just don't forget the cashew queso! It's so creamy and provides a cheese-like component, without any dairy! Once you've prepped these burritos, you'll be able to keep them in the freezer for up to 3 months.

Serves 5

1 medium head cauliflower, trimmed and cut into small florets

1 (15-ounce) can black beans, drained and rinsed

1 medium sweet potato, scrubbed and cut into small pieces

1 medium red onion, chopped

3 tablespoons olive oil

1 tablespoon chili powder

1 teaspoon ground cumin

½ teaspoon garlic powder

¼ teaspoon paprika

1½ teaspoons fine sea salt

¾ teaspoon ground black pepper

¼ cup chopped fresh cilantro

Juice of ½ lime

5 burrito-size tortillas, gluten-free or grain-free if desired

5 tablespoons Cashew Queso (page 245)

1. Preheat the oven to 400°F.

2. In a large bowl, toss the cauliflower florets, black beans, sweet potato, and onion with the oil and seasonings.

3. Spread out the vegetable mixture in a single layer on one or two rimmed baking sheets. Roast for around 40 minutes, tossing halfway through, until the cauliflower and sweet potato are fork-tender and browned in places.

4. Remove from the oven, top with the cilantro and lime juice, and toss to combine. Allow to cool for 5 to 10 minutes.

5. Divide the veggie and black bean mixture evenly between the tortillas and top each with 1 tablespoon cashew queso. Fold the sides and ends of the tortillas over the filling and roll up.

Serve Immediately: Spray a skillet with nonstick cooking spray and heat over medium-high heat. Cook the burrito until brown on all sides and warm throughout, 3 to 4 minutes per side.

Meal Prep: Wrap each burrito in aluminum foil, place the burritos in a freezer bag, and freeze. When ready to serve, follow the reheat instructions and enjoy.

Store: In the freezer for up to 3 months.

Reheat: Thaw the burritos in the refrigerator overnight. Spray a skillet with nonstick cooking spray and heat over medium-high heat. Cook the burrito until brown on all sides and warm throughout, 3 to 4 minutes per side. You can also bake the thawed burritos in a 350°F oven for about 20 minutes, until the tortilla is lightly browned and the burrito is warm throughout.

To cook from frozen, remove the aluminum foil and wrap the burrito in a damp paper towel. Microwave until warm throughout, 2 to 4 minutes. Alternatively, you can bake the frozen burrito (still wrapped in foil) in a 350°F oven for about 1 hour.

NUTRITION FACTS —————————————————

Per serving: 1 burrito | Calories: 469 | Carbohydrates: 70g | Protein: 17g | Fat: 16g | Fiber: 12g | Sugar: 7g

Maple-Chipotle Veggies and Chickpeas

While I love the combo of roasted broccoli, Brussels sprouts, and chickpeas, the maple-chipotle glaze is what makes this meal shine. It has a nice depth of flavor and spiciness from the chipotle peppers, but it's balanced by a bit of sweetness from the coconut aminos and maple syrup. The fresh lemon juice adds a bit of brightness and the roasted sunflower seeds are the perfect crunchy topping. Plus, it's one of the quickest sheet pan meals you can make! **Serves 4**

1 medium head broccoli, cut into florets (about 2 cups)

1 pound Brussels sprouts, trimmed and quartered

1 (15-ounce) can chickpeas, drained and rinsed

1½ tablespoons olive oil, plus more for serving

¾ teaspoon fine sea salt

¾ teaspoon ground black pepper

3 cups cooked quinoa (see page 20; use 1 cup quinoa + 2 cups water)

Lemon wedges, for serving

¼ cup roasted salted sunflower seeds, for topping

Chipotle Sauce

2 tablespoons canned chipotle peppers in adobo sauce, chopped

2 cloves garlic, minced

2 tablespoons reduced-sodium tamari, reduced-sodium soy sauce, or coconut aminos

1 tablespoon pure maple syrup

2 teaspoons apple cider vinegar

1 teaspoon olive oil

1. Preheat the oven to 400°F. Line a rimmed baking sheet with parchment paper.

2. In a large bowl, toss the broccoli, Brussels sprouts, and chickpeas with the olive oil, salt, and pepper.

3. Spread out the veggies and chickpeas on the prepared baking sheet.

4. Bake for 20 minutes.

5. While the veggies and chickpeas are roasting, whisk together all ingredients for the chipotle sauce in a small bowl and set aside.

6. After 20 minutes, remove the veggies and chickpeas from the oven. Turn on the broiler. Add the sauce to the baking sheet and toss to coat the veggies and chickpeas. Broil for about 5 minutes, until the chickpeas are crisp.

Serve Immediately: Scoop ¾ cup quinoa into 4 bowls, then evenly divide the roasted veggie and chickpea mixture on top. Garnish each bowl with a squeeze of lemon, a drizzle of olive oil, and 1 tablespoon sunflower seeds and enjoy.

Meal Prep: Scoop ¾ cup cooked quinoa into 4 meal prep containers, then evenly divide the roasted veggie and chickpea mixture on top. Add a squeeze of lemon, a drizzle of olive oil, and 1 tablespoon sunflower seeds. Alternatively you can add the lemon, oil, and sunflower seeds just before serving. When ready to serve, follow the reheat instructions and enjoy.

Store: In the refrigerator for up to 4 days.

Reheat: Heat in a skillet over medium heat until warm, about 5 minutes, or microwave for 1 to 2 minutes.

NUTRITION FACTS

Per serving: ¼ recipe | Calories: 478 | Carbohydrates: 66g | Protein: 19g | Fat: 17g | Fiber: 15g | Sugar: 9g

Eat the Rainbow Sheet Pan Meal

Written as is, this recipe makes for a beautiful rainbow-colored meal, to be served with quinoa and tahini sauce. But most of the time it's my go-to template when I'm looking to use up whatever is left in the fridge at the end of the week...all the veggies, pre-cooked grains, and a sauce or dressing that's still hanging around. If you don't have grains or a sauce to pair with the veggies, feel free to roast them up and use them as a simple side or as a topping for salads, sandwiches and wraps, pasta, or omelets. **Serves 4**

2 red bell peppers, seeded and cut into ½-inch chunks

3 tablespoons olive oil, divided

4 carrots, cut into ½-inch-thick pieces

2 yellow squash, cut into ½-inch-thick pieces

3 cups broccoli florets

1 red onion, cut into ½-inch-thick wedges

1 (15-ounce) can chickpeas, drained and rinsed

1 tablespoon Italian seasoning

1 teaspoon fine sea salt, plus more to taste

½ teaspoon black pepper, plus more to taste

3 cups cooked quinoa (see page 20; use 1 cup quinoa + 2 cups water or vegetable broth)

1 recipe Creamy Tahini Sauce (page 142), for serving

1. Preheat the oven to 400°F.

2. In a large bowl, toss the red bell peppers with 1 teaspoon of the olive oil.

3. Place the peppers in a single layer in one section of a parchment-lined rimmed baking sheet.

4. Repeat with the remaining oil and the carrots, squash, broccoli, red onion, and chickpeas, arranging each ingredient next to the one before it to make a rainbow.

5. Sprinkle everything with the Italian seasoning, salt, and pepper.

6. Roast for 15 minutes, toss everything, then continue roasting for another 10 minutes or so, until the veggies are just starting to brown and the carrots are fork-tender.

Serve Immediately: Scoop ¾ cup cooked quinoa into each bowl, then evenly divide the veggie and chickpea mixture on top. Drizzle on the tahini sauce and season with salt and pepper.

Meal Prep: Scoop ¾ cup quinoa into 4 meal prep containers, then evenly divide the veggie and chickpea mixture on top. Store the tahini sauce in a small container. When ready to serve, follow the reheat instructions, drizzle with the tahini sauce, and season with salt and pepper.

Reheat: Heat in the microwave until warm, 1 to 2 minutes.

NUTRITION FACTS —————————————————————

Per serving: ¼ recipe | Calories: 239 | Carbohydrates: 33g | Protein: 7g | Fat: 12g | Fiber: 10g | Sugar: 15g

BRITTANY'S TIPS —————

As I mentioned above, this is a great recipe to use whatever leftover veggies you have in the fridge or what's in season. It doesn't necessarily need to follow the colors of the rainbow. I love swapping the yellow squash for butternut squash in the fall and winter months. Try to choose veggies that will finish cooking around the same time and be sure not to overcrowd your baking sheets so the veggies roast instead of steam. You may need to use two sheets!

One Pan Meals

176 Modern Broccoli Cheese Casserole

179 Pesto-Feta Pasta Bake

180 Tofu Shakshuka

183 Greek Green Beans and Potatoes

184 Italian-Style Stuffed Bell Peppers

187 Tofu Lettuce Wraps

188 Red Lentil and Sweet Potato Curry

191 Taco-Stuffed Zucchini Boats

192 Thai-Inspired Spaghetti Squash
    Noodles with Peanut Sauce

195 Creamy "No Cream" Broccoli
    Cheese Soup

196 The Best Baked Eggplant Parm

199 Add-the-Veggies Fried Rice

200 Butternut Squash and
    Black Bean Enchiladas

203 Slow Cooker Tuscan White
    Bean Soup

204 Quinoa Black Bean Burgers

207 Slow Cooker Chili Mac

208 Spaghetti Squash Pizza Bake

211 Mushroom Stroganoff

Modern Broccoli Cheese Casserole

Growing up, I was obsessed with broccoli cheese casserole...the one with instant rice and cream of mushroom soup. These days I'm all about making upgrades to my childhood comfort foods to make them healthier, and this updated version of broccoli cheese casserole still gives me all the nostalgic vibes. It's cheesy, comforting, and filling. Broccoli cheese casserole is traditionally served as a side dish, but I find that this version is hearty enough to enjoy as a main dish, with over 20 grams of protein per serving thanks to the combo of chickpeas, broccoli, and cheese. **Serves 6**

1 tablespoon olive oil

3 cloves garlic, minced

1 cup diced button mushrooms

½ teaspoon fine sea salt, plus more to taste

⅛ teaspoon ground black pepper, plus more to taste

1½ cups white rice

3 cups vegetable broth

2 cups unsweetened oat milk or other plant-based milk

1 (15-ounce) can chickpeas, rinsed and drained

2 medium-large heads broccoli, trimmed and cut into bite-size florets (7 to 8 cups)

2 cups shredded mild or sharp cheddar cheese or plant-based shredded cheese

1. Heat the oil in a Dutch oven or large pot over medium heat. Add the garlic and mushrooms and sauté, stirring occasionally, until fragrant, 3 to 5 minutes. Season with the salt and pepper.

2. Add the rice and let toast for about 2 minutes. Pour in the vegetable broth and milk stir to combine. Bring the liquid to a boil, then cover, reduce the heat, and simmer until the rice is cooked through and most of the liquid has been absorbed, 15 to 20 minutes.

3. Add the chickpeas and broccoli and stir everything together. Cover again and cook over medium-low heat until the broccoli is bright green and cooked to your desired firmness, 7 to 8 minutes. If the rice starts to stick to the bottom of the pan, add a splash of vegetable broth or water.

4. Reduce the heat to low and stir in the cheese until it's melted and incorporated with the rice and veggies. Turn off the heat, taste, and season with additional salt and pepper, if needed.

Serve Immediately: Evenly divide the casserole into 6 bowls or plates and serve warm.

Meal Prep: Evenly divide the casserole into 6 meal prep containers. When ready to serve, follow the reheat instructions.

Store: In the refrigerator for up to 4 days.

Reheat: Microwave until warm, 1 to 2 minutes.

NUTRITION FACTS

Per serving: ⅙ recipe | Calories: 423 | Carbohydrates: 55g | Protein: 21g | Fat: 16g | Fiber: 8g | Sugar: 5g

---

BRITTANY'S TIP

I prefer white rice over brown in this recipe because it cooks faster, but you can use brown rice if you prefer. You'll need to add an extra ½ cup vegetable broth and cook the rice for about 35 minutes before adding the chickpeas and broccoli.

Pesto-Feta Pasta Bake

Baked feta pasta was all the rage a few years ago, and I'm still hooked on baking feta until it becomes creamy enough to use as a pasta sauce. For this variation we're loading up the pan with colorful summer veggies and topping the pasta off with pesto for even more flavor! I recommend using chickpea pasta if it's available because of the added nutritional value, but any pasta will work. **Serves 6**

1 medium zucchini, cut into ½-inch pieces

1 medium yellow squash, cut into ½-inch pieces

2 cups chopped cherry or grape tomatoes

2 cloves garlic, minced

½ medium red onion, chopped

1 (8-ounce) block feta cheese

½ cup olive oil

½ teaspoon fine sea salt

½ teaspoon ground black pepper, plus more for serving

2 (8-ounce) boxes chickpea pasta

¼ cup jarred pesto

¼ cup chopped fresh basil, plus more for serving

1 teaspoon grated lemon zest

¼ teaspoon crushed red pepper, plus more for serving (optional)

Grated Parmesan cheese, for serving

1. Preheat the oven to 375°F.

2. Combine the zucchini, yellow squash, tomatoes, garlic, and onion in a 9 x 13-inch baking dish and nestle the block of feta in the middle. Drizzle the olive oil all over the veggies and feta. Sprinkle with the salt and pepper and use a spoon to toss until the veggies are nicely coated.

3. Bake for about 40 minutes, until the veggies are sizzling and the feta has softened.

4. Meanwhile, cook the pasta until al dente according to the package instructions. Drain.

5. Remove the baking dish from the oven. Add the pesto, basil, lemon zest, and crushed red pepper, if using, and stir until everything is well combined.

6. Add the pasta and toss to coat.

Serve Immediately: Evenly divide the pasta and veggies into 6 bowls and serve warm with additional basil, crushed red pepper, Parmesan, and black pepper.

Meal Prep: Evenly divide the pasta and veggies into 6 meal prep containers. Top with additional basil, crushed red pepper, Parmesan, and black pepper now or right before serving if you prefer. When ready to serve, follow the reheat instructions and enjoy.

Store: In the refrigerator for up to 4 days.

Reheat: Microwave until warm throughout, 1 to 2 minutes.

NUTRITION FACTS —————————————————————

Per serving: ⅙ recipe | Calories: 583 | Carbohydrates: 56g | Protein: 25g | Fat: 33g | Fiber: 9g | Sugar: 6g

Tofu
Shakshuka

3 tablespoons olive oil, divided

1 (14- to 16-ounce) package extra-firm tofu, drained, pressed, and cut into 8 large chunks

¾ teaspoon fine sea salt, divided

½ teaspoon ground black pepper, divided

1 large yellow onion, chopped

1 yellow, red, or orange bell pepper, seeded and chopped

4 cloves garlic, minced

½ teaspoon ground cumin

½ teaspoon paprika

¼ teaspoon cayenne pepper

1 (28-ounce) can diced tomatoes

½ cup crumbled feta cheese, plus more for garnish

¼ cup chopped fresh cilantro, for garnish

¼ cup chopped fresh parsley, for garnish

3 cups cooked brown rice, white rice, or quinoa (see pages 20–21; use 1 cup brown rice + 2½ cups water, 1 cup white rice + 2 cups water, or 1 cup quinoa + 2 cups water)

Toasted sourdough bread, pita, or naan, for serving (if desired)

There was a good stretch of time where Isaac and I would make shakshuka at least once a week. It was right after visiting Israel and we were totally enamored by how dynamic such a simple dish, made with minimal ingredients and one pan, could taste. Shakshuka is a classic Middle Eastern recipe with eggs cooked in tomato sauce, very similar to eggs in purgatory but with the addition of peppers, cumin, and paprika. It is traditionally served for breakfast, but for this version we're swapping the eggs for tofu, and I prefer to serve it for dinner. The tofu provides the perfect texture and a good amount of protein—and it soaks up all the tomato sauce flavor! **Serves 4**

1. Heat 1 tablespoon of the olive oil in a large skillet over medium heat. Add the tofu and sauté until lightly golden, about 2 minutes per side. Season with ¼ teaspoon each of the salt and black pepper while it cooks. Transfer the tofu to a plate.

2. Add the remaining 2 tablespoons oil to the skillet. Once hot, add the onion, bell pepper, and garlic and cook until the onion is soft and fragrant, 5 to 7 minutes.

3. Add the cumin, paprika, cayenne, and remaining ½ teaspoon each salt and black pepper. Give the mixture a stir and cook for 1 minute. Add the diced tomatoes and their juices and bring the sauce to a boil. Reduce the heat to a simmer and cook until the sauce thickens up a bit, about 10 minutes. Add the feta cheese and stir.

4. Gently add the tofu chunks to the tomato sauce, arranged around the pan. Cover and let the tofu cook until warm, about 5 minutes. Remove the skillet from the heat, uncover and let rest for a minute or two before serving.

Serve Immediately: Scoop ¾ cup brown rice or quinoa into 4 shallow dishes. Spoon 2 tofu chunks along with a big serving of tomato sauce on top. Garnish with extra feta cheese, cilantro, and parsley. Serve with toasted bread for dipping, if you like.

Meal Prep: Scoop ¾ cup brown rice or quinoa 4 meal prep containers. Spoon 2 tofu chunks along with a big serving of tomato sauce on top. When ready to serve, follow the reheat instructions, then garnish with extra feta cheese, cilantro, and parsley.

Store: In the refrigerator for up to 5 days.

Reheat: Heat in a skillet over medium heat until warm, about 5 minutes, or microwave for 1 to 2 minutes.

NUTRITION FACTS ———————————

Per serving: ¼ recipe without bread | Calories: 468 | Carbohydrates: 54g | Protein: 19g | Fat: 20g | Fiber: 6g | Sugar: 10g

Greek Green Beans and Potatoes

Every time I make this dish I'm reminded of the Richmond Greek Festival and my favorite side dish they serve featuring green beans slow-cooked in a tomato sauce. I look forward to it every year. My best friend's nanny is Greek and makes a similar dish called fasolakia, and it's what inspired this recipe. I love how this version turns the braised green beans into a meal with hearty potatoes and carrots. It's absolutely delicious served over brown rice or rice pilaf, and it's perfect to make ahead of time because it tastes even better after sitting in the fridge for a day or two. I should also note that it is super family friendly. Both Olivia and my friend's daughter gobble it up! **Serves 4**

⅓ cup olive oil

1 medium yellow onion, diced

8 cloves garlic, minced

1½ teaspoons fine sea salt

¼ teaspoon ground black pepper

2 teaspoons dried dill or parsley

¼ teaspoon ground cinnamon

4 Yukon Gold potatoes, cut into bite-size pieces

1 (28-ounce) can peeled whole tomatoes

2 cups vegetable broth

2 tablespoons tomato paste

1½ pounds fresh or frozen green beans, trimmed

2 carrots, peeled and chopped

3 cups cooked brown rice or rice pilaf (see page 21; use 1 cup brown rice + 2½ cups water, or follow package instructions for rice pilaf mix)

1. In a large pot or Dutch oven, heat the oil over medium-high heat. Add the onion and garlic and cook until fragrant, 5 to 7 minutes. Add the salt, pepper, dried dill or parsley, and cinnamon and cook for 1 minute, stirring frequently.

2. Add the potatoes, tomatoes and their juices, vegetable broth, tomato paste, green beans, and carrots. Use your spoon or spatula to break the tomatoes into small pieces.

3. Bring the mixture to a boil, then reduce the heat and simmer uncovered for 45 to 55 minutes or until the potatoes are fork-tender. Stir the mixture occasionally while also making sure the veggies are pressed down into the liquid so that they cook evenly.

Serve Immediately: Scoop ¾ cup rice or rice pilaf into 4 shallow dishes. Evenly divide the green bean mixture on top. Serve warm.

Meal Prep: Scoop ¾ cup rice or rice pilaf into 4 meal prep containers. Evenly divide the green bean mixture on top. When ready to serve, follow the reheat instructions and serve warm.

Store: In the refrigerator for up to 5 days.

Reheat: Heat in a skillet over medium heat until warm, about 5 minutes, or microwave for 1 to 2 minutes.

BRITTANY'S TIP

This dish is also really good with peas. Feel free to add 1 cup frozen peas at the same time you add the green beans and carrots if you have them on hand.

NUTRITION FACTS

Per serving: ¼ recipe | Calories: 531 | Carbohydrates: 82g | Protein: 12g | Fat: 20g | Fiber: 12g | Sugar: 16g

Italian-Style Stuffed Bell Peppers

We're putting a little spin on classic stuffed peppers by using a combination of veggie crumbles, mushrooms, and brown rice as the filling. Veggie crumbles are an easy plant-based substitute for ground meat, typically made with soy or pea protein. Don't skip the step of pre-baking the bell peppers, which helps soften them so that they cut easily without being too crunchy or tasting raw. Because this is a lighter meal, I recommend serving the peppers with a side of roasted or steamed vegetables and/or a side salad. **Serves 3**

6 bell peppers, any color

2 tablespoons olive oil

1 medium yellow onion, diced

2 cloves garlic, minced

1½ cups chopped button mushrooms

1 (13.5-ounce) package refrigerated or thawed frozen veggie crumbles (such as Lightlife)

2 teaspoons Italian seasoning

1 teaspoon fine sea salt, plus more to taste

1 teaspoon ground black pepper, plus more to taste

1 (14.5-ounce) can diced tomatoes

1 cup cooked brown rice (see page 21; use ⅓ cup rice + ¾ cup water)

1 cup shredded mozzarella cheese or plant-based shredded mozzarella, divided

1 tablespoon chopped fresh parsley

1. Preheat the oven to 400°F.

2. Slice off the top ¼ inch of each bell pepper and remove the ribs and seeds.

3. Pour about ½ inch water into a 9 x 13-inch baking dish. Place the peppers cut side down in the water, cover with aluminum foil, and bake for 30 minutes.

4. Meanwhile, heat the oil in a medium skillet over medium heat. Add the onion, garlic, and mushrooms and sauté until the onion is translucent and starting to brown and the mushrooms are soft, 7 to 10 minutes. Add the veggie crumbles, Italian seasoning, salt, and pepper.

5. Sauté for 3 to 4 minutes, then add the diced tomatoes and their juices. Stir to combine.

6. Add the cooked rice and ½ cup of the shredded mozzarella and mix until the cheese is melted. Taste and season with additional salt and pepper, if needed, and set aside.

7. When the peppers are done—they should be gently steamed, but not fully cooked—remove the foil and carefully discard the water, then let the peppers cool a bit.

8. Flip the peppers over and spoon the filling evenly into each one. Top with the remaining ½ cup mozzarella cheese.

9. Stand the stuffed peppers in the baking dish and bake, uncovered, for about 10 minutes, until the cheese is melted and the peppers are fully cooked through.

Serve Immediately: Put 2 stuffed peppers on each plate and garnish with the parsley. Serve warm.

Meal Prep: Put 2 stuffed peppers each in 3 meal prep containers. When ready to serve, follow the reheat instructions. Serve warm, garnished with parsley.

Store: In the refrigerator: Let cool, then store in an airtight container for up to 5 days.

In the freezer: Let cool, then wrap each pepper in two layers of plastic wrap and place in a freezer bag. Freeze for up to 3 months.

Reheat: From the fridge, place the peppers in a baking dish, cover with aluminum foil, and bake at 350°F for about 15 minutes, until warm throughout, or microwave for 1 to 2 minutes. From frozen, increase the bake time to 30 minutes, until thawed and warm throughout. You can also thaw overnight in the refrigerator, then bake as directed.

NUTRITION FACTS

Per serving: 2 stuffed peppers | Calories: 255 | Carbohydrates: 26g | Protein: 18g | Fat: 9g | Fiber: 7g | Sugar: 8g

Tofu Lettuce Wraps

  EF

If you're looking for a light and refreshing meal for spring and summer, these tofu lettuce wraps will hit the spot! Water chestnuts are a key ingredient in the tofu filling because they add a delightful crunch. Surprisingly, water chestnuts aren't a nut but instead a vegetable that's part of the tuber family (similar to a potato). They're grown in ponds, rice paddy fields, and/or shallow lakes and contain a high amount of fiber, vitamins, and antioxidants. Often you'll see lettuce wraps served with a dipping sauce, but I don't find one necessary with this recipe given how much flavor the homemade teriyaki sauce provides. However, if you'd like a sauce, the wraps would be delicious dipped in my Peanut Sauce (page 149). **Serves 3**

Teriyaki Sauce

3 tablespoons hoisin sauce

2 tablespoons reduced-sodium tamari, reduced-sodium soy sauce, or coconut aminos

2 tablespoons rice vinegar

1 teaspoon sriracha

1 teaspoon toasted sesame oil

Tofu Filling

¼ cup avocado or olive oil

2 (14- to 16-ounce) packages extra-firm tofu, drained, pressed, and cut into ¼-inch cubes

2 cups chopped button mushrooms

4 cloves garlic, minced

4 teaspoons minced fresh ginger

2 (8-ounce) cans water chestnuts, drained and sliced

5 green onions, sliced, plus more for garnish

Large romaine, butter, or iceberg lettuce leaves, for wrapping

¼ cup grated carrots

2 to 3 tablespoons chopped roasted peanuts

1. In a small bowl, whisk together all the teriyaki sauce ingredients. Set aside.

2. Heat the oil in a large skillet over medium-high heat. Add the tofu cubes and cook until all sides are golden, about 10 minutes. Add the mushrooms, garlic, ginger, water chestnuts, and green onions and cook for another 5 minutes.

3. Lower the heat to medium-low, pour in the sauce, and cook until the sauce is bubbly and starting to reduce, 1 to 2 minutes. Remove from the heat.

Serve Immediately: Portion 2 to 3 tablespoons tofu filling onto each lettuce leaf and top with the carrots, peanuts, and green onions. Enjoy warm.

Meal Prep: Transfer the tofu filling to a storage container and place the lettuce leaves, carrots, and green onions in a separate storage container. When ready to serve, follow the reheat instructions. Portion 2 to 3 tablespoons tofu filling onto each lettuce leaf and top with the carrots, peanuts, and green onions. Enjoy warm.

Store: In the refrigerator for up to 4 days.

Reheat: Heat the tofu filling in a skillet over medium heat until warm, 4 to 5 minutes, or in the microwave for 1 to 2 minutes.

BRITTANY'S TIP

Turn this recipe into a salad! Chop the lettuce, layer it on the bottom of your plate or bowl, and top with the tofu mixture, carrots, peanuts, and green onions. Use the Peanut Sauce (page 149) as a dressing.

NUTRITION FACTS

Per serving: ⅓ recipe | Calories: 335 | Carbohydrates: 25g | Protein: 18g | Fat: 19g | Fiber: 8g | Sugar: 13g

Red Lentil and Sweet Potato Curry

Red lentils are one of my favorite legumes to cook with because they don't require soaking and cook faster than any other lentil variety. They're loaded with nutrients, including ample fiber and protein, folate, iron, zinc, magnesium, and potassium. They also get amazingly soft and creamy while cooking, making them the perfect base for dips, curries, and stews. With this recipe we're combining sweet potatoes and red lentils to make a cozy stew with curry spices and coconut milk. The robust flavor will make it feel like the stew has been simmering for hours, but you'll only need to cook it for about 30 minutes! **Serves 6**

1½ teaspoons olive oil

1 medium yellow onion, diced

4 cloves garlic, minced

2 teaspoons yellow curry powder

2 teaspoons ground turmeric

1 teaspoon ground cumin

1 teaspoon chili powder

½ teaspoon garam masala

¼ teaspoon cayenne pepper

¼ teaspoon ground cinnamon

1 teaspoon fine sea salt

½ teaspoon ground black pepper

2 medium sweet potatoes, scrubbed and cut into bite-size pieces (about 5 cups)

2 cups vegetable broth

1 (14-ounce) can diced tomatoes

1 (13.5-ounce) can light coconut milk

1 cup red lentils, rinsed and drained

3 tablespoons tomato paste

2 to 3 teaspoons fresh lemon juice

3 cups cooked white or brown rice (see page 21; use 1 cup white rice + 2 cups water, or 1 cup brown rice + 2½ cups water)

Chopped fresh cilantro, for garnish

Sliced green onions, for garnish

1. Heat the oil in a large pot or Dutch oven over medium heat. Add the onion and garlic and sauté until fragrant, about 5 minutes. Add the curry powder, turmeric, cumin, chili powder, garam masala, cayenne pepper, cinnamon, salt, and black pepper and cook for an additional minute, stirring frequently.

2. Add the sweet potato, vegetable broth, tomatoes and their juices, coconut milk, lentils, tomato paste, and lemon juice.

3. Bring the mixture to a boil, then reduce the heat to medium, and simmer, stirring occasionally, until the sweet potatoes are fork-tender and the lentils are cooked through, 30 to 35 minutes.

Serve Immediately: Scoop ½ cup rice into each bowl, then evenly divide the curry on top. Serve warm, garnished with cilantro and green onions.

Meal Prep: Scoop ½ cup rice into 6 meal prep containers, then evenly divide the curry on top. When ready to serve, follow the reheat instructions. Serve warm, garnished with fresh cilantro and green onions.

Store: In the refrigerator: Let the curry cool, then transfer to a storage container and refrigerate for up to 4 days.

In the freezer: Let the curry cool, then transfer to a storage container and freeze for up to 3 months.

Reheat: From the fridge, heat the curry in a saucepan over medium heat until warm, 5 to 6 minutes. From frozen, thaw overnight in the refrigerator and reheat as directed.

NUTRITION FACTS

Per serving: ⅙ recipe | Calories: 368 | Carbohydrates: 80g | Protein: 13g | Fat: 13g | Fiber: 8g | Sugar: 18g

Taco-Stuffed Zucchini Boats

1½ teaspoons olive oil

½ small yellow onion, diced

1 clove garlic, minced

1 medium red bell pepper, seeded and diced

1 small sweet potato, scrubbed and diced (about 1½ cups)

¾ cup canned black beans

¾ cup salsa

1½ teaspoons taco seasoning

¾ cup cooked quinoa (see page 20; use ¼ cup quinoa + ½ cup water or vegetable broth)

4 medium-large zucchini

1 cup shredded Mexican cheese blend (plant-based, if needed)

Toppings: plain Greek yogurt or dairy-free sour cream, avocado, extra green onion, chopped fresh cilantro, sliced jalapeños, and/or hot sauce

Zucchini boats are one of my favorite savory dishes to make during the summer months. I've made many different versions, but these taco-inspired zucchini boats are some of the best because the blend of textures from the quinoa, veggies, and black beans is perfect. Similar to tacos, these boats are made even more flavorful with the toppings. I recommend yogurt (or sour cream), avocado, green onion, and cilantro, but your options are really endless. **Serves 4**

1. Preheat the oven to 400°F.

2. Heat the oil in a medium skillet over medium heat. Add the onion and garlic and cook until fragrant, 5 to 7 minutes. Add the bell pepper, sweet potato, black beans, salsa, and taco seasoning and cook, stirring frequently, until the sweet potato is fork-tender, about 15 minutes. Remove from the heat and stir in the quinoa.

3. As the veggies cook, cut each zucchini in half lengthwise. Use a spoon to scoop out the center of each zucchini half. You want the boats to be about ¼ inch thick along the bottom and sides. Save the zucchini pulp for another use, like soups, Chocolate–Peanut Butter Shake (page 95), or Zucchini Bread Breakfast Cookies (page 62).

4. Arrange the zucchini halves cut side up in two 9 x 13-inch baking dishes. Spoon the veggie mixture into the zucchini boats. Sprinkle each boat with a little shredded cheese. Cover the baking dishes with aluminum foil. Bake for 20 to 30 minutes, until the boats are heated throughout and the cheese is melted.

Serve Immediately: Serve the zucchini boats warm with your toppings of choice.

Meal Prep: When ready to serve, follow the reheat instructions and add your toppings of choice.

Store: In the refrigerator: Let cool and store in an airtight container for up to 5 days.

In the freezer: Let cool, place on a baking sheet, and freeze for at least 1 hour, then store in a freezer bag or airtight container for up to 3 months. To stack them, you can place a sheet of parchment paper between the layers.

Reheat: From the fridge, place the zucchini boats in a baking dish, cover with aluminum foil, and reheat in a 350°F oven for 15 to 20 minutes, until warm throughout. From frozen, let the boats thaw overnight in the refrigerator, then reheat as directed.

NUTRITION FACTS

Per serving: 2 zucchini boats | Calories: 344 | Carbohydrates: 45g | Protein: 15g | Fat: 12g | Fiber: 8g | Sugar: 13g

Thai-Inspired Spaghetti Squash Noodles with Peanut Sauce

While I love all sorts of veggie noodles, including zoodles (aka zucchini noodles), my favorite vegetable noodle is definitely the kind made from spaghetti squash. You don't need a fancy spiralizer gadget to make them, and I really enjoy their texture and subtly sweet flavor. As a bonus, spaghetti squash is low in calories but plenty filling thanks to its fiber content. It also contains a good amount of vitamin C, vitamin B$_6$, and potassium. If you haven't tried my ring method for roasting spaghetti squash, get ready for a total game-changer! By cutting your squash this way, you'll end up with long, spaghetti-like strands that aren't watery at all. This noodle dish is inspired by Thai peanut noodles, and the creamy peanut sauce is the perfect blend of sweet and savory. I know I shouldn't pick favorites, but it's definitely one of my preferred dishes in this book. **Serves 3**

1 large spaghetti squash

1 tablespoon plus 2 teaspoons olive oil, divided, plus more for coating squash

Fine sea salt to taste

Ground black pepper to taste

1 (14- to 16-ounce) package extra-firm tofu, drained, pressed, and cut into 1-inch cubes

½ teaspoon minced fresh ginger

½ medium yellow onion, sliced

1 red bell pepper, seeded and sliced

1 cup matchstick carrots

1 recipe Peanut Sauce (page 149)

2 tablespoons chopped salted peanuts or almonds (optional)

Sliced green onions, for garnish

Fresh cilantro, for garnish

Lime wedges, for garnish

1. Preheat the oven to 400°F.

2. Slice off the ends of the squash, then cut crosswise into 1-inch-thick slices. Use a spoon to scrape out the seeds from the center to make rings. Place the squash rings on a rimmed baking sheet. Use your hands to coat each ring with a tiny bit of olive oil, salt, and pepper.

3. Roast for 15 minutes, flip the rings, then continue roasting for another 15 to 25 minutes, until the squash is fork-tender and brown in spots.

4. Allow the squash to cool for about 15 minutes, then peel away the skin and use a fork to separate the strands into long spaghetti noodles.

5. Heat 1 tablespoon of the oil in a large skillet over medium heat. Add the tofu and season liberally with salt and pepper. Cook, stirring often, until all sides are golden and the tofu is starting to crisp, 8 to 12 minutes. Transfer to a plate.

6. Add the remaining 2 teaspoons oil to the same skillet. Once hot, add the ginger, onion, bell pepper, and carrots and sauté until the veggies are starting to soften and become fragrant, 7 to 8 minutes. Season with salt and pepper.

7. Reduce the heat to low. Add the tofu, spaghetti squash strands, and peanut sauce to the skillet and mix everything together thoroughly. (If your skillet isn't large enough, you can mix everything in a large bowl instead.)

BRITTANY'S TIP

● This dish is delicious with mushrooms in place of the tofu. Heat 1½ teaspoons oil in the skillet over medium heat, add 10 ounces sliced shiitake mushrooms, and season with salt and pepper. Cook until they brown and crisp up a bit, about 7 minutes. Transfer to a plate and cook the rest of the veggies as instructed on page 192. Return the mushrooms to the skillet when you add the spaghetti squash strands and peanut sauce.

Serve Immediately: Evenly divide into 3 bowls and top with the chopped peanuts (if using), green onions, cilantro, and a lime wedge. Serve warm.

Meal Prep: Evenly divide into 3 meal prep containers. When ready to serve, follow the reheat instructions. Serve warm with chopped peanuts (if using), green onions, cilantro, and a lime wedge for garnish.

Store: In the refrigerator for up to 5 days.

Reheat: Reheat in a skillet over medium heat until warm throughout, about 5 to 6 minutes, or in the microwave for 1 to 2 minutes.

NUTRITION FACTS

Per serving: ⅓ recipe | Calories: 538 | Carbohydrates: 35g | Protein: 28g | Fat: 33g | Fiber: 7g | Sugar: 15g

Creamy "No Cream" Broccoli Cheese Soup

There isn't anything better than a warm bowl of cheesy broccoli soup on a cold day. And did you know that blended cauliflower can make things extra creamy? I use it as a base for my dairy-free Alfredo sauce, and frozen cauliflower rice gives smoothies the best texture. Try the Coffee Date Smoothie (page 83) to test it out. The cauliflower does wonders for making this broccoli cheese soup feel super rich and decadent, while also packing it with veggies and nutrients. **Serves 6**

1 tablespoon olive oil

1 medium yellow onion, chopped

4 cloves garlic, minced

1 head cauliflower, trimmed and cut into small florets

¼ teaspoon ground nutmeg

½ teaspoon fine sea salt, plus more to taste

1 teaspoon ground black pepper, plus more to taste

Pinch cayenne pepper (optional)

4 cups vegetable broth

5 cups fresh or frozen small broccoli florets

1 cup diced carrots

2 cups shredded cheddar cheese, plus more for sprinkling (plant-based, if needed)

Sliced green onions, for garnish

1. Heat the oil in a large pot or Dutch oven over medium heat. Add the onion and garlic and sauté until the onion is translucent, 5 to 7 minutes. Add the cauliflower, nutmeg, salt, black pepper, and cayenne (if using) and sauté for a minute or two.

2. Add the broth and bring to a boil. Reduce the heat to a simmer, cover, and cook until the cauliflower is very tender (soft enough to mash with a fork), 15 to 20 minutes.

3. Use an immersion blender to puree the soup until it's smooth.

4. Add the broccoli and carrots, bring the soup back to a simmer, and cook until the broccoli is tender, 20 to 25 minutes. If you use frozen broccoli (which is already parcooked), you'll only need to cook until the broccoli is thawed and heated through.

5. Reduce the heat to low and stir in the cheese a little at a time. The soup will be pretty thick. If you want a thinner soup, add additional broth or water to reach a desired consistency. Taste and season with more salt and pepper.

Serve Immediately: Evenly divide the soup into 6 bowls. Sprinkle with additional shredded cheese (if desired) and green onions and serve warm.

Meal Prep: Let the soup cool, then evenly divide into 6 meal prep containers. When ready to serve, follow the reheat instructions. Serve sprinkled with shredded cheese (if desired) and green onions.

Store: In the refrigerator for 3 to 4 days or in the freezer for up to 3 months.

Reheat: From the fridge: Reheat the soup in a saucepan over medium-low heat until warm, 5 to 6 minutes, or in the microwave for 2 to 3 minutes. From frozen: Thaw in the fridge overnight and reheat as directed.

BRITTANY'S TIP

If you don't have an immersion blender for step 3, you can transfer the cauliflower soup base to a regular blender for pureeing, but do so carefully and in batches so the soup doesn't splash out. Alternatively, you can use a potato masher to mash the cauliflower. This will result in a chunkier soup, but it will still be delicious.

NUTRITION FACTS

Per serving: ⅙ recipe | Calories: 269 | Carbohydrates: 16g | Protein: 20g | Fat: 16g | Fiber: 5g | Sugar: 4g

The Best Baked Eggplant Parm

I created this recipe because eggplant parm is one of Isaac's favorite foods and I was determined to make a baked version that is a bit healthier and easier for those of us who want to get dinner on the table fast. With this method, we're skipping the sweating of the eggplant, instead simply coating it with an almond flour and Parmesan cheese mixture and baking it up, before layering it with mozzarella cheese and tomato sauce. If you're looking for a home-run dinner that doesn't taste like "health food" at all, this eggplant parm is where it's at. I highly recommend making a double batch, one to eat right away and one to freeze. I also suggest serving it with crusty bread and a side salad.
Serves 6

1 cup almond flour

1 cup grated Parmesan cheese, divided

2 teaspoons Italian seasoning

½ teaspoon fine sea salt, plus more to taste

Ground black pepper

2 large eggs

2 tablespoons water

2 medium eggplants, sliced into ¼-inch-thick rounds

1 (24-ounce) jar marinara sauce

2 cups shredded mozzarella cheese

⅓ cup thinly sliced fresh basil, plus more for serving

Crusty bread, for serving (optional)

1. Preheat the oven to 425°F. Line two rimmed baking sheets with parchment paper and coat the parchment with nonstick cooking spray.

2. In a shallow bowl, whisk together the almond flour, ½ cup of the Parmesan, the Italian seasoning, the salt, and a sprinkle of pepper.

3. In another shallow bowl, whisk together the eggs and water and sprinkle with salt and pepper.

4. Dip each eggplant slice into the egg wash, then sprinkle the almond flour–Parmesan mixture over both sides. Place on the prepared baking sheets. Spray the tops lightly with cooking spray.

5. Roast for 15 minutes, flip the eggplant slices, and continue roasting for another 15 minutes or so, until soft inside and golden and crisp on the outside.

6. Spread 1 cup of the marinara in a 9 x 13-inch baking dish and spread evenly. Add a layer of baked eggplant slices. Top with another 1 cup sauce. Sprinkle with 1 cup of the mozzarella, ¼ cup of the remaining Parmesan, and about half of the basil. Add another layer of baked eggplant slices and top with the remaining 1 cup sauce. Sprinkle with the remaining 1 cup mozzarella cheese, remaining ¼ cup Parmesan, and remaining basil.

7. Bake until the top is bubbly and golden, 15 to 20 minutes. Cut into 6 pieces.

Serve Immediately: Divide evenly onto 6 plates. Top with additional chopped basil and serve with crusty bread, if desired.

Meal Prep: Divide evenly into 6 meal prep containers. When ready to serve, follow the reheat instructions. Top with additional chopped basil and serve with crusty bread, if desired.

BRITTANY'S TIPS

I don't recommend freezing this dish after baking. Instead, after step 6, cover the dish with aluminum foil and freeze. Let thaw overnight in the refrigerator, then uncover and bake as instructed in the recipe. Note that if you're planning to freeze this dish, you may want to prepare it in a disposable aluminum pan so you won't miss your baking dish while it's in the freezer.

● If you have a nut allergy, feel free to use 1 cup breadcrumbs instead of the almond flour.

● To make this dairy-free, use plant-based Parmesan and mozzarella.

Store: In the refrigerator for up to 5 days or in the freezer for up to 3 months.

Reheat: Reheat in the microwave until warm throughout, 1 to 2 minutes.

NUTRITION FACTS

Per serving: ⅙ recipe | Calories: 391 | Carbohydrates: 27g | Protein: 25g | Fat: 23g | Fiber: 9g | Sugar: 8g

Add-the-Veggies Fried Rice

 DF GF

Fried rice is one of my daughter's favorite meals, and since we can't order from our favorite Vietnamese restaurant every night, I created a really simple recipe to make at home. It's one of those meals that we all enjoy equally, and I love seeing Olivia gobble up all the added veggies. This is also a great place to use up that leftover rice you have sitting in the fridge! I like to use brown rice to amp up the nutrition a bit, but white rice works well for this recipe too. It's important to note that both brown and white rice are a good source of carbohydrates and similar in terms of calorie content, but brown rice is a whole grain so it's naturally higher in fiber and other nutrients—including magnesium. Often white rice is enriched or fortified to add vitamins and minerals back in, but even then brown rice is still considered a healthier choice in most cases.

Serves 3

1 tablespoon avocado or coconut oil

1 cup diced carrot

1 cup diced yellow onion

1 tablespoon minced garlic

1 tablespoon minced fresh ginger

1 cup diced red bell pepper

1 cup bite-size broccoli florets

1 cup frozen peas, thawed

1 cup frozen corn kernels, thawed

3 large eggs, beaten

3 cups cooked brown or white rice (see page 21; use 1 cup brown rice + 2½ cups water, or 1 cup white rice + 2 cups water)

¼ cup reduced-sodium tamari, reduced-sodium soy sauce, or coconut aminos

1 tablespoon toasted sesame oil

Ground black pepper to taste

Sriracha, for serving (optional)

1. In a wok or deep skillet, heat the oil over high heat. Add the carrot, onion, garlic, and ginger and cook until the onion is translucent, 7 to 10 minutes.

2. Add the bell pepper, broccoli, peas, and corn and cook for an additional 3 to 4 minutes. Push all of the cooked vegetables to one side of the pan.

3. Pour the beaten eggs into the empty side of the pan. Scramble the eggs briefly, then mix with the vegetables.

4. Add the rice, tamari, sesame oil, and pepper. Mix well and let the rice cook until slightly crispy, 5 to 6 minutes.

Serve Immediately: Evenly divide onto 3 plates. Serve warm with a drizzle of sriracha, if desired.

Meal Prep: Evenly divide into 3 meal prep containers. When ready to serve, follow the reheat instructions. Serve warm with a drizzle of sriracha, if desired.

Store: In the refrigerator for up to 4 days.

Reheat: Reheat in a skillet over medium heat until warm, about 5 minutes, or microwave for 1 to 2 minutes. If the rice seems a little dry, you can add a tablespoon or two of water or vegetable broth to rehydrate.

NUTRITION FACTS

Per serving: ⅓ recipe | Calories: 531 | Carbohydrates: 80g | Protein: 20g | Fat: 17g | Fiber: 11g | Sugar: 12g

Butternut Squash and Black Bean Enchiladas

Gooey, warm enchiladas right out of the oven are such a treat, and I love that you can prep and freeze them in advance! If you're feeling ambitious, you can double this recipe and make one batch of enchiladas to enjoy right away and one batch to freeze for an easy meal a few weeks from now. Feeling strapped for time? You can totally buy pre-chopped butternut squash. It's more cost effective to chop your own, but the pre-chopped version can sometimes be worth the slight upcharge when you're busy. If you do end up chopping your own butternut squash, you can use the leftover squash and yellow onion to make Lemony Fall Harvest Sheet Pan Meal (page 157). **Serves 3**

1 tablespoon olive oil

1 cup yellow onion, diced

2 cloves garlic, minced

2 cups ¼-inch butternut squash cubes

1 (15-ounce) can black beans, drained and rinsed

1 tablespoon chili powder

1 teaspoon ground cumin

½ teaspoon fine sea salt

2 tablespoons chopped fresh cilantro

½ cup water

1 (10-ounce) jar red enchilada sauce

6 (6-inch) whole-wheat flour tortillas

1½ cups shredded Mexican cheese (plant-based, if needed)

Topping options: sliced green onions, additional chopped fresh cilantro, salsa, sliced jalapeños, sliced avocado, plain Greek yogurt or sour cream

1. Preheat the oven to 400°F.

2. Heat the oil in a large skillet over medium heat. Add the onion and garlic and sauté until fragrant, about 5 minutes. Add the butternut squash, black beans, chili powder, cumin, salt, cilantro, and water. Cover and cook until the butternut squash is fork-tender, 12 to 15 minutes. Remove from the heat.

3. Spread a thin layer of enchilada sauce in the bottom of a 9 x 13-inch baking dish.

4. Fill each tortilla with the butternut–black bean mixture and a sprinkle of shredded cheese. Roll the tortilla up and place seam side down in the baking dish. Once all the tortillas are filled, cover with the remaining enchilada sauce and sprinkle the remaining cheese on top.

5. Bake for about 20 minutes, until the cheese is melted and the enchiladas are warm throughout.

Serve Immediately: Place 2 enchiladas on each plate and serve with your toppings of choice.

Meal Prep: Place 2 enchiladas each in 3 meal prep containers. Store the toppings separately. When ready to serve, follow the reheat instructions. Serve warm with your toppings of choice.

Store: In the refrigerator for up to 5 days or in the freezer for up to 3 months.

Reheat: Reheat in the microwave until warm throughout, about 1 minute.

NUTRITION FACTS

Per serving: 2 enchiladas without toppings | Calories: 741 | Carbohydrates: 93g | Protein: 31g | Fat: 30g | Fiber: 17g | Sugar: 13g

BRITTANY'S TIP

I don't recommend freezing this dish after baking. Instead, after step 4, cover the dish with plastic wrap and then aluminum foil and freeze. Thaw in the fridge overnight, then uncover and bake as instructed in the recipe. Note that if you're planning to freeze the enchiladas, you may want to prepare them in a disposable aluminum pan so you won't miss your baking dish while it's in the freezer.

Slow Cooker Tuscan White Bean Soup

2 (15-ounce) cans white cannellini beans, drained and rinsed

6 cloves garlic, minced

½ cup quinoa

1 (13.5-ounce) can full-fat coconut milk

4 cups vegetable broth

½ cup oil-packed sun-dried tomatoes, chopped

⅔ cup grated Parmesan cheese, plus for more topping

1 tablespoon Italian seasoning

1 teaspoon fine sea salt

¼ teaspoon ground black pepper

½ teaspoon crushed red pepper (optional)

2 cups (packed) chopped lacinato kale

BRITTANY'S TIP

● Feel free to swap chickpeas for the white beans or use 1 can of each.

I love a good slow cooker meal, and this white bean soup doesn't disappoint, especially when you can simply set it and forget it! Because the sun-dried tomatoes are preserved in oil with fresh herbs, they give the soup a robust flavor, and the Parmesan cheese adds a satisfying touch. I know coconut milk may seem like an unusual addition to a Tuscan-inspired soup, but it gives the soup the same creaminess that heavy cream would provide, and you can't taste the coconut flavor at all.
Serves 6

1. Combine everything except the kale in a slow cooker and stir. Cover and cook on high for 3 to 4 hours or low for 6 to 8 hours.

2. Add the kale about 20 minutes before serving. If you're worried about the quinoa getting overcooked you can add it into the slow cooker when you have about 1 hour left of cooking.

Serve Immediately: Evenly divide the soup into 6 bowls and top with Parmesan and pepper, if desired. Serve warm.

Meal Prep: Evenly divide the soup into 6 meal prep containers. When ready to serve, follow the reheat instructions. Serve warm topped with Parmesan cheese and pepper, if desired.

Store: In the refrigerator for up to 5 days or in the freezer for up to 3 months.

Reheat: From the refrigerator: Reheat the soup in a saucepan over medium heat until warm, 5 to 10 minutes. From frozen: Let the soup thaw overnight in the refrigerator, then reheat as directed.

NUTRITION FACTS ——————————————————

Per serving: ⅙ recipe | Calories: 403 | Carbohydrates: 50g | Protein: 19g | Fat: 15g | Fiber: 9g | Sugar: 4g

Quinoa Black Bean Burgers

There's no need to buy frozen bean burgers when you can easily make your own with this simple, flavorful recipe! The combo of black beans and quinoa gives these burgers the perfect texture and a good amount of protein. The recipe suggests serving these with traditional burger fixins like buns and condiments, but feel free to get creative. Sometimes I love making a big salad and chopping up one of these bean burgers as a topping. If you decide to try them on a salad, throw some baked sweet potato fries on there for a burger and fries salad! **Serves 5**

1 teaspoon olive oil

⅓ cup chopped yellow onion

1 clove garlic, minced

1 (15-ounce) can black beans, drained and rinsed

1½ cups cooked quinoa, cooled (see page 20; use ½ cup quinoa + 1 cup water)

2 tablespoons tomato paste

1 tablespoon ground flaxseed

½ teaspoon chili powder

½ teaspoon ground cumin

½ teaspoon fine sea salt

Ground black pepper to taste

4 whole-grain burger buns

Toppings of choice: sliced red onion, sliced tomato, lettuce, sliced cheese (plant-based, if needed), ketchup, and mustard

1. Heat the oil in a medium skillet over medium heat. Add the onion and garlic and sauté until fragrant, 5 to 7 minutes. Remove from the heat and let cool, then transfer to a food processor.

2. Add the black beans and cooled quinoa to the food processor and pulse a couple times. The beans should be broken up but still have some small chunks. Don't overprocess, as you want your bean burgers to be a little chunky.

3. Transfer the bean mixture to a large bowl and stir in the tomato paste, flaxseed, chili powder, cumin, salt, and pepper. Combine fully.

4. Using your hands, scoop the bean burger mixture and form into 5 patties. You can use a 1-cup measuring cup, peanut butter jar lid, or cookie cutter to "cut" the patties into a perfectly round shape and make them even in size. (Or just use your hands if you're not too concerned with the shape!)

5. Spray a large skillet with nonstick cooking spray and heat over medium heat. Add the patties and cook until browned on both sides, 6 to 7 minutes total.

Serve Immediately: Put each burger on a bun and serve with your toppings and condiments of choice.

Meal Prep: Let the burgers cool and place parchment paper between the patties so they don't stick together. When ready to serve, follow the reheat instructions. Put each burger on a bun and serve with your toppings and condiments of choice.

Store: In the refrigerator: Let the burgers cool completely, then put them in a storage container, using parchment paper between the patties so they don't stick together. Store for up to 5 days.

In the freezer: Let the burgers cool completely on a baking sheet lined with parchment. Once cool, place the sheet in the freezer until the burgers are frozen solid, 2 to 4 hours. Transfer to a storage

container or freezer bag, using parchment paper between the patties so they don't stick together. Store for up to 3 months.

Reheat: From the fridge, heat the burger in a skillet over medium heat for 5 to 7 minutes, flipping halfway, or in a 350°F oven for 8 to 10 minutes, flipping halfway, just until warm throughout. From frozen, thaw the burger in the microwave for 60 to 90 seconds, then reheat as directed.

NUTRITION FACTS ——————————————————————————

Per serving: 1 burger without bun or condiments | Calories: 172 |
Carbohydrates: 29g | Protein: 8g | Fat: 3g | Fiber: 8g | Sugar: 2g

Slow Cooker Chili Mac

When a friend mentioned to me that she serves chili over noodles, I was intrigued. We always serve our chili straight up with cornbread or tortilla chips on the side, but I had to try this new way, and the results were what inspired this chili mac. Is it chili? Is it mac and cheese? It's the best of both worlds, and it's surprisingly healthy and packed with veggies! **Serves 6**

1 medium yellow onion, chopped

2 cloves garlic, minced

1 red or orange bell pepper, seeded and chopped

1 (15-ounce) can pinto beans, drained and rinsed

1 (15-ounce) red kidney beans, drained and rinsed

1 cup frozen sweet corn kernels

1 (28-ounce) can diced tomatoes

2 cups vegetable broth

2 tablespoons chili powder

1 teaspoon ground cumin

1 teaspoon dried oregano

½ teaspoon fine sea salt

¼ teaspoon ground black pepper

1 (8-ounce) box chickpea elbow pasta noodles

1 cup shredded cheddar cheese, plus more for serving (plant-based, if needed)

Sliced green onions, for garnish

1. Add the onion, garlic, bell pepper, beans, corn, tomatoes and their juices, broth, and seasonings to a slow cooker. Stir to combine. Cover and cook on high for 3 to 4 hours or on low for 6 to 8 hours.

2. Add the pasta, cover, and continue cooking on low for 20 minutes, until the pasta is cooked through. Add the cheese and stir to combine.

Serve Immediately: Evenly divide the chili mac into 6 bowls and serve warm, topped with more cheese and green onions.

Meal Prep: Evenly divide the chili mac into 6 meal prep containers. When ready to serve, follow the reheat instructions. Serve warm, topped with more cheese and green onions.

Store: In the refrigerator for up to 5 days or in the freezer for up to 3 months.

Reheat: Reheat the chili mac in a saucepan over medium heat until warm throughout, 5 to 10 minutes, or in the microwave for 1 to 2 minutes.

NUTRITION FACTS

Per serving: ⅙ recipe | Calories: 424 | Carbohydrates: 59g | Protein: 25g | Fat: 13g | Fiber: 14g | Sugar: 7g

Spaghetti Squash Pizza Bake

This is such a fun way to serve spaghetti squash! It has all the flavor of a vegetarian pizza, but with even more veggies since we're using spaghetti squash noodles as the base. Once the squash and veggies are cooked, the prep is really simple. Just toss everything together, bake until the cheese is melted, and serve. My family loves this with black olives on top, but if you're not a fan you can certainly leave them off. We're using my spaghetti squash ring method to cook the spaghetti squash so it will come out roasted to perfection and not watery! **Serves 4**

1 medium-large spaghetti squash

2 teaspoons olive oil, plus more for coating squash

½ teaspoon fine sea salt, divided

½ teaspoon ground black pepper, divided

2 cloves garlic, minced

1 medium yellow onion, chopped

½ teaspoon Italian seasoning

1 green or red bell pepper, seeded and chopped

1 cup chopped button mushrooms

1 cup chopped baby spinach

1 cup pizza sauce (I like Rao's Homemade)

½ cup whole-milk ricotta cheese

1 large egg, whisked

1 teaspoon dried basil

2 cups shredded mozzarella cheese, divided

1 (2.25-ounce) can sliced black olives, drained

Chopped fresh basil, for garnish

Grated Parmesan cheese, for topping (optional)

Crushed red pepper, for topping (optional)

1. Preheat the oven to 400°F. Coat a 9 x 13-inch baking dish with nonstick cooking spray.

2. Slice off ends of the squash, then cut crosswise into 1-inch-thick slices.

3. Use a spoon to scrape out the seeds from the center to make rings.

4. Place the squash rings on a rimmed baking sheet. Use your hands to coat each ring with a tiny bit of olive oil, salt, and pepper.

5. Roast for 15 minutes, flip the rings, then continue roasting for another 15 to 25 minutes, until the squash is fork-tender and brown in spots. Leave the oven on. Allow the squash to cool for about 15 minutes, then peel away the skin and use a fork to separate the strands into long spaghetti noodles.

6. Meanwhile, in a medium skillet, heat 2 teaspoons oil over medium heat. Add the garlic and onion and cook until fragrant, about 5 minutes. Add the Italian seasoning and ¼ teaspoon each salt and pepper. Add the bell pepper and mushrooms and cook until softened, 8 to 10 minutes. Add the baby spinach and cook just until wilted, 1 to 2 minutes. Remove from the heat.

7. In a large bowl, combine the pizza sauce, ricotta, egg, basil, and remaining ¼ teaspoon each salt and pepper. Stir to combine, then add the spaghetti squash strands. Toss to coat.

8. Add the cooked veggies and 1 cup of the mozzarella to the spaghetti squash mixture and toss to combine.

9. Transfer the mixture to the prepared baking dish and spread evenly. Top with the remaining 1 cup mozzarella and sprinkle on the olives. Bake for about 15 minutes, until the cheese is melted.

Serve Immediately: Evenly divide onto 4 plates and serve warm, topped with chopped basil, Parmesan cheese, and crushed red pepper (if using).

Meal Prep: Evenly divide into 4 meal prep containers. When ready to serve, follow the reheat instructions. Serve warm, topped with chopped basil, Parmesan cheese, and crushed red pepper (if using).

Store: In the refrigerator for up to 5 days.

Reheat: Reheat in the microwave until warm throughout, 1 to 2 minutes.

NUTRITION FACTS

Per serving: ¼ recipe | Calories: 444 | Carbohydrates: 35g | Protein: 22g | Fat: 25g | Fiber: 6g | Sugar: 10g

Mushroom Stroganoff

This is my go-to recipe when I'm craving cozy, noodly comfort food! It's a true classic, but made a bit more nutritious (and gluten-free) with chickpea pasta instead of egg noodles. It has a ton of rich, creamy flavor but without any dairy as we're using coconut milk in place of sour cream. I like using a combo of baby bella mushrooms and fancy mixed mushrooms, but feel free to use whatever you have access to! Different mushroom varieties offer different varieties of nutrients, but they're all packed with fiber, vitamins, and minerals so you really can't go wrong. This is truly a family favorite at my house and I think it will quickly become part of your regular meal rotation too! **Serves 4**

1 tablespoon olive oil

1 small yellow onion, chopped

4 cloves garlic, minced

8 ounces baby bella mushrooms, sliced

4 ounces fancy mixed mushrooms, sliced

1 (8-ounce) box chickpea rotini pasta

2½ cups vegetable broth

1 (13.5-ounce) can full-fat coconut milk

1 tablespoon apple cider vinegar or fresh lemon juice

1 tablespoon vegan Worcestershire sauce

1 tablespoon reduced-sodium tamari, reduced-sodium soy sauce, or coconut aminos

2 tablespoons nutritional yeast

½ teaspoon ground black pepper, plus more to taste

¼ cup chopped fresh parsley

Fine sea salt to taste

1. Heat the oil in a large nonstick skillet over medium heat. Add the onion and garlic and sauté until fragrant, 2 to 3 minutes. Add the mushrooms and cook for another 3 to 4 minutes.

2. Add the pasta, broth, coconut milk, vinegar, Worcestershire sauce, tamari, nutritional yeast, and pepper and stir well.

3. Cover the skillet and increase the heat to medium-high so the liquid is bubbling. Cook until the liquid is creamy and the pasta is cooked, 10 to 12 minutes.

Serve Immediately: Evenly divide into 4 bowls, top with the parsley, and season with salt and pepper.

Meal Prep: Evenly divide into 4 meal prep containers. When ready to serve, follow the reheat instructions. Top with the parsley and season with salt and pepper.

Store: In the refrigerator for up to 5 days.

Reheat: Reheat in the microwave until warm throughout, 1 to 2 minutes.

NUTRITION FACTS ——————————————————————

Per serving: ¼ recipe | Calories: 482 | Carbohydrates: 47g | Protein: 18g | Fat: 25g | Fiber: 8g | Sugar: 6g

Snacks
+ Treats

214   Cheesy Almond Crackers

217   Pizza Trail Mix

218   Greek Yogurt Peanut Butter Dip

221   Edamame Hummus

222   Bird Food Granola Bars

225   Coconut Protein Balls

226   Tamari Roasted Almonds

229   Carrot-Raisin Oat Bars

230   Chocolate Chip Cookie Dough Bites

233   Crispy Peanut Butter Cups

234   No-Bake Coconut-Lemon Macaroons

237   Brownie Hummus

238   Trail Mix Cookies

241   Pecan Cookie Butter

242   Coconut Butter

245   Cashew Queso

246   Coconut Bacon

Cheesy Almond Crackers

1 cup fine blanched almond flour

1 cup shredded cheddar cheese

¼ teaspoon fine sea salt

1 tablespoon water (if needed)

Flaked sea salt (optional)

Craving a salty, cheesy snack? These crackers totally fit the bill, and you're going to be shocked at how easy they are to whip up. Everyone in our house loves these so much they never last long, and I feel good about the fact that they're made with nutrient-rich almond flour and real cheese, which means you can have a few and feel totally satisfied! We love snacking on these plain, but they are absolutely delish dipped in Edamame Hummus (page 221). **Serves 6**

1. Preheat the oven to 350°F.

2. Combine the almond flour, shredded cheese, and salt in a food processor and process until combined. If the mixture seems a little dry, add the water.

3. Transfer the dough to a piece of parchment paper and cover with a second piece of parchment.

4. Pat the dough with your hands and then use a rolling pin to roll it about ¹/₈ inch thick. Try to form the dough into a rectangular shape, but it's OK if it's not perfect.

5. Remove the top sheet of paper and sprinkle a bit of flaked sea salt over the dough if you like. Use your hands to press the salt down to help it stick. This step is optional, but the flaked sea salt makes the crackers really pretty and adds more saltiness.

6. Use a pizza wheel or knife to cut the dough into small squares. I make mine ½ to 1 inch big and usually get around 60 crackers. Use a toothpick to poke a little hole in the center of each cracker.

7. Carefully transfer the crackers (still on the parchment paper) to a baking sheet and bake for 18 to 20 minutes, until they are golden brown and crispy. The pieces on the outer edges will get brown faster than the center pieces. You can transfer those that are done to a cooling rack and put the rest back in the oven, if needed.

8. Let the crackers cool completely, either on the baking sheet or on a cooling rack. Break apart and enjoy or store.

Serve Immediately: Enjoy plain or with a dipping sauce of choice.

Meal Prep: Put the crackers in a storage container.

Store: In the pantry for up to 5 days.

NUTRITION FACTS ————————————————————————

Per serving: about 10 crackers | Calories: 180 | Carbohydrates: 5g | Protein: 10g | Fat: 14g | Fiber: 3g | Sugar: 1g

Pizza Trail Mix

Snack mixes are one of my favorite things to make (and eat), and I love to come up with fun flavor combos like this savory mix of roasted nuts with sun-dried tomatoes and Italian seasonings, which tastes like pizza. Most trail mixes are packed with dried fruit and tend to have a lot of sugar, but this one has only 3 grams per serving. It's the ultimate snack mix for lunch, hikes, and road trips. **Serves 8**

1 cup raw cashews

½ cup raw almonds

¼ cup raw walnuts

2 teaspoons olive oil

1 tablespoon nutritional yeast

½ teaspoon garlic powder

½ teaspoon onion powder

½ teaspoon dried oregano

½ teaspoon dried thyme

½ teaspoon dried basil

½ teaspoon fine sea salt

⅓ cup dry-packed sun-dried tomatoes, cut into bite-size pieces

1. Preheat the oven to 350°F. Line a rimmed baking sheet with parchment paper.

2. In a large bowl, toss the nuts with the oil, nutritional yeast, and all the seasonings in a large bowl. Spread the nut mixture out on the lined baking sheet.

3. Bake for 10 to 12 minutes, tossing every 5 minutes. You'll know the nuts are done when they are golden brown and fragrant. Remove from the oven, toss, then let the nuts cool.

4. Stir in the sun-dried tomato pieces.

Serve Immediately: Measure out a ¼-cup portion and enjoy.

Meal Prep: Measure out ¼-cup portions into small containers or reusable bags.

Store: In the pantry for up to 1 week.

NUTRITION FACTS

Per serving: ¼ cup | Calories: 215 | Carbohydrates: 19g | Protein: 7g | Fat: 14g | Fiber: 8g | Sugar: 3g

Greek Yogurt Peanut Butter Dip

DF* GF EF

1 cup plain full-fat Greek yogurt

⅓ cup natural peanut butter

2 tablespoons honey

⅛ to ¼ teaspoon ground cinnamon

Fresh apple slices, berries, or graham crackers, for dipping

This has to be one of my favorite protein-packed snacks. The creamy whipped peanut butter dip is the perfect complement to crisp, fresh apples, but it also pairs well with berries or graham crackers. Another option is to turn this into a yogurt bowl and add chopped fruit and granola on top. If your family loves this dip as much as we do, it won't last long! **Serves 5**

Combine the yogurt, peanut butter, honey, and cinnamon in a bowl. Mix until combined.

Serve Immediately: Serve ¼ cup dip with fresh apple slices, berries, or graham crackers for dipping.

Meal Prep: Portion ¼ cup dip into one side of 5 divided meal prep containers and apple slices, berries, or graham crackers in the other.

Store: In the refrigerator for up to 4 days.

NUTRITION FACTS

Per serving: ¼ cup dip without dippers | Calories: 175 | Carbohydrates: 12g | Protein: 8g | Fat: 11g | Fiber: 1g | Sugar: 9g

BRITTANY'S TIPS

● I prefer full-fat Greek yogurt because it's more filling and creamier, and doesn't taste as tart, but feel free to use 2 percent or even nonfat Greek yogurt if you want the dip to be lighter or if that's what you normally have on hand.

● Use a plant-based Greek-style yogurt to make this dip dairy-free.

● For graham crackers, I really like Simple Mills Honey Cinnamon Sweet Thins.

Edamame Hummus

While I can never resist traditional creamy hummus made with chickpeas, it's really fun to experiment with different legumes, and this edamame hummus has quickly become a household favorite. Unlike many other plant-based protein sources, edamame is a complete protein, containing all nine essential amino acids, and it's the least processed option when it comes to soy protein. It's a wonderful addition to your diet and a great option for healthy snacking. **Serves 8**

1 (12-ounce) bag frozen shelled edamame

¼ cup extra-virgin olive oil

3 tablespoons tahini

3 tablespoons fresh lemon juice

2 medium cloves garlic, peeled

1 teaspoon fine sea salt

¼ teaspoon ground black pepper

¼ teaspoon onion powder

Crackers and/or cut-up raw veggies (such as carrots, tomatoes, bell peppers, snap peas), for dipping

1. Cook the edamame according to the package instructions. Drain, reserving ½ cup of the cooking liquid.

2. Transfer the edamame to a food processor and add the oil, tahini, lemon juice, garlic, salt, pepper, and onion powder.

3. Process until smooth, gradually adding the reserved cooking liquid, a tablespoon at a time, to thin the dip, and scraping down the sides of the bowl as needed.

Serve Immediately: Serve ¼ cup hummus with crackers and/or veggies for dipping.

Meal Prep: Portion ¼ cup hummus into one side of several divided meal prep containers and crackers and/or veggies in the other.

Store: In the refrigerator for 1 week.

NUTRITION FACTS ——————

Per serving: ¼ cup without dippers | Calories: 139 | Carbohydrates: 5g | Protein: 4g | Fat: 11g | Fiber: 2g | Sugar: 1g

Bird Food Granola Bars

DF* GF EF

Homemade granola bars are so easy to make and tend to be much healthier than the bars you'll find on store shelves. With all the nuts and seeds, I couldn't resist naming these bars after a snack you would put outside for your feathered friends! Jokes aside, these bars are simply the best for on-the-go snacking. Whether you're running errands or going out for a hike, you'll be so grateful you have these on hand for an energizing treat. **Serves 16**

2 cups old-fashioned rolled oats

¼ cup sliced raw almonds

¼ cup chopped raw walnuts

¼ cup raw pepitas

¼ cup raw sunflower seeds

¼ cup unsweetened shredded coconut

2 tablespoons pure maple syrup or honey

1 tablespoon plus 1 teaspoon coconut oil, melted

1 teaspoon vanilla extract

1 teaspoon ground cinnamon

½ teaspoon fine sea salt

1½ cups pitted Medjool dates (about 15 dates)

1½ cups raisins

⅓ cup dark chocolate chips (dairy-free, if needed)

1. In a large bowl, toss the oats, almonds, walnuts, pepitas, sunflower seeds, and shredded coconut with the maple syrup, 1 tablespoon of the coconut oil, the vanilla, cinnamon, and salt.

2. In a food processer, process the dates and raisins until the mixture is completely chopped and forms into a big, sticky ball.

3. Scrape the dried fruit from the processor and break into small pieces using your hands. Add it to the bowl with the oat mixture and use your hands to combine everything together.

4. Line an 8-inch baking dish with parchment paper. Press the mixture into the pan.

5. In a small bowl, melt the chocolate chips with the remaining 1 teaspoon coconut oil in 30-second increments in the microwave. It shouldn't take more than 2 minutes. Spread the melted chocolate mixture evenly over the bars. Place the pan in the fridge for 20 minutes to let the chocolate set. Cut into 16 bars.

Serve Immediately: Enjoy 1 bar as a snack.

Meal Prep: Leave the bars in the pan and cover, or transfer the bars to small containers or a reusable bag.

Store: In the refrigerator for up to 2 weeks or in the freezer for up to 3 months. If frozen, thaw the bars for 10 to 15 minutes before enjoying.

BRITTANY'S TIPS

  I recommend raw nuts and seeds for this recipe to avoid added oils and salt, but if you have roasted nuts/seeds on hand and want to use those, it's totally fine.

The dates can easily be swapped for dried figs if you'd prefer a fig bar!

NUTRITION FACTS

Per serving: 1 bar | Calories: 244 | Carbohydrates: 43g | Protein: 4g | Fat: 8g | Fiber: 6g | Sugar: 26g

Coconut Protein Balls

1½ cups old-fashioned rolled oats

1 cup cashew butter

¼ cup Coconut Butter (page 242), melted or at room temperature

¼ cup pure maple syrup

2 scoops (50 grams) plant-based vanilla protein powder

1 tablespoon chia seeds

¼ cup unsweetened shredded coconut

¼ cup mini chocolate chips (dairy-free, if needed)

BRITTANY'S TIP

⬤ My favorite brands of plant-based protein powder are Nuzest and Sunwarrior.

If there's one thing you can always find in my fridge, it's some sort of protein ball. They're so easy to make, and I love that they satisfy my craving for something sweet after a meal but also provide a bit of protein and healthy fats. They're also great if you are in need of a light and easy-to-digest snack before or after a workout! I have so many protein balls on my website that you'd think it would be hard for me to come up with another variation, but no need to worry...this one was inspired by an EBF team member's favorite protein ball combo and is perfect for this cookbook given there's a recipe for homemade coconut butter on page 242. **Serves 24**

1. In a large bowl, mix together all the ingredients and stir to combine. Getting the mixture to combine takes a little arm muscle, and it may seem too thick at first, but it will come together as you keep mixing. I like to use my hands to knead the dough near the end.

2. Once combined, use a small cookie scoop to form the dough into 24 balls.

Serve Immediately: Enjoy 1 or 2 balls.

Meal Prep: Store the balls all together in one storage container or portion into small containers or reusable bags.

Store: In the fridge for up to 10 days or in the freezer for up to 3 months. If frozen, thaw the balls for 5 to 10 minutes before enjoying.

NUTRITION FACTS ───────────

Per serving: 1 ball | Calories: 145 | Carbohydrates: 12g | Protein: 4g | Fat: 9g | Fiber: 1g | Sugar: 4g

Tamari Roasted Almonds

2 cups raw whole almonds

2 tablespoons reduced-sodium tamari

½ teaspoon coconut sugar

Nuts, especially almonds, are a nutritious and easy snack to have on hand, but plain almonds can get kind of boring. Tamari roasted almonds were one of the first things I discovered when I started shopping at my local natural food store years ago. (If you're not familiar, tamari is essentially just gluten-free soy sauce.) They had these almonds in the bulk bin and I would stock up every time I went to the store, each time getting a few ounces more. I couldn't resist giving my own version a bit of sweetness by adding the coconut sugar. Watch out, they're addictive! **Serves 8**

1. Preheat the oven to 350°F. Line a rimmed baking sheet with parchment paper.

2. On the lined baking sheet, toss the almonds with the tamari and coconut sugar. Spread them out in a single layer. Roast for 10 minutes, toss, continue roasting for another 5 minutes, then remove from the oven and toss one more time. Set aside to cool; the almonds will crisp up as they cool.

Serve Immediately: Measure out a ¼-cup portion and enjoy.

Meal Prep: Portion ¼ cup almonds into small containers or a reusable bag.

Store: In the pantry for up to 2 weeks.

NUTRITION FACTS ———————————————————

Per serving: ¼ cup | Calories: 186 | Carbohydrates: 8g | Protein: 7g | Fat: 16g | Fiber: 3g | Sugar: 2g

Carrot-Raisin Oat Bars

Maybe it's because my dad's favorite cake is carrot cake, but I've always been a huge fan, and it's inspired a lot of different recipe creations over the years. While these oat bars aren't as sweet as carrot cake (mainly because there's no frosting), they go a long way to satisfy a similar craving, and the raisins add a nice touch of sweetness. Plus, you can feel good about the nutrients you'll be getting by adding veggies into your snack! **Serves 8**

3 cups quick oats, divided

1 teaspoon baking powder

1 teaspoon ground cinnamon

½ teaspoon fine sea salt

½ cup unsweetened applesauce

½ cup pure maple syrup or honey

¼ cup orange juice

2 tablespoons ground flaxseed

2 teaspoons coconut oil, melted

1 teaspoon vanilla extract

1 cup grated carrots

¼ cup chopped walnuts

¼ cup raisins

1. Preheat the oven to 375°F. Line an 8-inch baking dish with parchment paper.

2. Put 2 cups of the oats in a blender or food processor and blend until you've created oat flour.

3. Transfer to a large bowl.

4. Add the remaining 1 cup oats, baking powder, cinnamon, and salt. Stir to combine, then add the applesauce, maple syrup, orange juice, flaxseed, coconut oil, and vanilla and mix well. Gently fold in the grated carrots, walnuts, and raisins.

5. Pour the batter into the prepared baking dish.

6. Bake for about 30 minutes, until the bars are cooked through and hold their shape.

7. Let cool, then cut into 8 bars.

Serve Immediately: Enjoy 1 bar.

Meal Prep: Leave the bars in the pan and cover, or transfer to small containers or reusable bags.

Store: In the refrigerator for up to 1 week.

BRITTANY'S TIP

If you like coconut, these bars are delicious with ½ cup unsweetened shredded coconut added to the mix. Simply fold it in along with the carrots, walnuts, and raisins.

NUTRITION FACTS

Per serving: 1 bar | Calories: 269 | Carbohydrates: 48g | Protein: 6g | Fat: 6g | Fiber: 5g | Sugar: 22g

Chocolate Chip Cookie Dough Bites

There are times when I'm craving cookies, but in reality what I really want is the cookie dough. That's where these little bites come in. They taste like cookie dough but are made without flour or eggs so they're totally safe to eat raw. These bites are inspired by one of my favorite store-bought treats. The base is almond flour and unsweetened shredded coconut, so they're almost like a coconut macaroon, but a bit more moist—and there's no baking involved! I love the fact that they're nutrient-rich and filling so you can have one or two for a dessert and feel totally satisfied. **Serves 18**

1 cup fine almond flour

1 cup unsweetened finely shredded (desiccated) coconut

¼ cup pure maple syrup

2 tablespoons melted coconut oil

1 teaspoon vanilla extract

⅛ teaspoon fine sea salt

3 tablespoons mini chocolate chips (dairy-free, if needed)

In a medium bowl, combine all the ingredients. Scoop the dough using a small cookie scoop and place on a parchment-lined baking sheet. Place in the refrigerator to set for at least 30 minutes.

Serve Immediately: Once set, enjoy 1 bite.

Meal Prep: Transfer the bites to a large storage container or portion into small containers or reusable bags.

Store: In the refrigerator for up to 1 week or in the freezer for up to 1 month. If frozen, thaw the bites for 5 to 10 minutes before enjoying.

NUTRITION FACTS

Per serving: 1 bite | Calories: 126 | Carbohydrates: 19g | Protein: 2g | Fat: 10g | Fiber: 1g | Sugar: 5g

Crispy Peanut Butter Cups

Chocolate Layer

¾ cup chocolate chips (dairy-free if needed)

2 teaspoons coconut oil

Peanut Butter Layer

½ cup natural peanut butter

1 tablespoon honey or pure maple syrup

1 tablespoon coconut oil

Pinch fine sea salt (if peanut butter isn't salted)

½ cup crispy rice cereal

Imagine if Reese's peanut butter cups and Krackel chocolate bars had a baby...you'd end up with these crispy peanut butter cups! They're made with just a few ingredients that you probably already have in your pantry, they'll keep for a long time in your fridge or freezer, and they're the perfect cool treat on a hot day. **Serves 12**

1. Line a 12-cup muffin tin with silicone liners.

2. In a small bowl, melt the chocolate chips and coconut oil in the microwave in 30-second increments until the chocolate is melted and smooth, 1 to 2 minutes total. Stir to combine.

3. Divide the melted chocolate evenly into the lined muffin cups, using a spoon to completely cover the bottom and about ⅓ inch up the sides. Place the muffin tin in the freezer for 5 to 10 minutes for the chocolate to set.

4. In another bowl, melt the peanut butter, honey or maple syrup, coconut oil, and salt (if using) in the microwave until the mixture is slightly melted and pourable, 15 to 20 seconds. Add the crispy rice cereal and mix to combine.

5. Remove the muffin tin from the freezer and spoon about 1½ teaspoons of the peanut butter mixture into each cup. Place back in the freezer to set for about 30 minutes.

Serve Immediately: Once the cups have set in the freezer, they're ready to enjoy.

Meal Prep: Store the cups all together in one storage container or portion into small containers or reusable bags.

Store: In the refrigerator for up to 1 week or in the freezer for up to 1 month. If frozen, thaw the cups for 5 to 10 minutes before enjoying.

NUTRITION FACTS ———————————————————

Per serving: 1 cup | Calories: 163 | Carbohydrates: 13g | Protein: 3g | Fat: 11g | Fiber: 2g | Sugar: 10g

No-Bake Coconut-Lemon Macaroons

There's something about a lemon dessert that screams spring, but these freezer-friendly macaroon bites can be eaten all year long! They're super easy to whip up and there's no need to turn on your oven. Just process, form into balls, and enjoy. Doesn't get much easier than that. For the coconut cream, you can scoop this off the top of a chilled can of coconut milk or buy a can of coconut cream. Use leftovers to make Tiramisu Overnight Oats (page 47). **Serves 13**

½ cup Coconut Butter (page 242), melted or at room temperature

3 pitted Medjool dates

1 tablespoon canned coconut cream

2 teaspoons grated lemon zest

⅛ teaspoon fine sea salt

⅛ teaspoon ground ginger

⅛ teaspoon ground cinnamon

½ cup unsweetened finely shredded coconut

1. In a food processor, process the coconut butter, dates, coconut cream, lemon zest, salt, ginger, and cinnamon until combined.

2. Add the coconut and process until just combined.

3. Line a rimmed baking sheet with parchment paper. Use a tablespoon to scoop the dough onto the lined baking sheet and place in the freezer for at least 1 hour.

Serve Immediately: Enjoy 1 bite after freezing.

Meal Prep: Put the macaroons in a large storage container or portion into small containers or reusable bags.

Store: Store the macaroons in the freezer for up to 1 month. Thaw the bites for about 5 minutes before enjoying.

NUTRITION FACTS ─────────────

Per serving: 1 bite | Calories: 116 | Carbohydrates: 7g | Protein: 1g | Fat: 10g | Fiber: 2g | Sugar: 4g

Brownie Hummus

1 (15-ounce) can chickpeas, drained and rinsed

⅓ cup pure maple syrup

⅓ cup cashew butter

3 tablespoons unsweetened cocoa powder

2 tablespoons unsweetened cashew milk or other plant-based milk

1 teaspoon vanilla extract

¼ teaspoon fine sea salt

¼ cup chocolate chips (dairy-free if needed; optional)

Apple slices, strawberries, pretzels, and/or graham crackers, for dipping (optional)

When dessert hummus first came out, I practically ran to the store to try it, I was that excited about the idea. I was already hooked on incorporating beans into dessert recipes, as with my black bean brownies and chickpea cookie dough. One taste and I knew I wanted to make my own version. It tastes like a thick chocolate frosting or fudge, but it isn't nearly as sweet so you can eat it by the spoonful without getting a sugar rush. Don't worry, you can't taste the beans at all and they give this dip a good amount of protein and fiber. Serve it up to your family and simply forget to mention the secret ingredient: I guarantee no one will guess! **Serves 16**

Combine the chickpeas, maple syrup, cashew butter, cocoa powder, milk, vanilla, and salt in a food processor and process until the chickpeas are completely undetectable. Stir in the chocolate chips or sprinkle them on top, if desired.

Serve Immediately: Serve 2 tablespoons with apple slices, strawberries, pretzels, and/or graham crackers for dipping or just grab a spoon and dive in.

Meal Prep: Portion 2 tablespoons into one side of divided meal prep containers and apple slices, strawberries, pretzels, and/or graham crackers in the other.

Store: In the refrigerator for up to 1 week.

NUTRITION FACTS

Per serving: 2 tablespoons without dippers | Calories: 167 | Carbohydrates: 22g | Protein: 4g | Fat: 7g | Fiber: 3g | Sugar: 11g

Trail Mix Cookies

1 flax egg (see tip)

⅓ cup coconut oil, melted

¼ cup pure maple syrup

¼ cup coconut sugar

1 teaspoon vanilla extract

2 cups quick oats, divided

½ cup old-fashioned rolled oats

1 teaspoon ground cinnamon

½ teaspoon fine sea salt

⅓ cup chocolate chips (dairy-free if needed)

¼ cup raisins

I originally came up with the name for my blog, Eating Bird Food, thanks to all of the trail mix I used to eat in college. One of my roommates said I was "eating bird food" all the time, and when brainstorming ideas for my blog name, I immediately thought back to that moment and the name just stuck! I've clearly been a huge fan of trail mix since my college days, and to be honest, I'm surprised it took me this long to develop a trail mix cookie recipe, but it was well worth the wait. These cookies are essentially a loaded oatmeal cookie with a chewy component from the dried fruit and chocolate chips studded throughout. **Serves 12**

1. Preheat the oven to 350°F. Line a rimmed baking sheet with parchment paper or a silicone baking mat.

2. In a large bowl, whisk together the flax egg, coconut oil, maple syrup, coconut sugar, and vanilla.

3. Put 1 cup of the quick oats in a blender or food processor and blend until you've created oat flour. Transfer to a medium bowl. Add the remaining 1 cup quick oats, rolled oats, cinnamon, and salt.

4. Add the dry ingredients to the wet and mix until just incorporated. Fold in the chocolate chips and raisins.

5. Use an ice cream scoop to scoop 2 to 3 tablespoons of dough onto the prepared baking sheet. Press each one down with your fingers. You may need to wet your hands slightly so the dough doesn't stick.

6. Bake for 10 to 12 minutes, until golden brown on the bottom and edges but still soft on the top. Allow the cookies to cool on the baking sheet for about 5 minutes before transferring to a wire rack to cool completely.

Serve Immediately: Enjoy 1 cookie.

Meal Prep: Put all the cookies in one storage container or portion into small containers or reusable bags.

Store: In the pantry for up to 1 week.

BRITTANY'S TIPS

 To make a flax egg, whisk together 1 tablespoon flaxseed and 3 tablespoons water. Let the mixture sit for 5 minutes to thicken.

Feel free to use regular or golden raisins, whichever you have on hand—or even dried cranberries.

NUTRITION FACTS

Per serving: 1 cookie | Calories: 209 | Carbohydrates: 28g | Protein: 4g | Fat: 10g | Fiber: 3g | Sugar: 14g

Pecan Cookie Butter

This recipe was a happy accident that came together when I was working on a pecan pie crust recipe. I was processing the mixture, got distracted, and before I knew it, my pie crust turned into a creamy pecan butter. One spoonful and I knew I had created something brilliant: It smells like the holidays and tastes just like cookie butter, but is made with whole, real foods instead of processed cookies. You can use it the same way you'd use any nut butter—as a topping for oatmeal, a dip for apples, or a spread for toast and/or pancakes. **Serves 10**

1½ cups chopped pecans

1 cup old-fashioned rolled oats

2 tablespoons coconut sugar

¼ cup coconut oil, partially melted

½ teaspoon ground cinnamon

½ teaspoon fine sea salt

1. Preheat the oven to 350°F.

2. Spread out the pecans and oats on a rimmed baking sheet and bake until golden and fragrant, 10 to 15 minutes. Let cool completely.

3. Transfer the toasted pecans and oats to a food processor, add the coconut sugar, coconut oil, cinnamon, and salt, and process until the mixture turns into a nut butter consistency.

Serve Immediately: Grab a spoon and dig in.

Meal Prep: Transfer the cookie butter to a glass jar.

Store: In the pantry for up to 2 weeks.

NUTRITION FACTS

Per serving: 2 tablespoons | Calories: 180 | Carbohydrates: 9g | Protein: 3g | Fat: 14g | Fiber: 1g | Sugar: 3g

Coconut Butter

1 (8-ounce) package unsweetened shredded coconut (about 3 cups)

1 to 2 tablespoons coconut oil (optional)

Coconut butter is simply dehydrated coconut that's blended into a smooth spread, just like other nut/seed butters you might be more familiar with. You'll see coconut butter pop up in a few recipes in this cookbook, including my Coconut Protein Balls (page 225) and No-Bake Coconut-Lemon Macaroons (page 234), but I had to include it as a recipe of its own because it's quite delicious by the spoonful as a snack. Additional ideas include drizzling it over fruit or oatmeal, spreading it on baked goods, and/or adding a scoop to coffee in place of traditional creamer. Although coconut butter can be an expensive ingredient to buy at the store, it's incredibly easy (and way less inexpensive) to make at home with a bag of unsweetened shredded coconut. All you need is a food processor or high-powered blender. **Serves 12**

Process the shredded coconut in a high-powered blender on high or food processor until a smooth, runny butter forms. It will take about 2 minutes in a high-powered blender and about 15 minutes in a food processor. (I've found that my Vitamix blender works best for this.) You may need to scrape the sides of your food processor or blender midway through the processing. If you're having trouble getting a smooth consistency, add the coconut oil and this should help!

Serve Immediately: Grab a spoon and dive in.

Meal Prep: Transfer the coconut butter to a glass jar.

Store: In the pantry for up to 3 months.

NUTRITION FACTS

Per serving: 1 tablespoon | Calories: 106 | Carbohydrates: 8g | Protein: 1g | Fat: 8g | Fiber: 7g | Sugar: 1g

BRITTANY'S TIPS

Coconut butter becomes solid at room temperature, so you'll want to soften or melt it for measuring. I recommend using a warm water bath. Place the sealed jar in a pan of hot tap water until it's melted and you're able to stir it, 5 to 10 minutes. Another option is to microwave the coconut butter for 20 to 30 seconds to melt. If it still seems too thick, you can always add a little coconut oil. Start with 1 to 2 teaspoons and add more if needed to get the desired consistency.

Make your coconut butter ultra nutty and flavorful by toasting the shredded coconut. Spread out the coconut on a rimmed baking sheet and bake in a 325°F oven for 5 to 10 minutes, until lightly golden and fragrant. Watch it closely so it doesn't burn and toss the coconut once or twice while baking to ensure it browns evenly.

Cashew Queso

½ cup creamy cashew butter

¼ cup nutritional yeast

½ cup water

3 tablespoons salsa

1 clove garlic, peeled

1 teaspoon chili powder

¼ teaspoon salt, plus more to taste

⅛ teaspoon cayenne pepper (optional)

BRITTANY'S TIP

The cashew queso will thicken up as it sits in the fridge. You can warm it up to thin and add additional water, if needed.

You'll never believe this creamy queso is made with cashew butter. It's amazing as a sauce for my Black Bean and Cauliflower Burritos (page 169) and Portobello Mushroom Fajitas (page 158), but it's also delicious as a dip with tortilla chips for snacking. Just warm up the queso in a saucepan on the stovetop or in the microwave and serve. **Serves 8**

Combine all the ingredients in a high-powered blender and blend until smooth. Taste and add additional salt, if desired.

Serve Immediately: Enjoy with tortilla chips or raw veggies for dipping.

Meal Prep: Transfer to a storage container.

Store: In the refrigerator for 1 week.

NUTRITION FACTS

Per serving: 2 tablespoons | Calories: 104 | Carbohydrates: 6g | Protein: 4g | Fat: 8g | Fiber: 1g | Sugar: 0g

Coconut Bacon

1½ tablespoons reduced-sodium tamari, reduced-sodium soy sauce, or coconut aminos

1 tablespoon pure maple syrup

1½ teaspoons liquid smoke

½ teaspoon smoked paprika

2 cups unsweetened large-flake coconut

Crunchy, smoky sweet bacon...made from coconut flakes? Oh yes! The bacon flavor is pretty much spot-on and the coconut flakes get perfectly crispy, similar to the best pieces of bacon. Both tamari and liquid smoke provide a ton of flavor, so the taste of coconut is pretty much undetectable, which means even if you don't typically like coconut this recipe is still worth trying. I'm a huge fan of crunchy snacks, so I munch on this coconut bacon by the handful, but it has so many uses. It's amazing as a topping for salads, sprinkled on savory oatmeal, mixed into a tofu scramble, or added to a plant-based BLT sandwich. Of course you can also use it in my Cobb Salad with Coconut Bacon (page 111) and Coco-Bacon Loaded Sweet Potatoes (page 138). **Serves 16**

1. Preheat the oven to 325°F.

2. In a medium bowl, whisk together the tamari, maple syrup, liquid smoke, and paprika. Add the coconut flakes and stir gently until all the pieces are evenly coated with the sauce. Pour the coconut flakes onto a rimmed baking sheet and spread out in a single layer.

3. Bake for 14 to 15 minutes, stirring every 5 minutes. Make sure to keep a close eye on it at the end of the cooking process because it can easily burn.

4. Transfer the coconut bacon to a large plate to cool. It will continue to crisp as it cools and should be perfectly crunchy at room temperature.

Serve Immediately: Snack on a handful or sprinkle on your favorite savory dish.

Meal Prep: Transfer to a storage container.

Store: In the pantry for up to 2 weeks.

BRITTANY'S TIP

 Colgin liquid smoke is plant-based, but some other brands are not, so check the label carefully if you're looking for a vegan option.

NUTRITION FACTS

Per serving: 2 tablespoons | Calories: 74 | Carbohydrates: 4g | Protein: 0g | Fat: 6g | Fiber: 2g | Sugar: 2g

Meal Prep
for Littles

250 Broccoli Tots

253 English Muffin Pizzas

254 Apple-Cinnamon Mini Balls

257 French Toast Cups

258 Spinach Muffins

261 Veggie Pancakes

Broccoli Tots

 DF * GF

1 (12-ounce) bag broccoli florets or 2 medium heads broccoli, cut into florets

¼ cup quick oats

¼ cup diced yellow onion

⅓ cup shredded mild cheddar cheese (plant-based, if needed)

1 large egg, whisked

½ teaspoon fine sea salt

BRITTANY'S TIP

Switch up the veggies in these tots by using cauliflower instead of broccoli.

I don't know what it is about tater tots, but every child seems to love them, and I've found that they're an easy way to get kids to eat other veggies beyond potatoes! These veggie tots get extra flavor (and protein) from the shredded cheese and can be made with broccoli or cauliflower.
Serves 9

1. Preheat the oven to 375°F. Line a rimmed baking sheet with parchment paper.

2. Bring a large pot of water to a boil. Add a steamer basket, fill with the broccoli, and cover. Steam the broccoli until bright green, about 5 minutes. Drain well and let cool.

3. Meanwhile, process the oats in a blender or food processor until you've created oat flour. Transfer to a large bowl.

4. Transfer the broccoli to a food processor and pulse 4 to 6 times, until the broccoli is riced. Be careful not to overprocess.

5. Add the cooled riced broccoli to the bowl with the oat flour and add the onion, cheese, egg, and salt. Stir to combine.

6. Use your hands to form the mixture into small oval tots, using a heaping tablespoon for each. You should get about 18 tots.

7. Place the tots on the lined baking sheet and bake for 20 to 25 minutes, flipping halfway through, until the tots are golden brown in spots. Let cool.

Serve Immediately: Serve the tots warm with dipping sauce of choice. The classic kid-approved choice would be ketchup, but they're also tasty with Greek Yogurt Ranch Dressing (page 116).

Meal Prep: Put the tots in a storage container.

Store: In the refrigerator for up to 4 days.

NUTRITION FACTS

Per serving: 2 tots | Calories: 82 | Carbohydrates: 11g | Protein: 6g | Fat: 2g | Fiber: 4g | Sugar: 2g

English Muffin Pizzas

EF

1 teaspoon olive oil

4 button mushrooms, chopped

4 sweet mini bell peppers, seeded and sliced or chopped

¼ cup diced yellow onion

4 whole-grain English muffins, split

½ cup marinara or pizza sauce

¾ cup shredded mozzarella cheese

Italian seasoning to taste

These pizza muffins make for an easy after-school snack or can even be served for dinner. I've topped these mini pizzas with veggies (of course), but feel free to swap the veggies or skip them all together, if you know your kiddo won't eat them. That said, it doesn't hurt to make them as is and see what happens. **Serves 4**

1. Preheat the oven to 350°F.

2. Heat the oil in a medium skillet over medium heat. Add the mushrooms, bell peppers, and onion and sauté until softened and the onion is translucent, 3 to 4 minutes. Remove from the heat.

3. Place the English muffin halves on a rimmed baking sheet. To build each pizza, spread on 1 tablespoon pizza sauce, top with 1½ tablespoons cheese and an equal amount of the veggies, and add a sprinkle of Italian seasoning.

4. Bake for about 9 minutes, until the cheese is melted.

Serve Immediately: Serve the pizzas warm.

Meal Prep: Put 2 pizzas each in 4 meal prep containers. When ready to serve, follow the reheat instructions and serve warm.

Store: In the refrigerator for up to 5 days or in the freezer for up to 1 month.

Reheat: From the fridge, bake the pizzas in a 350°F oven or toaster oven for 5 to 6 minutes, until warm. From frozen, let the pizzas thaw in the refrigerator overnight and reheat as directed.

NUTRITION FACTS ————————————————————————

Per serving: 2 English muffin halves | Calories: 231 | Carbohydrates: 29g | Protein: 11g | Fat: 8g | Fiber: 4g | Sugar: 4g

Apple-Cinnamon Mini Balls

1½ cups raw walnuts

1 cup pitted Medjool dates (10 to 12)

½ cup soft dried apple

2 teaspoons coconut flour

1 teaspoon ground cinnamon

Pinch fine sea salt

These little balls are such a great snack to have on hand for the week for little ones. The base is walnuts, which are loaded with health benefits, including lots of antioxidants and trace minerals. They also contain folate and omega-3, both of which help in the development of a child's brain. Plus, kids love the apple-cinnamon flavor. **Serves 20**

1. Put the walnuts in a food processor and pulse until they are chopped into small pieces. Transfer to a bowl.

2. Put the dates in the food processor and pulse until a paste forms. If the dates form a sticky ball, break it apart with your hands.

3. Return the nuts to the processor with the dates.

4. Add the dried apples, coconut flour, cinnamon, and salt. Pulse until everything is well combined.

5. Scoop the dough from the food processor with your hands or ½-tablespoon measure and form into small balls.

Serve Immediately: Enjoy 1 ball.

Meal Prep: Put the balls all together in a storage container or portion into small storage containers or reusable bags.

Store: In the fridge for up to 1 week or in the freezer for up to 3 months. If frozen, let the bites thaw before eating.

BRITTANY'S TIPS

● If you don't have coconut flour, you can use 1 tablespoon almond flour or oat flour instead.

● My daughter has loved these since she was about 16 months old. The walnuts are chopped small enough for toddlers, and if needed, you can break the balls into smaller pieces rather than offering them whole. They're also yummy crumbled over yogurt for a protein-packed snack.

NUTRITION FACTS

Per serving: 1 mini ball | Calories: 97 | Carbohydrates: 13g | Protein: 2g | Fat: 6g | Fiber: 2g | Sugar: 10g

French Toast Cups

This recipe took a ton of testing to get just right, but I'm so glad I stuck with it because these French toast cups are such a hit with Olivia, and Isaac and I love them too. They have all the flavor you'd expect from traditional French toast, but packaged in an easy-to-serve muffin cup. I have a bag of these in my freezer at all times for busy mornings! **Serves 12**

4 large eggs

½ cup unsweetened vanilla almond milk

¼ cup pure maple syrup

1 teaspoon vanilla extract

½ teaspoon ground cinnamon

7 slices honey-oat bread, cut into ½-inch cubes (4 cups loosely packed)

¾ cup blueberries

1. Preheat the oven to 350°F. Coat a 12-cup muffin tin with nonstick cooking spray or line with silicone liners.

2. In a large bowl, whisk together the eggs, almond milk, maple syrup, vanilla, and cinnamon.

3. Add the bread cubes and let sit for 5 minutes.

4. Divide the mixture evenly into the prepared muffin cups.

5. Top each cup with a few blueberries, gently pressing them down so they stick once the cups bake.

6. Bake for 25 to 30 minutes, until set. Remove from the oven and let cool completely.

Serve Immediately: Serve 1 or 2 cups. You can cut them into smaller pieces for early eaters.

Meal Prep: Put the French toast cups in a storage container or freezer bag. When ready to serve, follow the reheat instructions and enjoy.

Store: In the refrigerator for up to 5 days or in the freezer for up to 3 months.

Reheat: From the fridge, wrap the French toast cup in a paper towel and microwave until warm, 30 seconds to 1 minute. From frozen, wrap in a paper towel and microwave in 30-second increments until warm, 1 to 2 minutes total.

NUTRITION FACTS ———————————————

Per serving: 1 cup | Calories: 96 | Carbohydrates: 15g | Protein: 4g | Fat: 2g | Fiber: 1g | Sugar: 6g

Spinach Muffins

 DF GF

These green muffins are not only fun, they're a breeze to whip up because everything is combined in your blender. Have your kiddos help you add all the ingredients to the blender—if they're old enough, they can even pour the batter into the muffin tin! These muffins are lightly sweetened with maple syrup and bananas and made with nutrient-dense almond flour and rolled oats. Olivia loves it when I cut the muffin in half and spread a little nut butter on each side. **Serves 12**

1 cup fine blanched almond flour

1 cup old-fashioned rolled oats

¼ cup pure maple syrup

¼ cup unsweetened almond milk

2 cups baby spinach

2 bananas (about 1 cup mashed)

2 large eggs

2 tablespoons coconut oil, melted

1 teaspoon vanilla extract

1 teaspoon baking soda

½ teaspoon fine sea salt

Pinch ground cinnamon

1. Preheat the oven to 350°F. Line a 12-cup muffin tin with silicone liners.

2. Combine all the ingredients in a blender and blend until smooth.

3. Pour or scoop the batter into the lined muffin cups. Bake for about 25 minutes, until the tops are golden brown and a toothpick comes out clean. Cool completely and enjoy.

Serve Immediately: Cool and serve.

Meal Prep: Put the muffins in a storage container or freezer bag. When ready to serve, follow the reheat instructions and enjoy.

Store: In the pantry for up to 3 days, in the refrigerator for up to 5 days, or in the freezer for up to 3 months.

Reheat: From the fridge, wrap the spinach muffin in a paper towel and microwave until warm, 30 seconds to 1 minute. From frozen, wrap the muffin in a paper towel and microwave in 30-second increments until warm, 1 to 2 minutes total.

NUTRITION FACTS

Per serving: 1 muffin | Calories: 155 | Carbohydrates: 17g | Protein: 5g | Fat: 8g | Fiber: 3g | Sugar: 7g

Veggie Pancakes

Have you noticed that I'm all about adding veggies to food that kids love? It's a bit sneaky, but it's such an easy way to incorporate nutrient-dense vegetables into your child's diet. My daughter loves pancakes and would eat them for breakfast, lunch, and dinner if she could, which is what inspired me to make a more savory pancake that's perfect for lunch, snacks, or even dinner. If your kiddos like to dip, serve the pancakes with Greek Yogurt Ranch Dressing (page 116) or marinara sauce. **Serves 9**

2 teaspoons olive or avocado oil, divided

½ cup frozen or fresh cauliflower rice

½ cup frozen sweet corn kernels, thawed and drained

¼ cup diced bell red pepper

¼ teaspoon fine sea salt, plus a pinch

Pinch ground black pepper

3 large eggs

¼ cup unsweetened plant-based milk

½ cup whole-wheat pastry flour, whole-wheat flour, or all-purpose flour

2 tablespoons shredded cheddar cheese

1 teaspoon baking powder

1. Heat 1 teaspoon of the oil in a medium skillet over medium heat. Add the cauliflower rice, corn, and bell pepper and sauté until the veggies are soft, about 5 minutes. Season with a pinch of salt and pepper. Remove from the heat.

2. In a large bowl, whisk the eggs. Add the cooked veggies, milk, flour, cheese, baking powder, and ¼ teaspoon salt and mix to fully combine.

3. Heat the remaining 1 teaspoon oil in the same skillet over medium heat. Pour in 1½ to 2 tablespoons batter for each pancake. Cook until bubbles start to form, 2 to 3 minutes, then flip and cook until the pancakes are golden on both sides, another 2 to 3 minutes.

Serve Immediately: Serve warm or at room temperature with dip, if desired.

Meal Prep: Put the pancakes in a storage container.

Store: In the refrigerator for up to 5 days or in the freezer for up to 1 month.

BRITTANY'S TIP

 Make the pancakes dairy-free by using plant-based cheese.

NUTRITION FACTS

Per serving: 1 pancake | Calories: 71 | Carbohydrates: 8g | Protein: 4g | Fat: 3g | Fiber: 1g | Sugar: 1g

Sauce and Dressing Inspiration

Here's a handy list of the sauces and dressings used in the cookbook to help you pull together your own sheet pan meals, bowls, and salads. You can mix and match and use these as you see fit!

- Avocado Green Goddess Dressing (page 111)
- Cashew Queso (page 245)
- Chipotle Sauce (page 170)
- Cilantro-Lime Dressing (page 120)
- Creamy Balsamic Dressing (page 113)
- Creamy Tahini Sauce (page 142)
- Greek Yogurt Ranch Dressing (page 116)
- Lo Mein Sauce (page 129)
- Peanut Sauce (page 149)
- Red Wine Vinaigrette (page 108)
- Southwest Chipotle Dressing (page 115)
- Teriyaki Sauce (page 187)
- Walnut Pesto (page 107)
- White Balsamic Dressing (page 123)
- Zesty Almond Dressing (page 119)

Acknowledgments

A big loving thank-you to Isaac, Olivia, and Tucker. You're my world and you'll always be my #1 taste testers.

To my agents, Sharon Bowers and Jan Baumer: Thank you for pushing me out of my comfort zone and encouraging me to finally turn my dream of writing a cookbook into a reality. I am so grateful Sharon sent that initial email back in June 2020.

To my editor, Thea Diklich-Newell: Thank you for believing in me and the concept for this cookbook from the beginning. It's been an honor to work with you and the whole Voracious team. Special thanks to Nyamekye Waliyaya and Ben Allen in production, Gregg Kulick for the cover design, Katherine Akey in marketing, and Lauren Ortiz in publicity and promotion. I also want to thank Mia Johnson for the gorgeous interior design.

To Kristin Tieg: I'm so happy we connected and were able to work together. You truly brought the recipes in this cookbook to life through your stunning photos. I'm still in awe of your ease behind the camera and those foliage shadows. Special thanks to David Peng and Caroline Hwang for food styling, Nidia Cueva for prop styling, and Jessica Darakjian for all her help in the kitchen. The photo shoot wouldn't have been possible without such an epic team! And thank you to Kirsty Wingfield, my hairstylist and makeup artist for the lifestyle shoot. You made me feel so glam!

To the Eating Bird Food team: Emily Leikam, Kate Pyle, and Maria Scott: This book simply wouldn't have been possible without each of you. Thank you for helping me bring *Mostly Veggies* to life, tirelessly testing recipes until they were perfect, and managing all the things that keep EBF running behind the scenes.

To my loving parents: Thank you for raising me to believe that I could accomplish anything I set my mind to and encouraging me to follow my own path. I am forever grateful and I wouldn't be here without you. Mom, thank you for letting me help you in the kitchen at a young age. I still remember sitting on the kitchen counter watching you cook. It's where my love of food began and many of my favorite recipes are inspired by things you taught me how to make.

To my mother-in-law: Thank you for being on the forefront of all the health trends, inspiring me to become a health coach, and taking such good care of Olivia. The days she spent with you afforded me the time and energy to focus on writing a cookbook.

To all of my family members and amazing friends: Your endless support over the years means the world to me. I am surrounded by the best people! To each of you who has made an EBF recipe, inspired one of my recipes, or shared my website with someone, know that I appreciate you so much.

Of course, my biggest thanks go to all of the Eating Bird Food readers. Whether you've been following along for over ten years or just found my site a few days ago, thank you so much for being here. The support and kindness I've received from the EBF community is truly overwhelming, and I think of you all as my friends. You allow me to have my dream job of creating and sharing healthy recipes with the world. This cookbook was created for you. I hope you enjoy it!.

Index

A

almond flour
  cheesy cheddar crackers with, 214
  chocolate chip cookie dough with, 230
  eggplant Parmesan with, 196
  spinach muffins with, 258
almond milk
  chia pudding with, 43
  French toast cups with, 257
  oatmeal with, 47–49, 73–74
  smoothies with, 80, 83–84, 87–88, 91–92
  spinach muffins with, 258
  squash oatmeal cups with, 50
  sweet potato pancakes with, 58
almonds
  granola bars with, 222
  instant oatmeal with, 57
  kale salads with, 112, 119
  pizza trail mix with, 217
  tamari roasted, 226
anise, star, 126
antioxidants, 84
apples, 28
  balls with cinnamon and, 254
  harvest kale salad with, 112
  instant oatmeal with, 57
applesauce, oat bars with, 229
artichoke hearts, farro salad with, 108
arugula, salads with
  breakfast, 77
  Greek couscous, 123
  Mediterranean farro, 108
  walnut pesto pasta, 107
avocado, 28
  burrito bowls with, 134–35
  dressing with, 111, 143
  smoothie with mango and, 96
  sweet potatoes with, 138–39
  white bean quinoa salad with, 103

B

bananas, 29
  chia pudding with, 42
  oatmeal with, 48, 74

  smoothies with, 80, 83–84, 87–88, 92, 95
  spinach muffins with, 258
barbecue sauce, jackfruit with, 145
bars
  bird food granola, 222
  carrot-raisin oat, 229
basil
  walnut pesto with, 107
  white bean quinoa salad with, 103
batch-cooking, 19, 20–21
beans
  canned, 18
  chili mac with, 207
beans, black
  burgers with, 204–5
  burrito bowls with, 134–35
  burritos with, 169
  enchiladas with, 200–201
  kale quesadillas with, 53
  mason jar salads with, 120
  sweet potatoes with, 138–39
  Tex-Mex casserole with, 133
  zucchini boats with, 191
beans, green, 29
  potatoes and Greek, 183
beans, white
  grain bowls with lemony, 142
  salads with, 103, 123
  Tuscan soup with, 203
beets, smoothie with, 92
berries. *See* blueberries; raspberries; strawberries
blueberries, 29
  chia pudding with, 43
  compote with, 70–71
  French toast cups with, 257
  instant oatmeal with, 57
  smoothies with, 84, 91
bread, French toast cups with, 257
  See also sandwiches
broccoli, 29
  casserole with cheese and, 176
  fried rice with, 199
  lo mein bowl with, 129
  maple-chipotle chickpeas and, 170
  orange tempeh and, 154–55

  rainbow meal with, 173
  soup with cheese and, 195
  tots, 250
broth, coconut curry, 150–51
  See also soups
brown sugar
  BBQ jackfruit with, 145
  instant oatmeal with, 57
Brussels sprouts
  breakfast salad with, 77
  grain bowls with, 142
  lemony fall harvest meal with, 157
  maple-chipotle chickpeas and, 170
buffalo sauce, tofu with, 116–17
burgers, quinoa and black bean, 204–5
burrito bowls, spicy chipotle tofu, 134–35
burritos, black bean and cauliflower, 169

C

cabbage, 29
cabbage slaw
  BBQ jackfruit with, 145
  tofu egg roll with, 141
cacao powder, smoothie with, 84
  See also chocolate chips; cocoa powder
carbohydrates, 13
  batch-cooking, 19
carrots, 29
  broccoli cheese soup with, 195
  fried rice with, 199
  Greek beans and potatoes with, 183
  lo mein bowl with, 129
  oat bars with, 229
  rainbow meal with, 173
  salads with, 111, 116, 119–20
  smoothie with, 88
  Thai lentil meatballs with, 150
  Thai spaghetti squash with, 192
  tofu curry with, 130
  tofu egg roll with, 141
  tofu lettuce wraps with, 187

cashew butter
    brownie hummus with, 237
    protein balls with, 225
    queso with, 158, 169, 245
cashews
    curried tofu salad with, 100
    pizza trail mix with, 217
casseroles
    broccoli cheese, 176
    cauliflower rice Tex-Mex, 133
cauliflower, 29
    broccoli cheese soup with, 195
    burritos with, 169
    gnocchi with, 166
    grain bowls with, 142
    shawarma pita pockets with, 165
    tikka masala with, 146
cauliflower rice
    bean and sweet potato salads
      with, 120
    coffee date smoothie with, 83
    Tex-Mex casserole with, 133
    tofu curry with, 130
    veggie pancakes with, 261
celery, 29
    salads with, 100, 104, 116
    Thai lentil meatballs with, 150
cheese
    Cobb salad with blue, 111
    enchiladas with Mexican, 200
    harvest kale salad with goat,
      112
    parfaits with cottage, 70–71
    zucchini boats with Mexican, 191
cheese, cheddar
    broccoli tots with, 250
    casserole with broccoli and, 176
    chili mac with, 207
    crackers with, 214
    kale and egg hash with, 161
    soup with broccoli and, 195
    veggie pancakes with, 261
cheese, feta
    egg cups with, 65
    pasta baked with, 179
    salads with, 103, 107, 123
    tofu shakshuka with, 180
cheese, mozzarella
    eggplant Parmesan with, 196
    farro salad with, 108
    pizzas with, 208, 253
    stuffed peppers with, 184
cheese, Parmesan
    eggplant Parmesan with, 196
    savory baked oatmeal with, 73
    white bean soup with, 203

cheese, pepper Jack
    breakfast sandwiches with, 69
    kale quesadillas with, 53
    "tuna" melt with, 104
chia seeds
    oatmeal with, 47–49, 57
    protein balls with, 225
    puddings with, 42–43
    raspberry jam with, 54
    smoothies with, 88, 91
chickpea pasta
    chili mac with, 207
    mushroom stroganoff with, 211
    pesto-feta baked, 179
    walnut pesto salad with, 107
chickpeas
    broccoli cheese casserole with,
      176
    brownie hummus with, 237
    EBF power bowl with, 149
    jerk, 137
    lemony fall harvest meal with, 157
    maple-chipotle veggies and, 170
    rainbow meal with, 173
    salads with, 104, 108, 111
    shawarma pita pockets with, 165
    stewed quinoa and, 126
chiles. See peppers, chile
chili mac, slow cooker, 207
chives, egg cups with, 65
chocolate chips
    brownie hummus with, 237
    cookie dough bites with, 230
    granola bars with, 222
    overnight oats with, 49
    peanut butter cups with, 233
    protein balls with, 225
    squash oatmeal cups with, 50
    trail mix cookies with, 238
    zucchini cookies with, 62
cinnamon roll baked oatmeal, 74–75
Cobb salad, 111
cocoa powder
    brownie hummus with, 237
    chocolate-peanut butter shake
      with, 95
    overnight oats with, 47, 49
coconut
    avocado mango smoothie with,
      96
    carrot-raisin oat bars with, 229
    chocolate chip cookie dough with,
      230
    granola bars with, 222
    macaroons with, 234
    protein balls with, 225

coconut bacon, 246
    Cobb salad with, 111
    sweet potatoes with, 138–39
coconut butter, 242
    cinnamon roll oatmeal with, 75
    macaroons with, 234
    protein balls with, 225
    smoothie with, 92
coconut milk
    broth with, 151
    cauliflower tikka masala with, 146
    chia puddings with, 42
    lentil and sweet potato curry with,
      188
    mushroom stroganoff with, 211
    tofu curry with, 130
    Tuscan white bean soup with, 203
coffee, smoothie with, 83
compote, blueberry, 70–71
cookies
    chocolate chip dough bite, 230
    coconut-lemon macaroon, 234
    trail mix, 238
    zucchini breakfast, 62
corn, 29
    BBQ jackfruit bowls with, 145
    chili mac with, 207
    fried rice with, 199
    salads with, 111, 115, 120–21
    sweet potatoes with, 138
    Tex-Mex casserole with, 133
    veggie pancakes with, 261
cottage cheese, parfaits with, 70–71
couscous, Greek salad with, 123
crackers, cheesy cheddar, 214
cucumbers
    pita pockets with, 165
    salads with, 111, 123
curry paste
    broth with, 151
    tofu with, 130
curry powder
    lentils and sweet potatoes with, 188
    tofu salad with, 100

D
dairy-free recipes, 14, 15
dates
    apple-cinnamon balls with, 254
    granola bars with, 222
    macaroons with, 234
    smoothies with, 83–84, 88, 95
dill, chickpea salad with, 104
dips
    brownie hummus, 237
    cashew queso, 245

dips *(Cont.)*
    edamame hummus, 221
    Greek yogurt peanut butter, 218
    pecan cookie butter, 241
dressings
    avocado green goddess, 111, 143
    batch-cooking, 19
    cilantro-lime, 115, 120
    creamy balsamic, 113
    Greek yogurt ranch, 116
    red wine vinaigrette, 108
    southwest chipotle, 115, 138
    white balsamic, 123
    zesty almond, 119

E

Eating Bird Food (EBF; blog), 14, 17, 74
edamame
    hummus with, 221
    salad with, 119
egg-free recipes, 14, 15
eggplant Parmesan, 196–97
eggs
    boiled, 20
    breakfast sandwiches with, 69
    broccoli tots with, 250
    eggplant Parmesan with, 196
    flaxseed, 51, 58, 62, 238
    French toast cups with, 257
    fried rice with, 199
    hash with kale and, 161
    kale quesadillas with, 53
    pancakes with, 58, 261
    potato and feta cups with, 65
    salads with, 77, 111
    spinach muffins with, 258
    squash oatmeal cups with, 50
    veggie quiche with, 66–67
enchiladas, squash and black bean, 200–201

F

fajitas, portobello mushroom, 158
farro
    batch-cooking, 20
    salads with, 108, 117
fats, healthy, 13
flaxseed
    egg substitute with, 51, 58, 62, 238
    granola with, 61
    instant oatmeal with, 57
food storage, 23, 28–30
French toast cups, 257
frozen foods, 18, 27, 28
fruit, 13
    storing, 28–30

G

garam masala, cauliflower tikka
    masala with, 146
garlic, 18, 29
ginger, 18
gluten-free recipes, 14, 15
gnocchi, cauliflower, 166
grains, whole, 13, 14
granola, crunch factor, 61
    parfaits with, 70–71
    yogurt jars with, 54
granola bars, bird food, 222
grapes, 29
    curried tofu salad with, 100
greens, 29
    See also arugula; kale; lettuce;
        spinach
grocery shopping, 18, 31

H

hash, kale and egg, 161
healthy eating, 13, 22
hemp seeds
    berry oat smoothie with, 91
    instant oatmeal with, 57
    parfaits with, 70–71
herbs, 28
hummus
    brownie, 237
    edamame, 221

J

jackfruit, BBQ, 145
jam, raspberry chia, 54
jerk seasoning, chickpeas with, 137

K

kale
    breakfast quesadillas with, 53
    cauliflower gnocchi with, 166
    EBF power bowl with, 149
    green smoothie with, 80
    hash with eggs and, 161
    salads with, 112–13, 119
    sweet potatoes with, 138
    Tuscan white bean soup with, 203

L

legumes, 14
lemons, 29
    fall harvest meal with, 157
    macaroons with, 234
    white beans with, 142
lentils
    batch-cooking, 20
    curry with sweet potato and, 188

taco salad with, 115
    Thai meatballs with, 150–51
lettuce, 29
    burrito bowls with, 134–35
    pita pockets with, 165
    salads with, 111, 115–16, 120
    tofu wraps with, 187
limes, 29
liquid smoke, 246
lo mein bowl, 20-minute veggie, 129

M

macaroons, coconut-lemon, 234
mango, 29
    smoothies with, 80, 96
maple syrup
    brownie hummus with, 237
    carrot-raisin oat bars with, 229
    chipotle sauce with, 170
    chocolate chip cookie dough with, 230
    coconut bacon with, 246
    French toast cups with, 257
    granola with, 61
    oatmeal with, 47–49, 74
    protein balls with, 225
    spinach muffins with, 258
    squash oatmeal cups with, 50
    zucchini cookies with, 62
mayonnaise (vegan)
    cabbage slaw with, 145
    curried tofu salad with, 100
    seaside chickpea salad with, 104
    yogurt ranch dressing with, 116
meal plans, 31–39
    including treats in, 22
    strategy for, 12, 17
meal prep, 12, 31
    EBF method for, 17–19
    recipe instructions for, 15
    tools for, 23–24
meatballs, Thai lentil, 150–51
meat substitutes, 13, 14
    Italian sausage, 162
    veggie crumbles, 184
melons, 29
milk, plant-based
    berry oat smoothie with, 91
    broccoli cheese casserole with, 176
    overnight oats with, 47
    veggie pancakes with, 261
    See also almond milk; coconut
        milk

muffins
butternut squash oatmeal, 50
chive, potato, and feta egg, 65
spinach, 258
muffins, English
breakfast sandwiches with, 69
pizzas with, 253
mushrooms
broccoli cheese casserole with, 176
egg cups with, 65
fajitas with portobello, 158
lo mein bowl with shiitake, 129
pizzas with, 208, 253
savory baked oatmeal with, 73
spaghetti squash noodles with
shiitake, 193
stroganoff with, 211
stuffed peppers with, 184
tofu egg roll with shiitake, 141
tofu lettuce wraps with, 187

N

nori (seaweed), seaside chickpea
salad with, 104
nutrition facts, 13

O

oats, rolled
baked cups with squash and, 50
berry smoothie with, 91
broccoli tots with, 250
carrot and raisin bars with, 229
cinnamon roll oatmeal with, 74–75
granola bars with, 222
granola with, 61
instant oatmeal packets with, 57
overnight oats with, 47–49
pecan cookie butter with, 241
protein balls with, 225
savory baked oatmeal with, 73
spinach muffins with, 258
sweet potato pancakes with, 58
Thai lentil meatballs with, 150
trail mix cookies with, 238
zucchini cookies with, 62
olives
Greek couscous salad with, 123
spaghetti squash pizza with, 208
onions, 29
cauliflower gnocchi with, 166
enchiladas with, 200
fried rice with, 199
kale and egg hash with, 161
lentil meatballs with, 150, 151
portobello fajitas with, 158
quiche with, 66

rainbow meal with, 173
savory baked oatmeal with, 73
tofu shakshuka with, 180
veggie sausage with, 162
onions, salads with
bean and sweet potato, 120
breakfast, 77
buffalo tofu, 116
Cobb, 111
kale edamame, 119
lentil taco, 115
seaside chickpea, 104
white bean quinoa, 103
orange juice, tempeh and broccoli
with, 154
oranges, 30

P

pancakes
sweet potato, 58–59
veggie, 261
pantry staples, 18, 27
parfaits, cottage cheese, 70–71
pasta. See chickpea pasta;
couscous; spaghetti
peaches, smoothie with, 87
peanut butter
chocolate shake with, 95
cups with chocolate and, 233
dip with yogurt and, 218
overnight oats with, 48
yogurt jars with, 54
peanuts, tofu lettuce wraps with, 187
peanut sauce
EBF power bowl with, 148–49
spaghetti squash noodles with,
192–93
tofu lettuce wraps with, 187
pears, 30
peas
fried rice with, 199
green beans and potatoes with,
183
lo mein bowl with snow, 129
tofu curry with, 130
walnut pesto pasta salad with, 107
See also chickpeas
pecans
cookie butter with, 241
oatmeal with, 50, 74
pepitas, granola bars with, 222
peppers, bell, 30
cauliflower gnocchi with, 166
chili mac with, 207
coconut curry broth with, 151
fried rice with, 199

Italian-style stuffed, 184–85
jerk chickpeas with, 137
kale and egg hash with, 161
kale edamame salad with, 119
lo mein bowl with, 129
pizzas with, 208, 253
portobello fajitas with, 158
quiche with, 66
rainbow meal with, 173
spaghetti squash noodles with,
192
tofu shakshuka with, 180
veggie pancakes with, 261
veggie sausage with, 162
zucchini boats with, 191
peppers, chile, 30
burrito bowls with, 134–35
cauliflower tikka masala with, 146
sauce with chipotle, 170
pesto
cauliflower gnocchi with, 166
feta pasta bake with, 179
pasta salad with walnut, 107
pineapple, green smoothie with, 80
pita pockets, cauliflower and
chickpea shawarma, 165
pizza
English muffin, 253
spaghetti squash, 208–9
trail mix seasoned like, 217
plantains, 136
jerk chickpeas with, 137
potatoes, 30
egg cups with, 65
Greek green beans and, 183
kale and egg hash with, 161
tofu curry with, 130
veggie sausage with, 162
See also sweet potatoes
processed foods, 13, 14
protein
batch-cooking, 19
plant-based, 13, 14
protein powder
overnight oats with, 48
protein balls with, 225
smoothies with, 83, 92, 95
pudding, chia, 42–43
pumpkin seeds, granola bars with,
222

Q

quesadillas, kale breakfast, 53
queso, cashew, 245
burritos with, 169
portobello fajitas with, 158

quiche, veggie, 66–67
quinoa, 18
    batch-cooking, 20
    BBQ jackfruit bowls with, 145
    burgers with beans and, 204–5
    rainbow meal with, 173
    salads with, 77, 103, 117, 119
    stewed chickpeas and, 126
    Tuscan white bean soup with, 203
    veggies and chickpeas with, 170
    zucchini boats with, 191

R

raisins
    curried tofu salad with, 100
    granola bars with, 222
    oat bars with, 229
    trail mix cookies with, 238
raspberries, 29
    chia jam with, 54
    chia pudding with, 43
    smoothie with, 91
refrigerated foods, 18, 27, 28
reheating foods, 19, 28, 30
rice, 18
    add-the-veggies fried, 199
    batch-cooking, 21
    broccoli cheese casserole with, 176
    buffalo tofu salads with, 116
    burrito bowls with, 134–35
    cauliflower tikka masala with, 146
    EBF power bowl with, 149
    grain bowls with, 142
    Greek beans and potatoes with, 183
    jerk chickpeas with, 137
    kale salad with wild, 112–13
    lemony fall harvest meal with, 157
    lentil and sweet potato curry with, 188
    orange tempeh and broccoli with, 154
    stuffed peppers with, 184
    Thai lentil meatballs with, 151
    tofu egg roll with, 141
    tofu shakshuka with, 180
    See also cauliflower rice
rice cereal, peanut butter cups with, 233

S

salads
    black bean and sweet potato, 120
    buffalo tofu mason jar, 116–17
    cabbage slaw, 141, 145
    Cobb, 111
    curried tofu, 100
    Greek couscous, 123
    harvest kale, 112–13
    kale edamame, 119
    lentil taco bowl, 115
    Mediterranean farro mason jar, 108
    roasted veggie breakfast, 77
    seaside chickpea, 104
    tofu lettuce, 187
    walnut pesto pasta, 107
    white bean quinoa, 103
salsa
    burrito bowls with, 134
    Tex-Mex casserole with, 133
    zucchini boats with, 191
sandwiches
    freezer breakfast, 69
    quinoa and black bean, 204–5
    shawarma pita pocket, 165
    "tuna" melt, 104
sauces
    batch-cooking, 19
    cashew queso, 158, 169, 245
    chipotle, 170
    creamy tahini, 142, 165, 173
    jackfruit with barbecue, 145
    lo mein, 129
    oat bars with apple-, 229
    peanut, 148–49, 187, 192–93
    teriyaki, 187
    tofu with buffalo, 116–17
    walnut pesto, 107, 166
    See also tomato sauce
sausage, veggie, 162
shake, chocolate-peanut butter, 95
    See also smoothies
shakshuka, tofu, 180
smoothies
    antioxidant boost, 84
    avocado mango, 96
    back-on-track green, 80
    berry oat, 91
    coffee date, 83
    peaches and green, 87
    red velvet cake batter, 92
    24 carrot gold, 88
snacks, 19, 22
soups
    creamy broccoli cheese, 195
    Tuscan white bean, 203
spaghetti, veggie lo mein with, 129
spaghetti squash
    pizza bake with, 208–9
    Thai-inspired noodles of, 192–93
spinach, 30
    breakfast sandwiches with, 69
    chickpea quinoa bowl with, 126
    coconut curry broth with, 151
    muffins with, 258
    quiche with, 66
    savory baked oatmeal with, 73
    smoothies with, 80, 84, 87, 91
    spaghetti squash pizza with, 208
    white bean quinoa salad with, 103
squash, 30
squash, butternut
    enchiladas with, 200–201
    lemony fall harvest meal with, 157
    oatmeal cups with, 50
squash, spaghetti
    pizza bake with, 208–9
    Thai-inspired, 192–93
squash, yellow
    pesto-feta pasta bake with, 179
    rainbow meal with, 173
    See also zucchini
star anise, 126
stew, chickpea quinoa, 126
strawberries, 29
    chia pudding with, 43
    smoothie with, 91
stroganoff, mushroom, 211
sunflower seeds
    granola bars with, 222
    granola with, 61
    veggies and chickpeas with, 170
sweet potatoes
    burritos with, 169
    chia pudding with, 42
    coco-bacon loaded, 138–39
    curry with red lentils and, 188
    EBF power bowl with, 149
    pancakes with, 58–59
    quiche crust with, 66–67
    salads with, 77, 112, 120
    24 carrot gold smoothie with, 88
    zucchini boats with, 191

T

taco seasoning
    lentil taco salad with, 115
    zucchini boats with, 191
tahini
    creamy sauce with, 142, 165, 173
    seaside chickpea salad with, 104
tamari
    almonds roasted with, 226
    coconut bacon with, 246

tempeh
  broccoli and orange, 154–55
  kale salad with balsamic, 112–13
teriyaki sauce, tofu lettuce wraps
    with, 187
Tex-Mex casserole, cauliflower rice,
    133
tikka masala, cauliflower, 146
tiramisu overnight oats, 47
tofu
  broccoli and orange, 154
  burrito bowls with, 134–35
  curried, 130
  egg roll in a bowl with, 141
  lettuce wraps with, 187
  salads with, 100, 116–17
  shakshuka with, 180
  spaghetti squash noodles with, 192
tomatoes, 30
  cauliflower tikka masala with,
      146
  chickpea quinoa bowl with, 126
  chili mac with, 207
  Greek beans and potatoes with,
      183
  lentil and sweet potato curry with,
      188
  pesto-feta pasta bake with, 179
  shawarma pita pockets with, 165
  stuffed peppers with, 184
  tofu shakshuka with, 180
tomatoes, salads with
  bean and sweet potato, 120
  buffalo tofu, 116
  Cobb, 111

lentil taco, 115
  Mediterranean farro, 108
  walnut pesto pasta, 107
  white bean quinoa, 103
tomatoes, sun-dried
  breakfast sandwiches with, 69
  Greek couscous salad with, 123
  pizza trail mix with, 217
  Tuscan white bean soup with, 203
tomato sauce
  eggplant Parmesan with, 196
  pizzas with, 208, 253
tortillas
  burritos with, 169
  enchiladas with, 200
  quesadillas with, 53
trail mix
  cookies with, 238
  pizza-flavored, 217

V
vegetables, 13
  cruciferous, 142
  pre-chopped, 18
  prepping, 19
  storing, 28–30
veggie crumbles, stuffed peppers
    with, 184
vinaigrette, red wine, 108

W
waffles, sweet potato, 58
walnuts
  apple-cinnamon balls with,
      254

carrot-raisin oat bars with, 229
  granola bars with, 222
  instant oatmeal with, 57
  pesto with, 107, 166
  pizza trail mix with, 217
  smoothies with, 84, 88
  Thai lentil meatballs with, 150
  zucchini cookies with, 62
water chestnuts, tofu lettuce wraps
    with, 187
wild rice, kale salad with, 112–13

Y
yeast, nutritional
  cashew queso with, 245
  mushroom stroganoff with, 211
  pizza trail mix with, 217
  veggie quiche with, 66
yogurt
  cabbage slaw with, 145
  dip with, 218
  dressings with, 115, 116
  pb&j jars with, 54
  smoothie with, 87

Z
zucchini
  breakfast cookies with, 62
  chocolate-peanut butter shake
      with, 95
  pesto-feta pasta bake with,
      179
  taco-stuffed, 191

About the Author

Brittany Mullins is a recipe developer, photographer, and founder of Eating Bird Food. She has a marketing degree, a health coaching certification, and a knack for creating simple, nutrient-dense recipes that have been featured in *Shape*, *Good Housekeeping*, *HuffPost*, Self.com, and more. She lives with her husband, daughter, son, and pup in Richmond, Virginia.

Unlock the simplicity of planning and prepping your way to healthy, delicious, veggie-forward eats at every meal.

Plant-focused meal prep means a fridge stocked with healthy snacks ready to grab on your way out the door. It means having an easy answer every time the question "What's for dinner?" pops into your head. It means saving time and money while you enjoy flavorful, nutritious meals that come together in minutes.

Brittany Mullins has perfected the art of flavor-filled holistic cooking for the whole family while tackling a busy to-do list and a hectic schedule: now, *Mostly Veggies* brings you the same tools and tricks Brittany herself uses every day.

Mostly Veggies focuses on wholesome ingredients and prioritizes fruits and vegetables, whole grains, and plant-based proteins as the foundation for healthy, filling meals that everyone in your family will love. Here you'll find over 100 recipes that are easily adaptable to countless diets and lifestyles, including:

- Customizable overnight oats, chia puddings, and energizing smoothies for busy mornings

- Batched meals, sheet pan dinners, and meal-size salads for satisfying lunches and dinners you can pull right out of the fridge or freezer

- Healthy snacks and treats for when those cravings hit

- Nourishing prep-ahead dishes for kiddos that they can even help you make

- And so much more!

With four weekly meal plans laid out for you based on maximizing fresh produce for each season, as well as guidelines to create your own meal plan, *Mostly Veggies* is your key to eating healthy all week long, no matter how many other things you have on your plate.